Parties, Conflicts and Coalitions in Western Europe

Parties, Conflicts and Coalitions in Western Europe explores the impact intraparty conflicts have on a political party's ability to bargain with other parties and enter into coalitions. Focusing on the UK, Italy, France, Denmark and Norway, it investigates whether the organisational imperatives of political parties play a role in party strategy and interparty competition.

Maor shows that the degree of centralisation or decentralisation of a party and the nature of the intraparty conflict affect the party elite's ability to neutralise and pacify internal opposition. He challenges the traditional view that centralised party structures make it easier to remain in coalitions. Crucially, he finds that decentralised models provide a variety of ways to manage such conflict without members leaving the party or voicing dissent outside the party.

Using extensive empirical evidence and drawing on numerous interviews with parliamentary elites, this study challenges traditional theory to show that, in practice, those parties able to contain internal conflict retain the strongest bargaining power within coalition governments.

Moshe Maor is a Senior Lecturer at The Hebrew University of Jerusalem.

Books published under the joint imprint of LSE/Routledge are works of high academic merit approved by the Publications Committee of the London School of Economics and Political Science. These publications are drawn from the wide range of academic studies in the social sciences for which the LSE has an international reputation.

Parties, Conflicts and Coalitions in Western Europe

Organisational determinants of coalition bargaining

Moshe Maor

London and New York

First published 1998
by Routledge
11 New Fetter Lane, London EC4P 4EE

Simultaneously published in the USA and Canada
by Routledge
29 West 35th Street, New York, NY 10001

Typeset in Times by Routledge
Printed and bound in Great Britain by Antony Rowe Ltd,
Chippenham, Wiltshire

British Library Cataloguing in Publication Data
A catalogue record for this book is available from the British Library

Library of Congress Cataloguing in Publication Data
Maor Moshe. Parties, conflicts, and coalitions in Western Europe:
organisational determinants of coalition bargaining / Moshe Maor.
p.cm. Includes bibliographical references and index. 1. Coalition
governments–Europe, Western. 2. Political parties–Europe, Western.
I. Title. JN94.A979M36 1998 324.2′ 094–dc21 97–14940 CIP

ISBN 0–415–11602–3

Contents

Illustrations

Appendices

Preface

The effectiveness of centralised, highly articulated parties in coalition games is often taken for granted. Many scholars believe that the more centralised the party structure, the easier it is for the party to remain in the coalition. The reason for this lies in the ability of 'strong' organisations to impose themselves upon internal actors, channelling their strategies into specific and obligatory paths. With reference to the negative impact of factions on their host parties, in particular, some argue that highly centralised parties can present a threat to decentralised, loosely-structured parties. Deepening an internal crisis in a loosely-organised party, they argue, may lead to a change in its policies which, in turn, destabilises the party. One of the main reasons I have for writing this book is to challenge these traditional views and change the widespread (negative) image of loosely-organised parties.

In the book I try to understand the impact intraparty conflicts have on a party's coalitional strategy. I investigate whether organisational imperatives of political parties play a role in interparty competition and, if so, how the relationship between the two could be addressed on theoretical and empirical grounds. This question is subdivided into four, namely:

1 How can 'claims' be made by actors operating within the party on the party elites?
2 How can the party elites pacify and neutralise internal dissent?
3 What are the implications of successful as well as unsuccessful resolution of internal conflicts on the party's bargaining power in the parliamentary arena?
4 What are the implications of a relative change in a party's bargaining power in the parliamentary arena on its coalitional bargaining?

Explanations of intraparty conflicts can easily become 'historicist', favouring interpretations that stress the complexity and uniqueness of historical events. However, my attempt to provide answers to these and other questions means that this book is not simply a descriptive account of intraparty conflicts. Rather, I am trying to provide a theoretical account of intra- and interparty dynamics. Thus the study proceeds along three stages. First, I find paradoxical implications of straightforward rational principles. Second, I put these implications in the form of a simple model, and third, the model is later tested by a detailed cross-national comparison. This comparison reveals the presence of systemic patterns in the relationship between intra- and interparty politics.

The model developed here is based on the assumption that party elites are motivated, above all, by the desire to remain party leaders (Luebbert 1986). In other words, for party leaders who are in office, it is more important to remain party leaders than to remain in office. If intraparty conflict threatens their position, rather than stay in government they will leave office in order to remain party leaders. Party leaders, in short, will emphasise central features of party policy so as to minimise dissent within various sections of the party and secure their position. Broadly speaking, therefore, the model is driven by policy-based, rather than office-based preferences.

Let me briefly explain the paradox underlying the model. In much of the literature devoted to intraparty determinants of coalition bargaining, the impact is found to derive from the structural context within which party elites operate. Sven Groennings (1968: 454) has argued that, for example, when internal disputes occur, the more centralised the party structure, the easier it is for the party to remain in the coalition. A similar conclusion has been reached by Angelo Panebianco (1988: 219) – that a strongly institutionalised party can defend its stability better than a weakly institutionalised party, and that an alliance among parties inevitably destabilises the less institutionalised organisations. These arguments raise two problems. First, strongly organised parties are characterised by excessive rigidity in so far as policy-making is concerned, as they drastically limit their internal actors' margins of manoeuvrability. Once internal conflict emerges – which in itself is an indication of the political importance of the issue at stake – leaders of strongly organised parties may face severe organisational strains compared to those faced by leaders of parties which do not impose themselves upon party subgroups. Second, strongly organised parties are characterised by excessive rigidity, in so far as their ability to pacify and neutralise internal dissatisfaction is concerned, as they lack mechanisms for the diffusion of dissent (e.g., factions, factional activities, dissentions in parliament, etc.). Consequently, internal dissatisfaction – which in some cases may be politically important and not easily suppressed – can be only expressed outside the party (e.g., resignations of elite members and demonstrations of party activists and militants).

Based on these problems, the book posits a 'puzzle' in Panebianco and Groennings' arguments: why are centralised parties considered to be effective coalitional actors if they are prone to severe organisational strains once internal conflict emerges and lack structural mechanisms for the diffusion of dissent? Based on the view that internal relationships are not only a matter of democracy, but also a matter of manageability, the book aims to show that the way in which power is distributed among the different levels of leadership (i.e., the degree of centralisation and decentralisation) and the nature of intraparty conflict affect the elites' ability to neutralise and pacify internal opposition.

The parties selected are classified as centralised or decentralised organisations according to the distribution of control among party organs over the following dimensions: policy development, execution of party line, candidate selection, leadership selection, funding allocation, party press, and discipline (including expulsion). Centralised parties are those which feature the concentration of effective decision-making authority in the national party organs over most of the above-mentioned dimensions, with a premium placed on the smaller number of individuals participating in the decision. Mechanisms for the diffusion of dissent, such as factions, factional activities and dissensions in parliaments, are not likely to be found within such parties. Classic examples for such parties are the Italian and French Communist parties during the 1960s and 1970s.

The conclusion drawn is that, when intraparty conflicts occur, organisational decentralisation allows the party to handle intra-elite and elite-follower conflicts in a variety of manageable ways without forcing members to leave the party. As a result, the party can enter into conflict – inducing coalition negotiations with other parties without risking its hold on its own members. A centralised organisation, however, lacks the mechanisms necessary to adjust to dissent among its members, and is therefore at a disadvantage when it enters parliamentary negotiations. When interparty negotiations induce intra-elite or elite-follower conflicts, members may be forced to leave the party, or air their dissatisfaction outside the party as their primary mechanisms for the expression of dissent. A centralised, rigid organisation – especially when confronted with the latter conflict mode – can lead to party disintegration when such a party enters serious coalition negotiations with other parties.

Based on a systemic analysis of 143 interviews with party parliamentary elites which proceeds from careful historical research, the book analyses the relationship between intraparty conflicts and parties' coalition bargaining in nine west European parties operating in minority situations (i.e., when the governmental parties control less than half of the seats in parliament). The focus on conflicts which evolved within parties competing in minority situations is based on the presumption that acute intraparty conflicts seem most likely to occur due to the complexity of securing a parliamentary majority and the need to cooperate with untraditional partners. The cases chosen include the following:

1 three decentralised parties which faced intra-elite conflicts, namely the Italian Christian Democrats (DC) during 1976–79, the French Socialist Party (PS) during 1988–90 and the British Labour Party during 1977–78;
2 one decentralised party which faced elite-follower conflict, namely the British Liberal Party during 1977–78;
3 three centralised parties which faced intra-elite conflicts, namely the Danish Social Democratic Party (SD) during 1977–78, the Danish Radical Liberals (RV) during 1988–90, and the Norwegian Center Party (SP) during 1989–90; and
4 two centralised parties which faced elite-follower conflict, namely the Italian Community Party (PCI) during 1976–79 and the French Communist Party (PCF) during 1988–90.

Turning to the contents, Chapter 1 elaborates some essential concepts which are vital to the development of an organisational analysis of political parties. The theoretical framework is then built upon these concepts. Chapter 2 explores the organisational context of each party under examination and the constitutional context within which the party operates. The empirical analysis that follows (Chapters 3 to 7) is structured along three themes:

1 modes of conflict manifestation (Chapters 3 and 4);
2 modes of conflict resolution (Chapters 5 and 6); and
3 modes of coalition bargaining following successful and unsuccessful resolution of intraparty conflicts (Chapter 7).

Chapter 8 analyses modes of conflict manifestation, resolution and bargaining of the Danish RV during 1988–90. It illustrates a case where party elites, operating in a centralised organisation, have successfully withheld information regarding the coalition agreement from members of the parliamentary and extraparliamentary party, thus denying them a platform from which a challenge to the party strategy could be launched. Chapter 9 concludes by examining some of the practical and theoretical lessons that party strategists and scholars of political parties can learn from my findings.

Acknowledgements

As perhaps befits an effort to bring together such diverse elements as theories of coalitional behaviour and intraparty politics, a simple paradox, an historical analysis and interviews with party elites, this book has been long in the making. In the course of writing it, first as a PhD dissertation, I have enjoyed the stimulating environment of the Government Department at LSE, and have accumulated debts to a group of wonderful friends–teachers and teachers–friends. Over these years, I had the good fortune to enjoy the help, challenges and the converging or diverging comments of my supervisors, Gordon Smith and Howard Machin. In a very skilful way, they always knew how to interpret my broken English and how to gather meaningful insights from my thoughts and feelings. I was also fortunate to benefit from the criticism of Patrick Dunleavy and Desmond King whose rigorous thinking contributed a solid foundation for this work. Numerous people read separate chapters or gave comments when I presented them in various conferences and informal forums: Lars Bille, Erik Damgaard, Gianfranco Pasquino, Gideon Doron, Angelo Panebianco, John Madeley, Hilmar Rommetvedt, Vernon Bogdanor, Alan Beattie, Vincent Wright, Rob Elgie, Jan-Erik Lane, Knud Heidar, Lawrence Rose, Kaare Strøm, Rosa Mule, Razin Sally and Trevor Gunn. I am grateful to them for their advice and support.

No less important was the role of friends and colleagues in taking care of the logistic aspects of the visits to five European capitals. I would like to thank Hadasa Bezalel, Birte and Erik Haagh, Henry Valen, Ole Andersen, Søren Villadsen and Geoffrey Pridham. I would like to also acknowledge the help of Valeria de Bonis, Giovanni Orsina, Anita Ferraro and Christina di Pietro who tirelessly translated hours of interviews. Their work greatly improve the quality of the book. Michael Glass, Alan Barnes, Mitza Edge and Simon Hix read what I had considered the final draft of the manuscript and persuaded me that more iteration was necessary. The research was made possible by the joint financial support of Argov Fellowship, Overseas Research Studentships, The Central Research Fund of the University of London, the Anglo-Jewish Association, Mr Ian Karten and an anonymous Swiss fund.

Didi, my closest friend, was a prime partner in this work. Her sharp intellect and emotional support were the key for making this dream come true.

Abbreviations

CD	Centrum Democraterne
CERES	Centre d'etudes, de recherches et d'education socialiste
CDS	Centre des Démocrates-Sociaux
CDU	Christlich-Demokratische Union
CGIL	Confederazione Generale Italiana del Lavoro
CGT	Confédération Générale du Travail
CIR	Convention des Institutions Républicaines
CP	Høyre (Conservative Party, Norway)
CPP	Det Konservative Folkeparti
CSU	Christlich-Soziale Union
DC	Democrazia Christiana
DNA	Det Norske Arbeiderparti
EC	European Community
EEA	European Economic Area
EFTA	European Free Trade Area
EMS	European Monetary System
FLM	Federazione dei Lavoratori Metallurgia (Federation of Metalworkers)
FN	Front National
FrP	Fremskridtspartiet (Denmark)
FrP	Fremskrittspartiet (Norway)
IMF	International Monetary Fund
KrF	Kristeligt Folkeparti (Denmark)
KrF	Kristelig Folkeparti (Norway)
LO	Landsorganisationen i Denmark (Danish Federation of Trade Unions)
MP	Member of Parliament
MRG	Mouvement des Radicaux de Gauche
MSI-DN	Movimento Sociale Italiano – Destra Nazionale
NATO	North Atlantic Treaty Organisation

NEC	National Executive Committee
OECD	Organisation for Economic Co-operation and Development
PCF	Parti Communiste Français
PCI	Partito Comunista Italiana
PLI	Partito Liberale Italiano
PLP	Parliamentary Labour Party
PR	Proportional Representation
PRI	Partito Repubblicano Italiano
PS	Parti Socialiste
PSD	Parti Social Democrate
PSDI	Partito Socialista Democratico Italiano
PSI	Partito Socialista Italiano
PTT	Postes, Télégraphes et Téléphones
RPR	Rassemblement pour la République
RV	Det Radikale Venstre
SD	Socialdemokratiet
SF	Socialistisk Folkeparti
SFIO	Section Française de l'Internationale Ouvrière
SID	Specialarbejderforbundet i Denmark (General Workers' Union in Denmark)
SP	Senterpartiet
SPD	Sozialdemokratische Partei Deutschlands
SV	Socialistisk Venstreparti
TUC	Trades Union Congress
UDC	Union du Centre
UDF	Union pour la Démocratie Française
UGCS	Union des Groupes et Clubs Socialistes
V	Venstre (Liberal Party)
VS	Venstresocialisterne

1 The problem, the paradox, the model

This book began from two observations. One is commonplace or nearly so: there are many parties whose coalition strategies are easily disturbed by internal conflicts, forcing them to modify their coalition strategies. The second observation is somewhat more stimulating: there are many parties that maintain their coalition strategies under conditions of intense internal conflicts.

These observations are theoretically related because they treat the party as a political system (Katz and Mair 1992), and indicate that interparty competition in the parliamentary arena could be understood through the internal dynamics of party politics. For the premise that a party could be treated as a party system, members of the parliamentary party and its extra-parliamentary wings thrive on the hope of winning and the desire to influence party policy and strategy. Different coalitions of forces are being formed within the party and actors striving for dominance interact with each other in the struggle for relative influence within the organisation. The interplay between internal actors, each with his or her own agenda, is thus the driving force of party life. For the relationship between intra- and interparty politics, the choice of coalition partners, the type of interparty commitment, the content of the coalition agreement and the timing of the coalition formation, to mention only few, are often divisive issues within the party. Suffice it for now to indicate that members who becomes dissatisfied with the party strategy, policy or effectiveness have three basic choices. They can leave the party – the 'exit' option; or they can stay in and use their 'voice' option to try to change the party's performance by campaigning for new policies or a new leadership. Alternatively, dissatisfied members may opt for the 'loyalty' option, remaining within the party and keeping quiet about their dissatisfaction (Hirschman 1970). The interest of this study lies within the former two, that is, within the realm of intraparty conflicts which are visibly manifested within or outside the party organisation.

The interplay between intraparty politics and party strategy is a complex research topic. For not only does there exist conflict between parties, but there are also conflicts between individual actors or groups of actors within different party subsystems, with the resources of one area being employed as a weapon in the internal conflict inside another area, and the possibility that particular intraparty coalitions can cut across intra-organisational boundaries. Furthermore, there is little doubt that this interplay is what today defines the gap in the literature relating to coalition bargaining. There is a yawning gap between specialised and detailed enquiry into individual party organisations with an appropriate theoretical conceptualisation and the broad sweep of surveys involving a large number of cases. Where there surely ought to be a stock of middle-level, cross-national comparison of party organisations over a limited and carefully selected sample of party systems, there is very little at all. Given the complexity of the topic and the lack of a serious attempt to approach it, the aim of this book is to provide a theoretical framework and an empirical analysis of the impact intraparty conflicts have on a party's coalition bargaining. Before doing so I examine the insights provided by scholars of political parties and coalition bargaining.

PARLIAMENTARY COMPETITION AND INTRAPARTY DETERMINANTS

In multiparty systems a natural focus is on coalition bargaining and the process of government formation.[1] Yet despite the growing interest in explaining coalition bargaining and the government formation process in parliamentary systems little attention has been devoted to intraparty determinants. At the outset, there is a considerable general literature on the internal politics of parties. Much of this material, however, has no direct bearing on coalition bargaining. A substantial reason for this lies in the fact that most theorists see parties as anthropomorphic unitary actors. Notable exceptions are Hirschman's (1970) discussion of the impact on interparty competition of the divergent views that are likely to be held by party workers and party voters, Robertson's (1976) analysis of the impact of the divergent views of campaign contributors and voters, and Strøm (1990a) who incorporated propositions concerning parties' internal organisations into two causal models – permitting strategy to operate as a variable – to explain the mix of strategies pursued by competitive political parties.

Only recently Laver and Shepsle (1996) developed a theory of equilibrium cabinets which look at intraparty politics by replacing the unitary actor assumption with a view of parties as a coalition of factions, each supporting a set of cabinet-rank politicians. Consequently, they treated a political party as 'a holding company for a cadre of senior politicians, each credibly associated with a particular policy position' (Laver and Shepsle 1996: 249).

Gregory Luebbert was the first to devote exclusive attention to this topic by proposing a theory of coalitional behaviour which was based fundamentally upon the assumption that party leaders are motivated above all by the desire to remain party leaders (Luebbert 1986: 46). This assumption means that party leaders will always strive to minimise party disunity by attempting to base the party's attitude towards participation in a coalition on preferences that produce the least disunity. From this perspective:

> the leaders' task is to insist on preferences that are sufficiently focused that they generate the widest possible support within the party, but sufficiently vague and opaque that they do not engage in government formation the disagreements that are a constant feature of any party.
>
> (Luebbert 1986: 52)

Preferences that embody a party's fundamental principles of policy or programme direction are therefore decisive in government formation. The reason for this lies in their role in minimising party disunity by being derived from the most widely shared values within a party, and because they directly engage the party's most basic sense of purpose.

In Luebbert's view it is only when party leaders intend to bargain seriously that intraparty considerations significantly affect the selection of a few major programmatic issues as sticking points in the bargaining process. Negotiations concerning coalition formation are thus mainly about intraparty politics. As Luebbert notes:

> What makes the talks so long, difficult, and complex is generally not the lack of goodwill among elites, but the fact that negotiations must appear the way they do in order to satisfy the members whose orientation is still largely attuned to the vocal, symbolic, and ideological aspects characteristic of each respective political subculture. It is wrong to assume that, because interparty negotiations take a long time, much is being negotiated among the parties. Most negotiation in cases of protracted government formation takes place

between leaders and their followers and among rival factions within parties.

(Luebbert 1986: 52)

Luebbert's account could be challenged for its sole concentration on policy issues. According to Luebbert (1986: 249), one of the theory's central propositions is that decisive policy preferences can be discovered by studying the historical crises and challenges that shaped party profiles. In so doing, Luebbert ignores matters of internal politics which relate to genuine disagreements over party strategy and conflicts which represent a personal struggle for power between different leaders and their respective followers. Personal conflicts, which are actually about power, career, spoils and rewards rather than policy or ideology, explain how a party can be relatively divided without containing many significant policy differences.

The dynamics of intraparty politics can also be approached from an interparty perspective. Until the 1990s, political economists tended to approach the problem of legislative coalitions by formulating spatial models based on the assumption that all possible policy proposals are feasible. Those models allow for a continuum of potential alternatives to the *status quo* on each policy dimension. Their account of government coalition formation is, therefore, in the form of a game of weighted voting in a legislature in which the entire policy space constitutes the set of feasible policy outcomes (McKelvey and Schofield 1987; Schofield 1986). This approach raises a problem related to the assumption that all possible policy proposals are feasible. In the real world the set of feasible policy proposals is limited by various factors, such as, the 'legitimate' ideological spectrum which is defined by established parties to exclude anti-system parties from coalition bargaining, the constraints imposed on the party leadership by party members and supporters, the constraints imposed on party leadership by their choice of potential coalition partner and so on. Another problem with the spatial models was the inability to associate between alternative policy proposals (read alternative governments) and the ministers who are needed to implement them.

The linkage between these two variables proved immensely useful in predicting the government formation process on the basis of the credibility of policy proposals. This refreshing improvement in the study of coalitional behaviour came in the form of Laver and Shepsle's (1990a; 1990b) approach of modelling government formation. Two innovative ideas were raised by the authors: first, treating government coalitions as being governments as well as coalitions; second, considering the credibility of policy proposals made during coalition bargaining. These two important matters are linked by a common concern with the qualitative allocation of cabinet portfolios among parties, as the latter may be taken to imply a credible commitment to implement the ideal policy of the parties in the relevant policy jurisdiction:

> [The] characterisation of the workings of the division-of-labour cabinet system should lead actors to forecast that jurisdiction-specific policy outputs will tend toward those preferred by the party of the relevant minister. This means that a proposal that promises to enact the preferred policy position of the person (party) nominated for each relevant portfolio is *credible* in the sense that it depends only on giving ministers the power to do what they expressly want to do. Any proposal promising that a minister with wide-ranging power over the relevant policy jurisdiction will act against expressed preferences is less credible.
>
> (Laver and Shepsle 1990b: 874)

The credible policy promises that are made when governments are formed are therefore limited to those that can be implemented by placing portfolios in the hands of those politicians who are inclined to carry them out; no other policy promises are credible. In this sense, portfolio allocation becomes the mechanism by which prospective coalitions make credible promises.

The central point in Laver and Shepsle's analysis is that dealing with governments rather than merely with legislative coalitions gives them the freedom to consider a range of policy-related issues that are central to the operation of coalition government. However, this viewpoint overlooks the possibility that the issues at stake during the operation of legislative coalitions may transcend the ordinary range of legislative policy areas, and may involve questions of pure coalition strategy: the willingness to work with one set of parties rather than another. In multiparty systems where the choice of coalition partners – and their derived attributes in terms of past coalition experience, ideological flexibility, their hold on members and so on – is what determines the ability of a party to implement its programme, questions related to the coalition strategy tend to dominate the political agenda to the near exclusion of ordinary policy debates. Laver and Shepsle's (1990a; 1990b) accounts fall far short of dealing successfully with this issue.

An additional shortcoming of their approach relates to their implicit assumption that party debate ends after a coalition has been established. Specifically, Laver and Shepsle's approach focuses on the period of government formation, during which party discipline reaches a maximum. After this stage, however, intraparty conflicts may still evolve, undermining the 'credibility' of a proposal by exerting pressures on cabinet members. As each alliance partner re-commits itself to parliamentary co-operation by voting in favour of the coalition over critical divisions (e.g. no-confidence motions, budget approval, etc.), the 'credibility' of a proposal can be continuously evaluated. Hence, a partner's strategy will be dependent on the extent to which promises are implemented. Theoretically, only an approach that views coalition maintenance as a continuous process of alliance formation can effectively capture the notion of a 'proposal credibility' and intraparty dynamics.

Recently, Laver and Shepsle (1996) have challenged majority-rule models that ignore the structure of government decision-making thus failing to identify equilibrium outcomes which are common in the real political world. The model developed by Laver and Shepsle takes the institutional arrangements of parliamentary democracy – in particular, the departmental organisation of governmental decision-making – as its basic premise. In addition, they treat parties as if they are unitary actors. 'One of the most significant implications of the assumption that politicians behave as perfect agents of their parties is that each party can be treated as if it has a unique ideal policy position' (Laver and Shepsle 1996: 25) which it is forecast to implement if given the opportunity to do so. This is a realistic policy which the party would implement if elected. Laver and Shepsle argued that when politicians consider the making and breaking of governments they look ahead both to the most likely consequences of putting a particular cabinet in charge of running the country's affairs and to the most likely consequences of replacing that cabinet with some visible alternative. This leads to a theory of cabinet equilibrium.

Although the rationale of Laver and Shepsle's analysis is straightforward, significant aspects of their thesis remain unanswered. First, questions of coalition strategy may dominate the political agenda of coalition bargaining and government formation to the near exclusion of conventional policy issues. Second, personal conflicts may lead to party disintegration although the party may not contain many significant policy differences. Third, the impact intraparty conflicts have on credibility of proposals could not be assessed once parties are treated as unitary actors. The former two points were already elaborated in my criticism of Laver and Shepsle's (1990a, 1990b) analysis. The third aspect deserves attention.

The unitary actor assumption has been reviewed from the perspective of government formation by Laver and Schofield (1990: chap. 2, App. A). Their conclusions are based primarily on the empirical observation that it is almost always the case that parties both enter and leave cabinet coalitions as unified blocs. They take it to imply that, for the purpose of analysing cabinet formation and maintenance over a reasonably short timescale, nearly all Western European political parties can be treated as if they were unitary actors (Laver and Schofield 1990: 28). This evidence has been supplemented by a series of country studies collected by Laver and Shepsle (1994). These notable efforts to validate the argument that parties can be treated as if they are unitary actors manipulate the most important point: although parties enter and leave cabinet coalitions as unified blocs they may do so purely as a result of internal conflicts. In other words, a focus on parties that enter and leave cabinet coalitions is misleading. Party split – an indicator commonly used by rational theorists to validate the view that parties could be treated as unitary actors – is only one among many other manifestations of internal conflicts. Discussions in party bodies, resignation of elite members, violent demonstrations of party activists, to mention only few, can significantly affect the coalition bargaining and the process of government formation, and yet parties could enter or leave cabinet coalitions as unified blocs. Attention should therefore move away from the 'end-situation' of coalition bargaining towards analysing the 'process' which leads to the observed output. This, in turn, could be done only after the unitary actor assumption is excluded. Obviously, this line of argument escaped Laver and Shepsle (1996: 247) who 'heroically assumed that political parties approach the making and breaking of governments as if they are unitary actors'.

Considering the implications of their model, Laver and Shepsle (1996: 247) admit that 'to treat parties as unitary actors in the government formation process is, clearly a considerable oversimplification'. Consequently, they relax the unitary actor assumption by treating a political party as 'a holding company for a cadre of senior politicians, each credibly associated with a particular policy position' (Laver and Shepsle 1996: 249). The relaxation of the unitary actor assumption enables them to tap into the dynamics of change of party policy: 'any diversity in the policy positions associated with senior party politicians allows the party to change its overall policy profile by nominating different politicians as spokesperson for a particular area' (Laver and Shepsle 1996: 249).

Although Laver and Shepsle (1996) allow for the possibility that parties contain a group of ministerial-calibre politicians who do not share the same ideal point, as far as decision-making within the party is concerned, they still assume a very centralised decision-making regime. According to this regime, all strategic decisions are taken either by a single autocratic leader or within a leadership faction all members of which do share the same ideal policy point. Thus loosely organised parties, which are common in the real political world, are not within the scope of their analysis. In addition, although Laver and Shepsle's (1996) research is theoretically fascinating, their argument can be no more than suggestive because it is based – as they admit – on 'pencil-and-paper examples' (Laver and Shepsle 1996: 260).

To sum up, the above discussion suggests that intraparty conflicts have been largely dealt with on an *ad hoc* basis, and as such, have been treated as a constraint on coalition bargaining and the process of government formation. In other words, discussions of the topic have concentrated almost exclusively on the negative influences of party disunity and the strategies of party elites to cope with these (for instance, through the allocation of portfolios). Little attention has been devoted to the strategic advantages in a diversity of policy orientations among senior ministers, as well as among party subgroups. Most scholars have operated without a clear conception of the precise nature of internal conflicts; and how party elites can take advantage of the structural context in which they operate in order to neutralise internal dissent. To fill this gap, an attempt is made to account for the variability in the manifestation and resolution of intraparty conflicts as well as the modes of legislative behaviour based upon two explanatory variables, namely, the structural context within which intraparty politics take place and the nature of the internal conflict. The analysis sits squarely in the tradition of Strøm and Luebbert's works as it proposes a framework that is based fundamentally upon a differentiation of party organisations and assumptions about intraparty politics. It is, therefore, necessary to justify the choice of 'centralised' and 'decentralised' parties as the base point of the analysis, not least because with each contribution it seems that the parameters of the discussion change, resulting in a confusion and profusion of terms. This is unfortunate because the above differentiation is fundamental to our understanding of the dynamics of party politics; the type of party organisation being a key factor in promoting or inhibiting a change in the nature of coalition bargaining and the process of government formation.

DIFFERENTIATING PARTY ORGANISATIONS

Approaches to the study of party organisation have tended to deal with four analytically distinct themes. In the first place, various studies have sought to distinguish among types of party organisation (Duverger 1964; Neumann 1956). Second, a variety of analyses have addressed the question of party organisational strength (Wright 1971; Epstein 1980). Third, various attempts have also been made to measure and explain the extent of party organisational change and transformation (Kirchheimer 1966, Panebianco 1988). Fourth, a recent account sought to distinguish among faces of party organisation and, by that, to arrive at a classification of party organisations (Katz and Mair 1995). As a point of departure, each approach provides a very valuable base-line against which divergences among party organisations can be analysed. In addition, each theoretical model offers a variety of dimensions which constitutes a very useful guide from which to begin an evaluation of politics in the 'real' world.

Studying the interplay between intra- and interparty politics involves actors with widely different relationships to their political environment, as well as parties with widely different relationships to their social and political environment. To encompass this complexity, I use the concept of 'centralisation of power'. As a concept in the analysis of political parties, centralisation of power relates to Anderson's (1968: 392–6) dimension of 'control' as a concept in organisational theory. More specifically, Anderson means the distribution of control instead of the volume or sources of control. In this sense, it is identical with Duverger's (1964: 52) concepts of 'centralisation and decentralisation' which 'define the way in which power is distributed among the different levels of the party's leadership'. Viewing centralisation of power within the party, I define the national party organs as a reference point for 'central' location. Thus, a centralised party is one which features the concentration of effective decision-making authority in the national party organs, with a premium placed on a smaller number of individuals participating in the decision (Janda 1980: 108). Let us take two parties, *A* and *B*. In the first, *A*, the extra-parliamentary wings have no real prerogatives and the fundamental decisions are taken by the parliamentary party. In the second, *B*, the extra-parliamentary wings may affect party policy and strategy either through horizontal linking (i.e. party conference in which all tendencies/factions can find expression), or vertical linking (i.e. when authority at the subnational level is in the hands of a managing committee elected by a conference, itself made up of delegates nominated by the branches). The centralised party, *A*, drastically limits its internal actor's margins of manoeuvrability. The organisation imposes itself upon the actors, channelling their strategies into specific and obligatory paths. In contrast, the decentralised party, *B*, is one in which the actors have more autonomy in order to compete with each other; the competing organisational subunits are assured autonomous control over organisational resources. At the heart of this study therefore lies the notion that the difference in the way in which power is distributed among the different levels of party leadership matters in coalition bargaining.

THE INTERPLAY BETWEEN INTRA- AND INTERPARTY POLITICS IN MULTIPARTY SYSTEMS: A MODEL

In multiparty systems party elites will use tactical moves and counter-moves in the internal and the parliamentary arenas in an attempt to resolve their bargaining problem, i.e. to commit the party to co-operative relationships in such a way as to ensure party cohesion (Sjöblom 1968). This brings out very clearly the significance of two variables, namely, intraparty conflicts (the independent variable) and coalition bargaining (the dependent variable).[2]

Intraparty conflict is taken to signify intra-elite as well as elite-follower conflict, following an alliance, which results in organisational decline (i.e. a deterioration of the party's stability and/or cohesion). Two operational criteria, both of which are necessary to designate an internal dispute as an intraparty conflict, include:

1   party elites' perception of the intraparty strife as an attempt to change their legislative behaviour; and
2   patterns of organisational decline, i.e. exit and/or voice by party members.

(Hirschman 1970)

We have at our disposal at least seven indicators of organisational decline. Intra-elite conflicts, for example, may be manifested by resignation of elite members (i.e. the 'exit' option), dissension in parliament, and petitions or appeals to party elites with the intention of forcing a change in party strategy (i.e. the 'voice' option). Elite-follower conflict, by comparison, may be manifested by a decline in party membership (i.e. the 'exit' option), demonstrations of party activists, and petitions or appeals to party elites with the intention of forcing a change in party strategy (i.e. the 'voice' option).

For the distinction between elite-followers and intra-elite conflicts, in a genuinely factionalised party the two types are mixed as members of conflicting elites have their respective followers in the party organisation, party media and in auxiliary organisations. The power of the leadership of factions will, *inter alia*, be based on the relative resources of the followers of each faction. To minimise ambiguity in these terms, I define 'intra-elite conflicts', as those which occur within the parliamentary party, including those between members of parliament and the party representatives in government. 'Elite-follower conflicts' are taken to signify any other internal disputes. Regarding the actual evolution of conflicts, it is important to note that the analytical differentiation between intra-elite and elite-follower conflicts does not exclude evolution of both at the same time. It is reasonable to suggest, however, that in the case of any one particular party, either intra-elite, or elite follower will ordinarily be the dominant conflict mode. The subsidiary conflict is then likely to manifest itself to such a limited degree that it will never become destructive for the simple reason that, if the decrease in the level of party cohesion proceeds, the job of destruction is accomplished single-handedly by the dominant conflict mode.

Bargaining power refers to the power of a party to bind itself (Schelling 1960). Self binding is closely related to the credibility of threat which depends on how visible to the threatened party is the inability of the threatening party to rationalise its way into, or out of, its commitment. Most studies (Schelling 1960; Bacharach and Lawler 1981; Laver and Schofield 1990: 178) associate the ability of a party to commit itself to co-operative relationships with pivotal position, general *Koalitionsfähigkeit* and ideological closeness/distance to presumptive coalition partners. This treatment – commonly viewed as external bargaining power – explores part of the complex concept. The model developed here, however, focuses on internal bargaining power when internal conflicts emerge. It associates the ability of the party to commit itself to co-operative relationships with organisational attributes.

From an intraparty point of view, the credibility of a party's threats and proposals are significantly affected by the ability of its elites to establish and maintain control over the party.[3] In the parliamentary arena, both voice and exit are costly in terms of a party's bargaining power. The cost of devoting even a modicum of elites' time and resources to resolve internal conflict may undermine their bargaining power in the parliamentary arena. As parties can only estimate the resources and commitments of their opponents, perceptions are a crucial factor in such processes (Bacharach and Lawler 1981). Elites' perception of credibility of threats can therefore provide a relatively accurate picture of intra- and interparty dynamics. For operational purposes, therefore, *bargaining power* will be defined as the power of a party to commit itself to parliamentary co-operation over its 'decisive preference' (Luebbert 1986).

Figure 1.1 indicates that the fundamental relationships being considered here are those pertaining to a party's leadership, linkages between the leadership and the party base, and the effect of these considerations on coalition bargaining and the process of government formation. *A party is considered to be a political system* (Katz and Mair 1995). Members of the parliamentary group and its extra-parliamentary wings thrive on the hope of winning, and the desire to influence party policy and strategy. Different coalitions of forces are formed within the party and actors striving for dominance interact with each other in the struggle for relative influence within the organisation. Internal relationships, however, are not only a matter of democracy, but also a matter of manageability. Party elites attempt to establish conformity, whether a highly generalised decision to conform automatically, a disposition to support the party and its leadership 'in general', or an adherence to the elites' position on a particular piece of legislation (Barber 1960).[4] A failure of party elites to achieve such a conformity seems likely to impact coalition bargaining and the process of government formation. This evaluation is based on the assumption that party elites are motivated, above all, by the desire to remain party leaders (Luebbert 1986). In other words, for party leaders who are in office, it is more important to remain party leaders than to remain in office. If intraparty conflicts threaten their position, rather than stay

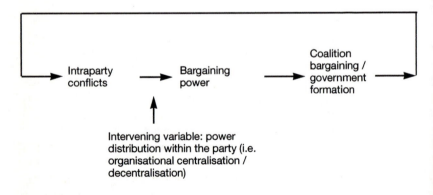

Figure 1.1 Coalition bargaining and the process of government formation

in government they will leave office in order to remain party leaders. Party leaders, in short, will emphasise central features of party policy so as to minimise dissent within various sections of the party, and secure their position.

Recognising this, one would expect those which operate within a decentralised party to be able to express their dissatisfaction within the party, whether through individual, or collective petition to the party elites with the intention of forcing a strategy change, or through various types of actions and protests. Those operating within a centralised party – where the organisation imposes itself upon the actors and limits their margins of manoeuvrability – seem more likely to express their dissatisfaction outside the party. In such cases, the exit and the voice (outside the party) options are the only ways in which dissatisfied members can react. Their decision whether to exit or express dissatisfaction within or outside the party is dependent, among other variables, on the way power and the instruments of control are distributed within the party leadership. Thus, centralisation/decentralisation becomes an intervening variable in the relationship between intraparty conflicts and bargaining power.

A paradox and derived hypotheses

Few scholars have considered the nature of the structural context in which party elites operate as a variable in coalition bargaining. Sven Groennings (1968) has argued that, when internal disputes occur:

> *the more centralised the party structure, the easier it is for the party to remain in the coalition.* The *a priori* hypothesis that a party weakened by factional dispute will find it difficult to formulate a coalition policy leads quickly to the hypothesis that the greater the organised dissensus within a party, the lesser is the tendency to coalesce, even if the dissensus has nothing to do with coalition policy. It should be noted, furthermore, that it is easier for a party with loose central control to coalesce with another party of the same character than one with tight discipline, because *a highly centralised party can present a threat to a loosely structured party.*
>
> (Groennings 1968: 454; my emphasis)

A similar conclusion has been reached by Angelo Panebianco (1988: 219), namely that:

1 a strongly institutionalised party can defend its stability better than a weakly institutionalised party; and

2 an alliance among parties inevitably destabilise the less institutionalised organisations.

These arguments raise two problems related to the excessive rigidity
of strongly organised parties in so far as policy-making and the ability
to diffuse internal dissent is concerned. For the former, in contrast to
weakly organised parties where internal actors have more autonomy in
order to compete with each other and competing subgroups are
assured autonomous control over their followers and resources,
strongly organised parties are characterised by excessive rigidity as
they drastically limit their internal actors' margins of manoeuvrability.
Once internal conflict emerges – which in itself is an indication of the
political importance of the issue at stake – leaders of strongly organised parties may face severe organisational strains compared to those
faced by leaders of parties which do not impose themselves upon party
sub-groups. For the ability to diffuse internal dissatisfaction, whereas
weakly organised parties are characterised by the availability of organisational mechanisms through which internal dissatisfaction can be
pacified and neutralised (e.g. factions, factional activities, dissensions
in parliament and so on), strongly organised parties are characterised
by excessive rigidity as they lack mechanisms for the diffusion of
dissent. Consequently, internal dissatisfaction – which in some cases
may be politically important and not easily suppressed – can be only
expressed outside the party (e.g. resignations of elite members and
demonstrations of party activists and militants).

Students of politics can posit therefore a logical problem in
Panebianco and Groennings' arguments: why are centralised parties
considered to be effective coalitional actors if they are prone to severe
organisational strains once internal conflict emerges and lack structural mechanisms for the diffusion of dissent? When interparty
negotiations induce internal conflicts, members may be forced to leave
the party or air their views outside the party as their primary mechanisms for expression of dissent. From the elites' point of view, once
dissatisfaction is mobilised outside the internal network, it cannot be
effectively monitored. The inability of such elites to pacify internal
opposition is likely to be translated into an inferior position in the
parliamentary bargaining arena. This, in turn, may contribute to the
termination of the coalition bargaining and the process of government
formation. Moreover, in cases of followers' hostility which is manifested by violent demonstrations, a rigid organisation can lead to party
disintegration when such a party enters serious coalition negotiations.

As noted earlier, the mechanisms for the diffusion of dissent allow a decentralised organisation to handle internal opposition in a variety of flexible ways without forcing members to leave the party. Such a party can enter into conflict – inducing coalition negotiations with other parties without risking its hold on its own elite and party members.[5] The traditional view of intraparty determinants of coalition bargaining, therefore, raises a paradox. *Everything else being equal, when intraparty conflicts occur, the strength of a party in the parliamentary bargaining arena (i.e. its relative bargaining power) lies in its organisational decentralisation.* 'Everything else being equal' refers, for instance, to the degree (amount) of internal conflicts, the behaviour of other parties, etc. 'The strength of the party' refers to its bargaining power over the decisive preference underlying the alliance or the preference underlying its actual strategy. If these two differ, the latter is paramount to our evaluation of a party's bargaining power.

In describing this interplay between the intra- and interparty environments, the intent is not to depreciate the nature of the conflict itself. On the contrary, precisely because political parties can be seen as actually divided into competing sub-groups (Duverger 1964), the nature of intraparty conflict retains a fundamental role in the ability of the party leadership (i.e. cabinet members and party leader) to cope with internal conflict. Party leaders differ in the extent to which they control parliamentary group members and party members. A substantial reason for this lies in the fact that rank and file members tend to be less divided – thus more susceptible to 'interest articulation' – than their leaders (McClosky *et al.* 1960). To understand why rank and file are less divided, it is important to appreciate that leaders often come from the more articulated segments of society and, on average, are politically more aware than their followers and far better informed about issues; differences in the degree of partisan involvement parallel the differences in knowledge and have similar consequences; the nature (selective versus non-selective) and size of the two types of groups differ remarkably; and, finally, the degree to which each group is exposed to political competition impacts the pressures exerted upon members to distinguish themselves from each other (McClosky *et al.* 1960).

From the leaders' point of view, such a division implies that members of the parliamentary group may respond much more constructively (in terms of conformity) to 'selective incentives' than to 'collective incentives' (Olson 1965). Rank-and-file members, on the other hand, may respond much more constructively to 'collective incentives'. The fact that members of parliament are interested primarily in 'selective incentives' emphasises their dependency on the top leadership (Panebianco 1988: 27). This, in turn, may enhance the elites' ability to control the behaviour of MPs. Less influence can be exerted on party members as they are primarily interested in 'collective incentives' (Panebianco 1988: 26). It is therefore reasonable to assume that the ability of the party leaders to cope with dissenting behaviour of the parliamentary group members is likely to be greater than their ability to cope with hostility of party activists. Given the above-mentioned paradox, one could hypothesise that this tendency will mostly be manifested in a centralised context.

The above discussion gives rise to the following set of hypotheses:

1 Conflicts within a decentralised party are most likely to be manifested by 'voices' within the parliamentary and party arenas whereas conflicts within a centralised party are most likely to be manifested by 'exit' or 'voices' outside these arenas.

2 Elites within a decentralised party are most likely to emphasise 'decisive preferences' during coalition life-span and tolerate factional activities and the formation of new factions in an attempt to pacify internal opposition. Elites within a centralised party which face intra-elite conflicts are most likely to emphasise 'decisive preferences', and impose structural constraints on the day-to-day operation of the government coalition or the party. Elites within a centralised party which face elite-follower conflicts are most likely to emphasise 'decisive preferences', initiate 'articulation of ends' and impose a transition period before a formal alliance is concluded.

3 A decentralised party is more likely than a centralised one to resolve conflicts successfully. When intraparty conflicts occur, a decentralised party is most likely to sustain its bargaining power over its decisive preference and, thus, to maintain its coalition strategy. A centralised party which faces internal conflicts is most likely to face a decline in its bargaining power over its decisive preference, leading to the break-up of the coalition bargaining and the process of government formation.

The preceding discussion – during which the reasoning underlying the above hypotheses was explored – has been pursued at a rather high level of abstraction. In the remainder of the book the theoretical argument will be illustrated by analysing nine case studies along three themes:

1 modes of conflict manifestation;
2 modes of conflict resolution, and

3 modes of coalition bargaining following successful and unsuccessful resolution of intraparty conflicts.

The cases include the following:

1 three decentralised parties which faced intra-elite conflicts, namely the Italian Christian Democrats (DC) during 1976–79, the French Socialist Party (PS) during 1988–90 and the British Labour Party during 1977–78;
2 one decentralised party which faced elite-follower conflict, namely the British Liberal Party during 1977–78;
3 three centralised parties which faced intra-elite conflicts, namely the Danish Social Democratic Party (SD) during 1977–78 and the Radical Liberals (RV) during 1988–90, and the Norwegian Centre Party (SP) during 1989–90; and
4 two centralised parties which faced elite-follower conflict, namely the Italian Community Party (PCI) during 1976–79 and the French Communist Party (PCF) during 1988–90.

Attention now turns to the methodological considerations underlying the analysis.

METHODOLOGICAL CONSIDERATIONS

The fundamental methodological premise of this inquiry is that the best way to study intraparty processes and legislative behaviour and to probe the formal and informal nuances of these aspects is to talk with party elites systematically and listen carefully (Putnam 1973; Aberbach *et al.* 1981). During 1989–91, 143 members of party parliamentary elites in France, Italy, the UK, Denmark and Norway were interviewed in open interviews lasting somewhat more than half an hour each (see Appendix 1.1).

The decision to use open-ended, unstructured interviews was taken because this research instrument has the virtue of greater response validity (Verba 1971: 321). The interviews were recorded and all the interviewees were told at the beginning that the interviews would be attributional. At the end of each interview, an informal unrecorded discussion was conducted in order to elicit sensitive data concerning intraparty power struggles and conflicts. In order to increase the reliability of the data gathered during the interview, a twofold strategy was implemented. First, any interviewee's perception of intraparty conflict was confirmed by at least another elite member. Second, attitudes of at least three elite members concerning aspects of coalitional behaviour were taken to signify the party's view on this matter.

The politicians were chosen according to three criteria:

1 formal position in the party hierarchy during the period under examination;
2 evaluation of local academics about the relevancy of the politician during the period under examination; and
3 recommendations by politicians.

Thus, the sampling net was targeted to interview politicians at the top of government and party hierarchy, such as prime ministers, ministers, party leaders and the leaders of parliamentary groups.

Naturally, the actual value of elite interviewing depends on whether they offer a central or secondary means of fulfilling a research project, and this depends not only on the kind of problems being examined, but also on the availability and quality of alternative sources. This general remark applies particularly to political parties in liberal democracies as a field of study. Since parties are relatively open institutions they are usually reported on in detail in the press and their own documentation may be reasonably available to researchers. Given the need of controlling for memory or political bias or situational problems in interviews, secondary sources, such as official statistics and newspapers, provide a useful basis for corroborating interview material.

As already noted, all cases involve party competition during minority situations (that is, when the governmental parties control less than half of all seats in the national legislature) as it is assumed that intraparty conflicts are most likely to occur under these circumstances, due to the complexity of the bargaining system and the probable need to co-operate with non-traditional partners. Recognising there are many variables which differentiate party systems, the decision to focus on party competition during minority situations requires the adoption of variables which were found to be helpful in explaining minority government formation.

The variables which explain the calculi leading to minority government formation were found to be two structural features of political systems, namely, the potential influence of the parliamentary opposition and the decisiveness of elections (Strøm 1990b). Oppositional influence 'which measures the benefits of governing (or, more precisely, the policy costs of being in opposition), represents the opportunities for legislative influence open to parliamentary opposition' (Strøm 1990b: 70). The decisiveness of elections 'taps the costs of governing in future elections' (Strøm 1990b: 72). According to Strøm (1990b: 74), 'as electoral decisiveness and oppositional influence increase, the parliamentary bases of the governments formed should diminish, and the likelihood of minority government formation increase'.

To differentiate between party systems I use Strøm's indexes of the above-mentioned variables. A five-dimension index which represents the potential for opposition influence aggregates the following indicators: the number of standing committees, areas of specialisation, correspondence to ministerial departments, number of committee assignments and the way committee chairs are distributed among parliamentary parties. The index which represents the decisiveness of elections for government formation aggregates the following four indicators: the identifiability of viable government alternatives, electoral volatility, electoral responsiveness and proximity. Five party systems, namely, Denmark, Norway, Italy, France and the UK, were found to be 'different' with respect to Strom's explanatory variables. On a 1 to 5 scale of oppositional influence, Norway scored 5, Italy and France 4, Denmark 3 and the UK 1 (Strøm 1990b: 73). On electoral salience – a measure combining two components of electoral decisiveness, UK scored the highest, France and Italy scored the lowest, and Denmark and Norway scored in between (Strøm 1990b: 75). The parties under investigation were thus selected from party systems which feature different structural characteristics in so far as minority government formation is concerned.

Having reduced the sample of minority governments under study to those operating within five different political systems enables a greater measure of analytical depth. The particular combination of Denmark, Norway, Italy, France, and the UK, furthermore, recommends itself for three reasons. First, it captures a possibly extreme leap in patterns of intra- and interparty politics found within the European context in moving, for example, from the Mediterranean to the Scandinavian arena. Second, precisely because some cases represent numerous examples of formal and informal minority governments, whereas other do not. Third, the fact that most countries chosen have illustrated both short- and long-lived minority governments, enhances the validity of any generalisation.

A comparative study like the present one obviously runs risks because methodological difficulties rise geometrically with the number of countries studied. These difficulties alert us to the need for constant sensitivity to the genuine peculiarities of each country. But if we are to understand the full complexity of intraparty conflicts and their impact on coalition behaviour, the benefits of explicit cross-national comparison far outweigh the perils.

2 The intraparty and constitutional contexts

This chapter examines the intraparty and constitutional contexts of the cases under investigation. The first section provides a classification of parties into 'centralised' and 'decentralised' organisations. Parties are classified according to the distribution of effective decision-making authority within the party over seven dimensions, namely policy development, execution of party line, candidate selection, leadership selection, funding allocation, party press, and discipline (including expulsion).[1] The criteria for this classification is the number of individuals who play a role in political processes over these dimensions because these privileged individuals are in a position to influence priorities for the attainment of party goals. The more restricted the organisational privilege to participate in a given process, the more highly centralised is the party.

A centralised party is therefore one which features the concentration of effective decision-making authority in the national party organs over a given dimension, with a premium placed on the smaller number of individuals participating in the decision. Put differently, the more individuals are allocated powers over a given dimension the more decentralised is the party over this dimension. The more dimensions the parties is found to be decentralised over (i.e. compared to other parties), the more decentralised it is.

The second section describes the institutional context in Denmark, Norway, the UK, Italy and France during the period under investigation. The rules of the government formation game 'create variations in the logic of coalition bargaining in parliamentary democracies' (Bergman 1993: 62). In addition, they encompass important considerations influencing the decision to initiate intraparty conflicts, the timing of conflicts, and the strategies employed by party elites to deal with them. This description may appear somewhat exhausted, yet it is crucial for the understanding of the behaviour of both intraparty actors as well as the parties themselves.

POWER DISTRIBUTION WITHIN PARTIES

The relatively high degree of centralisation of the French and Italian Communist Parties during the period under investigation is well recorded (for PCI see: Poggi 1968; Galli 1976; Bardi and Morlino 1994; for PCF, see: Bell and Criddle 1988). Indicative of the centralisation of these parties are four features. First, the principle of democratic centralism dictates the structure and the behaviour of both parties. Second, the absolute dominance of the PCF's Secretary General and the PCI's top executive bodies in the vertical organisation of the party is reflected in the horizontal relationship with the parliamentary party; the group in parliament remains in a subordinate position with respect to the extra-parliamentary party. Third, the mechanism of appointment in both parties is co-option from the leadership; posts of responsibility within these parties are allocated by the leadership with the central party hierarchy imposing candidates of its own. Fourth, any activity aiming at the formation of autonomous factions within the party is strictly forbidden and actively suppressed.

The Danish Social Democratic Party, the Radical Liberals and the Norwegian Centre Party are less centralised than the Italian and French communist parties for, among other reasons, they do not manifest features of democratic centralism, their top office-holders are elected by the national congress rather than by a central committee, and candidate selection is undertaken by constituencies and regional organisations. Furthermore, these parties' statutes stipulate that party congress is the highest authority in all matters. This stipulation however exists mainly on paper; effective decision-making authority in the national party organs of the Danish Social Democratic Party, the Radical Liberals, and the Norwegian Centre Party is concentrated around a relatively small number of individuals participating in decisions.

In the Danish Social Democratic Party, the leading party body in all organisational and policy matters is the national executive (*Forretningudvalg*) which has fourteen members including the party's top national officers: the chairman of the parliamentary group, representatives from associated organisations as well as six other representatives from the national board. Meeting twice a month, this party organ can expel members and must confirm all expulsions. It recommends the forty-nine members of the National Committee (*Hovedbestyrelsen*) candidates for the posts of chief treasurer, party secretary, one or more secretaries and five accountants. Although members of the National Committee may attend all meetings in the party they have no right to vote (Bille 1992, 1994).

The Radical Liberals share many similar features with the Social Democrats, such as a formal separation of the membership party and the parliamentary party, a position of primacy which the parliamentary parties have always enjoyed, and the fact that the real political leadership has always rested with the strong position of party leaders. The latter argument is valid even though, in the RV case, the two leadership posts of chairman of the national party organisation and party leader are held by different persons. Regarding policy development and the execution of party line, power in the Radical Liberals has always been concentrated with the parliamentary party. Furthermore the party's parliamentary group chooses its own chairman, who is normally the political leader of the party (unless its political leader is a government minister), and it is also given great freedom of manoeuvre by the national party organisation which cannot bind its decisions in any way. National politics has thus always been carried out by the parliamentary party without any significant interference from the national party organisation (Bille 1994: 149–50).

In the Norwegian Centre Party effective decision-making authority lies with two organs: The *Sentralstyret* and the *Landsstyret*. The former is composed of twelve members, namely, the party chairman and two vice-chairmen, the national studies leader and the leaders of the youth and women's organisations and six other members. As the party's top office-holders, this organ implements party policy. The *Landsstyret* is the highest party organ between Congresses with a responsibility to discuss the *Sentralstyret*'s reports and adopt party accounts. It consists of forty-three members of which twelve are members of *Sentralstyret* and nineteen are leaders of the county organisations. Although the biannual national congress elects the party's top office-holders and its central executives, it is the *Sentralstyret* which determines the agenda; proposals must be submitted to this organ at least two months in advance (Svåsand 1992, 1994). Effective decision-making over policy development and implementation is therefore undertaken by a rather small number of individuals, although it is important to note that some large national party organs – among which is the *Landsstyret* – reserve the right to discuss policies and proposals set by the *Sentralstyret*.

In decentralised parties effective decision-making is diffused among a relatively large number of individuals. The Italian Christian Democratic Party, for example, is a weakly institutionalised party

(Bardi and Morlino 1994). Parliamentary groups in the Senate and the Chamber of Deputies are relatively autonomous and factions, undercutting the power of the party secretary, direct much of the party energies into internal coalition building between faction leaders. These characteristics were reinforced after 1964 following the adoption of proportional representation in election to the *Consiglio Nazionale* (Bardi and Morlino 1992: Table VIII.D.2.f.i) which completed the process by which factions had become institutionalised (Leonardi and Wertman 1989: 109). This change in rules has resulted in the growing importance of provincial federations in determining parliamentary nominations which, in turn, contributed to the strengthening of the autonomy of the parliamentary groups. Following the 1976 elections, the DC parliamentary groups became even more autonomous as, for example, could be seen in the strong opposition in early 1970 to the Secretariat's strategy of favouring a formal alliance with the PCI.

The presence and dynamics between the different factions also explains the failure of party leaders to implement organisational reforms which would significantly change the party structure. As Bardi and Morlino (1994) note:

> At least formally, the DC organisational structures had been considerably strengthened during the 1970s and early 1980s, even though factionalism and patronage never ceased to play a role, thus rendering the formal organisation itself of little value in any attempt at centralisation.
>
> (Bardi and Morlino 1994: 255)

Put differently, no significant change in the formal power structure at the leadership level had been recorded in the mid-1970s.

A similar power structure at the leadership level is evident in the French Socialist Party. Since its creation at *Epinay*, where the various political clubs (such as the CIR of François Mitterrand and the UGCS of Jean Poperen) joined with the other components of the old SFIO, the PS has been organised in such a way that decentralisation of party structure has been its main features. The party's top leadership consists of a Directing Committee (*comité directeur*) and an Executive Committee (*comité exécutif*), which are both elected by the national congress, along with the party's first secretary. The party secretariat, its real organisational arm, is elected by the Executive Committee.

The presence and dynamics of 'tendencies' undercut the power of top office holders in the party. Despite a rule which actually forbids organised tendencies, the PS is one of the few parties in the world where different tendencies have a recognised, indeed institutionalised, place. According to Cole (1989a,b), throughout the 1970s there have been four major factions: Mitterrand, Mauroy, CERES, and, after October 1974, Rocard. The first two represent intraparty groups whose main strength lies within some aspect of the party organisation. The latter two, in contrast, refer to those groups which maintain a high level of independent factional organisation, in parallel to the party's official structure.[2] In the Directing Committee which controls the party and determines policy between congresses; the membership of 131 reflects the proportion of votes cast for each 'tendency'. For the Executive Committee, its membership of twenty-seven and thirteen substitutes is proportional to the size of each tendency. As in the DC, the autonomy of the parliamentary group is a prominent feature of the party; the Directing Committee meets the parliamentary group to secure its compliance with party policy (Bell and Criddle 1988; Frears 1991).

The British Liberal Party 'prides itself not only on its commitment to a decentralisation of government from Westminster and Whitehall but also on decentralisation in the party . . . This belief is reflected in the . . . party structure which is decentralised, democratically representative, and limits the powers of central committees' (Kavanagh 1983: 129). Indications to this belief is the election of the party leader directly by rank-and-file individual members and the selection of party candidates by constituencies with little effective central control due to a lack of applicants. Although the Party has a list of 'approved' candidates there is no requirement that the adoption should be confirmed. Regarding the locus of power, the party's top organs are the National Executive Committee which comprises of around 50–60 members responsible for directing the work of the party in matters other than policy. Party finance and administration is conducted by the Finance and Administration Board which has eight members. Policy is decided, according to the party constitution, by the Assembly but decisions are not binding on Liberal MPs. The Standing Committee, which comprises thirty-five members, oversees the development of party policy and, subject to the party leader's responsibility, prepares the manifesto. Added to the fragmented and cumbersome structure there is an independent Scottish Liberal Party, as well as twelve English Regional and the National Ulster and Welsh parties. The autonomy of these smaller national parties emphasises the decentralised nature of the Party.

Any discussion on the Liberal Party structure has to take into account the distinction between formal and informal organisation. As Kavanagh notes:

How the party works depends in part on the nature of the issues, personalities, and circumstances at any one time. But there is a recognisable leadership group, consisting of people who sit on various central bodies and others who have status but not office in the party. Many of them have been near the centre of the party's affairs for twenty years or so and are well known to one another. Their ability to keep in touch offsets the tendency to inertia induced by the plurality of bodies, checks and balances, and passion for consultation found in the party.

(Kavanagh 1983: 128–9)

For this reason, the *ad hoc* nature of political processes in the party may in some circumstances overshadow administrative procedures and structures provided by the party statutes. Thus, powers over organisational and policy matters shift between the recognisable leadership group and the national party organs depending on the issue at stake.

The British Labour Party has also manifested features of decentralised effective decision-making authority during the period under investigation. Although (prior to 1981) the Labour leader and deputy leader were selected by the parliamentary party, two limitations were faced by the parliamentary leadership. First, the party constitution avers the sovereignty of the party conference and legitimises the role of individual members to play a role in determining party policy. Second, the NEC has the responsibility for developing party policy between annual conferences and supervising the whole party organisation outside Parliament. The General Secretary, and other senior members of the party bureaucracy, are appointed by, and are answerable to, the NEC and not to the party leader. Under the Secretary, the party organisation is divided into various departments (e.g. press, finance and research) which are supervised by sub-committees of the NEC (Punnett 1994). In addition, seven out of the twenty-nine NEC places are reserved for representatives of the local party membership who are directly elected by the Constituency Labour Party delegates to annual conference. This power is used primarily to elect prominent members of the parliamentary party.

The presence of these two real limitations meant that, over the period observed, the party elite had needed to sustain a working relationship with certain key union leaders in order to dominate a consistent majority in the conference. Consequently, effective decision-making authority has generally been one of domination by 'a loose coalition of major union leaderships and parliamentary elites' (Webb 1994). Coalitions of parliamentary and trade union leaders have dominated the party, and even when delegates of the individual membership have succeeded in getting conference to adopt policies disapproved of by the leadership, the latter has been inclined to overlook such policies when drafting election manifestos (Hatfield 1978; Kogan and Kogan 1982).

To sum up, two party groups are depicted. The Italian and French Communist Parties, the Danish Social Democratic Party and the Radical Liberals, and the Norwegian Centre Party manifest features characteristic of centralised organisation. The Italian Christian Democratic Party, the British Labour and Liberal Parties and the French Socialist Party manifest features characteristic of decentralised organisation. The former group is furthermore divided into two subgroups: the French and Italian Communist Parties manifest a relatively high level of centralisation of power, whereas the Danish Social Democratic Party, Radical Liberals, and the Norwegian Centre Party manifest a lower level of centralisation of power compared to the former sub-group.

THE PARLIAMENTARY CONTEXT

Coalition theories have paid 'too little attention to the constitutional link between legislature and executive in European parliamentary systems' (Budge and Laver 1986: 488). This is very surprising because intra- and interparty considerations of party elites have no definitive meaning as a guide to action because their concrete meaning is always relative to the constitutional context within which party elites operate. The way in which winning is defined by the rules of the government formation game, for example, creates variations in the logic of coalition bargaining in parliamentary democracies (Bergman 1993). This implies that coalitions can be winning even if they do not control more than half of the legislators. To avoid a discrepancy between the model developed here and the empirical record of decentralised and centralised parties in dealing with intraparty conflicts, attention now turns to the institutional context in Denmark, Norway, the UK, Italy and France during the period under investigation.

Denmark

Danish politics, from the 1970s onwards, grew out of a major realignment which was manifested nationwide in the 1973 elections. It must be conceded, however, that from the 1920s the wider political system was characterised by stability in terms of voter support, legislative policy-making, a high predictability of cabinet formations, and governments in office for fairly long periods. A partial explanation for the unique long-term stability can be derived from the description of the Danish political system as a 'consensus system' (Damgaard 1974), which facilitated the development of a 'working multiparty system' (Rostow 1956), within a 'homogeneous and secularised' political culture (Almond and Verba 1963).

From its beginning, the parliamentary party system contained a core of four 'old' parties, namely the Social Democrats, the Radical Liberals, the Agrarian Liberals and the Conservatives, which could trace their history back to the nineteenth century. Additionally, a small and changing number of other parties, such as the Communist and the Justice party, were represented in the *Folketing* from 1932 to 1960, and from 1926 to 1960, respectively. Following World War Two, the four parties commanded almost 90 per cent of the seats, dominating the *Folketing*.

Before going any further, it is appropriate to clarify the factors that contributed to the defeat of five incumbent parties in the 1972 election. Among the most frequently cited long-term factors of change was the rapid shift to a 'service society' (Pedersen 1988: 265). This process bore a direct impact on the relationships among voters, social classes and parties, towards deteriorating bonds between the voter and the party 'in a way the old parties are suspended in the air, representing something which no longer exists' (Bendix 1974: 19). Equally important, are a number of relatively shorter-term factors operating in Danish politics during the late 1960s and early 1970s, such as tax reform, municipal reform, the liberalisation of pornography and abortion rights. These reforms met with heavy criticism from many sectors of the population, thus increasing polarisation among the parties in parliament and among voters and politicians. The defection of Erhard Jakobsen, the right-wing Social Democrat, led the Prime Minister to dissolve the *Folketing*, and the defector to form the Centre Democrats. Additionally, the formation of the Progress Party by Mogens Glistrup raised the need for change while intensifying the wave of political protest.

Yet, even among the parties riding the wave of political protest and social unrest in the 1972 election, few old-timers – the Communist and the Justice Parties – had succeeded in entering into the party system due to their principled and unrelenting opposition to European integration and to Denmark joining the EC. Beside the new Christian People's Party which was formed with the main purpose of objecting to 'moral decay and cultural nihilism' (Andersen 1975: 31), two new parties entered parliament representing a new party type. The Centre Democrats cast itself as a new party without a traditional programme, aimed mainly at defending private property without rejecting the basic principles of the welfare state and giving more emphasis to cultural issues. The Progress Party positioned itself as a popular movement operating against the 'old' parties.

The major realignment, however, did not preclude the formation of subsequent minority governments in the Danish polity. Understanding Danish post-war politics requires an explanation for the frequent occurrence of minority governments. Only three of 27 governments during 1945–91 have not been minority cabinets (Elklit 1991: 3). A partial explanation can be found in the Danish Constitution in which government formation rules are of a negative form (Bergman 1993). The underlying principle of this form is that a government must only be tolerated by the parliament. A government is formally appointed by the Head of State and, 'instead of requiring a positive vote of confidence from the legislature, can maintain itself in power so long as there is no vote of censure passed against it' (Bogdanor 1984: 55).

Indeed the Danish constitution does not elaborate much on the process of government formation. In a parliament as fragmented as the *Folketing* this leaves ample room for manoeuvre. Consequently, a gradual development of informal rules have filled the vacuum left by the Constitution. Six such rules have been summarised by Erik Damgaard (1990) on the basis of Tage Kaarsted's (1988) work:

1 If uncertainty about the appointment of a new government arises, the parties will have to give their advice to the Crown;
2 If this advice unambiguously points towards a majority government or a minority government supported by a majority, the Crown has to follow this advice;
3 If no majority can be found, the most viable minority must be found;
4 The interpretation of the advice of the parties is the responsibility of the acting Prime Minister, not of the Crown;
5 During the opening phases of the process, an *informateur* might be appointed;
6 The advice given by the parties is not subject to specific rules or norms as regards their framing or their wording.

For the frequency of minority government, Strøm (1990b) suggests that three factors – namely, strongly organised and future-oriented parties, decentralised and relatively non-hierarchical parliaments where opposition parties can be influential, and highly competitive elections – account for the predominance of the minority type by inducing political parties to 'defer the gratification of holding office'.

On the relationship between the legislative process and the willingness of members of parliament to follow the party line in votes in parliament, in the Danish case, as in other Scandinavian political systems, legislation is generally initiated by the presentation of the report of a royal commission representing all interested sections of opinion. It is then tendered for comment to the relevant interest groups, and is decided on by the deliberations of a parliamentary committee, whose major aim is to produce proposals which can be unanimously agreed by the plenary body (Castles 1978: 30). Differences of opinions and power struggles which occur within the parties are usually settled in party group meetings. Decisions are considered binding upon all the members of parliament of the party and non-compliance in important matters is met with sanctions (Damgaard 1973; Svensson 1982; Damgaard and Svensson 1989: 734). Not surprisingly, parties are disciplined in their legislative voting behaviour and function as relatively cohesive actors in final divisions.

In the mid-1970s, Denmark faced very serious economic problems which were triggered off by the first oil price increases during October–December 1973. In addition, following the 1975 general elections, political difficulties were created as the Danish political parties had to face a minority situation. Whereas the Liberal Party almost doubled its representation in the *Folketing*, the loss of support experienced by the RV, CPP and CD, together with the increase in the seats of the SD had the effect of perpetuating the pre-election absence of a majority for either of the two traditional blocs of the Danish spectrum (see Appendices 2.1 and 2.2). Following the subsequent resignation of the Liberals' minority government led by Poul Hartling, the parties had to confront another minority situation. This parliamentary situation provides the starting point for the analysis of the manifestation and resolution of conflicts within the SD during 1978–79.

Norway

Norway has a multiparty system where most parties are strongly linked to distinct social groups (Rokkan 1970; Powell 1982). Although it is a unitary state the political system is relatively decentralised (Eckstein 1966; Valen and Katz 1964). The system consists of seven parties which are, from left to right: the Socialist Left Party (SV), the Labour Party (DNA), the Liberals (V), the Christian People's Party (KrF), the Centre Party (SP), the Conservative Party (CP), and the

Progress Party (FrP). Whereas the oldest parties are the Liberals, the Conservatives and the Labour Party, which were formed in the 1880s, all the other parties emerged in the twentieth century.

Electorally, there have been a number of major changes during the post-war period. Whereas during 1945–61 the Labour Party enjoyed a predominant position in the Norwegian polity, it did not gain a parliamentary majority during 1961–73 because of the erosion of support on its left (by the emergence of the Socialist People's Party), and on its right (by the strengthening of the non-socialist parties). The Labour Party, for example, obtained around 47 per cent of popular support during the 1961–69 elections, but its share declined to around 35 per cent in the 1973 election. The SP and KrF, on the other hand, increased their share of the popular vote from around 10 per cent and 8 per cent, in 1965, to around 11 per cent and 12 per cent in 1973, respectively. The Socialist Left, moreover, gained around 11 per cent of popular support in the 1973 election (see Appendices 2.3 and 2.4).

It was, however, the EC referendum in 1972 which was the catalyst for the 'political earthquake' which manifested itself by short-term swings of popular support and long-term party system changes. The debacle, sustained in the 1972 referendum by those who advocated EC membership, was further reflected in the 1973 election when the DNA's strength was reduced from around 47 per cent in 1969 to 35 per cent. The DNA regained this ground in 1977 but that election also saw the CP gathering strength within the non-socialist bloc, from around 17 per cent of popular support to 25 per cent (see Appendix 2.3). Evidence of long-term party system changes were seen by increased fragmentation, volatility and polarisation (Heidar 1988). The starting point of the analysis is characterised therefore by the substantial weakening of the DNA, the growth of the extreme left and right, the Conservatives' resurgence and the atrophy of the non-socialist centre (Valen 1981; Kuhnle *et al.* 1986).

Among the most frequently cited factors which contributed to changes in the Norwegian party system is the country's cleavage structure. Six social cleavages, which are only partly cross-cut, have been identified as significant bases for the modern Norwegian party system (Urwin 1987; Valen and Rokkan 1974): first, a territorial cleavage between the centre and the periphery (Aarebrot 1982); second, a socio–cultural cleavage between the defenders of the two different versions of the Norwegian language; third, a moral cleavage that primarily concerns the production and consumption of alcohol; fourth, a religious cleavage between fundamentalist groups on the one hand and more liberal or secular groups on the other; fifth, a sectoral cleavage between the primary sector of the economy (agriculture and fisheries) and other industries, and finally, a class cleavage between unionised workers and private employers.

From the beginning, these cleavages have been politicised successively and formed a cumulative pattern of party conflict. However, there have been a number of major changes during the post-war period. Of the old cleavages, the language and cultural divisions have lost their importance as determinants of political preference. Additionally, the political individuality of the Southern and Western Norwegian periphery has become less distinct, although it still manifests itself by overall preference for the centre-right parties. Moreover, whereas the area around Oslo has shown a marked evolution to the right, the inner east of the North have retained a strong preference for the left (Jacobs 1989).

It is however misleading to exaggerate the saliency of the old divisions. Norway, in some respects, is a rather homogeneous country. Consensus orientation is reflected in the political and the public spheres (Olsen 1983). Indeed, the lack of wide policy differences between the main political parties on such key issues as the maintenance of the welfare state, foreign policy and Norway's membership in NATO, emphasises that interparty differences tended to be more over means than ends. Yet, the assertion of Lægreid and Olsen (1986) that 'there is a striking contrast between this willingness to co-operate within the *Storting* and the unwillingness to make co-operation formal to signal it to the environment', raises a central question regarding the scarcity of formal coalitions at cabinet level.

In fact, more than two-thirds of all Norwegian cabinets (during 1907–87) have been undersized. Of the thirty-nine cabinets formed in minority situations, thirty-two have been one-party minority governments, more than 82 per cent (Strøm 1990b). Whereas Strøm argues that the frequency of minority government in Scandinavia can be explained as a rational response to a peculiar set of institutional conditions, Bo Särlvik (1983) lays much stress on the impact of 'two-bloc' politics in creating a situation, analogous in some ways to two-party politics, which provides a considerable inducement for the parties not to split. In other words, it pits a governmental bloc with one set of incentives against an informal oppositional bloc with another, all of which are unlikely to change during an inter-election period. Two-bloc competition is, furthermore, a major factor in explaining the limited permutations of government formation. First, the Labour Party has eschewed coalition not only with non-socialist parties but also with any of the smaller parties to its left. Second, the non-socialist governments have tended to be coalitions (Strøm 1990b).

Undoubtedly, the Norwegian electoral system is a critical factor in the maintenance of 'two-bloc' politics. Since elections are by the *Saint Laguë* system of proportional representation, the overall effect of the Norwegian electoral system is not strictly proportional. According to Rokkan (1968), the electoral formula had a three-fold effect: it strengthened the middle-sized non-socialist parties by reducing the overall representation of the Social Democrats, it reduced the pay-offs of mergers within the opposition and, finally, it helped the established parties by discouraging the formation of splinter groups and new parties. Moreover, the fact that the *Storting* has a fixed election term of four years, combined with the existence of constituencies with few members, have been generally disadvantageous for the smaller parties.

Regarding party behaviour in parliament, Strøm (1990b) emphasises the 'high degree of control' that leaders exercise over their parties and Fitzmaurice (1986) emphasises the 'iron party discipline in Parliament'. A different explanation for the relatively unitary action of Norwegian parties in *Storting* was raised by Henry Valen (1988). His observation that party elites are not in a position to force their will by explicit threats, led him to conclude that the cohesion of the Norwegian parties arises because legislators accept the norm of party discipline.

After the 1977 elections Norway's parties had to face a minority situation due to the *Storting* ending up without one party or a bloc of parties controlling more than 50 per cent of the seats. Whereas the DNA gained seventy-six seats, the CP, SP and KrF had obtained forty-one, twelve, and twenty-two seats respectively. This parliamentary situation provides the starting point to the analysis of the manifestation and resolution of internal conflicts in the Centre Party during 1989–90.

Italy

Multiparty representation, based on the almost complete proportionality of the electoral system of preferential vote (Pasquino 1987), together with the strong heterogeneity of Italian coalitions (Di Palma 1977), characterised Italian post-war politics. Until the mid-1970s two unique political actors distinguished the Italian party system from the others; on the one hand, the uninterrupted dominance of the DC which has not been out of power since 1945 and, on the other hand, the role played by the PCI as the main opposition which has been operated within the system but has not shared control of the national government since May 1947. During 1958–72, where electoral stability and partisan continuity characterised the Italian political system, DC's strength in the Italian Parliament ranged between 42 per cent and 39 per cent respectively, while the PCI received between 23 and 27 per cent of the total votes respectively (see Appendices 2.5 and 2.6).

The dominance of the DC, however, did not preclude the possibility of changes in the composition of the Italian government coalitions. Since the end of the war, these government coalitions followed each other: 'centre' coalitions during the 1950s where the partners of the DC were the small centre parties, the Republican, the Liberals and Social-Democrats; and centre-left coalitions during the 1960s and 1970s where the Socialists became part of the DC dominated government. While 'over-sized' cabinets have predominated, there have also been intermittent minority governments, such as the DC minority governments during 1957–63 and Aldo Moro's minority governments during 1974–76. A partial explanation for the formation of minority governments in Italy focuses on the absence of an established coalition formula, that is, when parties have not been over-constrained by any specific coalition formula. The eight and two minority governments which were formed during 1953–62 and 1972–76, respectively, exemplify this tendency.

By the early 1970s, however, the DC's share of the vote declined while the PCI's electoral strength became increasingly evident. The PCI's potential for sharing power arose from the declining dominance of the DC. Electorally, it was first demonstrated by the latter defeat in the 1974 'divorce referendum' (around 41 per cent in favour of repealing the law, 59 per cent against). Politically, it was evident following the DC declining ability to retain the allegiance of its traditional alliance partners.

Three reasons are usually given credit for the evidence of such processes: first, the birth of the regions, in 1970, the intermediate level between the central state and local government; second, the electoral victory of the PCI in the regional and the administrative elections of 1975 in which it gained an outstanding 33 per cent of the total vote which provided it with the control of many local and regional administrations (LaPalombara 1977) and, third, the electoral growth of the PCI in the general election of 1976 in which it received around 34 per cent of the vote, reflecting a 27 per cent increase in its strength (see Appendix 2.5).

At the electorate level, moreover, the PCI's vote became more evenly distributed in the different geographic zones of the country than at any time before (Parisi and Pasquino 1980). At the level of party system on a left–right dimension, the DC constituted 76 per cent and 74 per cent of the total strength of the centrist forces in 1946 and 1976, respectively. But the PCI, which constituted only 45 per cent of the combined left percentage in 1946, had climbed to an impressive 73 per cent (Parisi and Pasquino 1980). This, in turn, suggests that a process of polarisation had taken place. Beyond the PCI's gain of control in several regions and municipalities where it had been absent earlier, it was the involvement in broader coalitions which emphasised the PCI's position as a political force compact and disciplined enough to assume the responsibility of governing.

The success of the PCI in the 1975 and 1976 elections is attributed mainly to the votes of the young with the lowering of the voting age in 1975 (Sani 1977). Other studies suggest that the electoral shifts among large sections of young voters had already began in 1968 producing their first effect in the elections of 1972 (Barbagli *et al.* 1979). A more comprehensive study, however, argues that two distinct factors contributed to the PCI electoral victories in 1975 and 1976: social movements of the previous years and the policy of the 'historic compromise' which was launched by the PCI in 1973. The former accounts for the increase in the percentage of young people and workers who voted PCI in 1975–76, while the latter accounts for sections of the middle-class, mainly clerks and craftsmen, moving towards the PCI (Barbagli *et al.* 1979, Barbagli and Corbetta 1982b: 86).

As one might question the conclusiveness of the electoral trends during the 1970s, attention should also be focused on the cleavage structure of the Italian polity. Basically, it is the left–right dimension in the Italian society along which one finds few cleavages that have animated political discourse during the twentieth century: capitalism versus socialism; democracy versus fascism; proletariat versus bourgeoisie; reform or revolution versus reaction, and church versus state (Mannheimer and Sani 1987). Consequently, the dynamics of formal and tacit interparty alliances has been influenced by the fact that a number of the important socio–economic cleavages – such as: developed versus underdeveloped areas; city versus periphery; agriculture versus industry, and workers versus owners – run through the DC rather than separating it from the other parties in the political spectrum. From this perspective, the PCI and PSI also represent mass parties through which socio–economic cleavages run. The national stance that DC, PCI and PSI assumed in the post-war period, the multiclass nature of these parties and the common legacy of antifacism shared by all these mass parties, were given credit for their diverse composition (Leonardi and Wertman 1989).

However, even though all the mass parties are, to a great extent, interclass in nature, the leftist parties differ significantly from the DC in the pattern of associations that are part of the subcultures which support each of the parties. Whereas, to a great extent, the Communist and Socialists grew out of the same Marxist subculture or community, the DC partook of the Catholic subculture (Barnes 1977). Not surprisingly, 'Italian Communist politicians are radical, programmatic and ideologically committed Marxists', but at the same time, 'they are sensitive to the need to bargain and compromise' (Putnam 1975: 209–10).

These restraints did not damage the DC advantage over other parties since the party is also rooted in the international arena. Beyond the DC's electoral strength lies the unqualified support of the USA which identified in the DC the party that could guarantee political stability and, thus, favoured the eventual success of the DC. However, among the most cited factors which predict the DC's eventual decline are the centrifugal drives which dominated the Italian multiparty system (Sartori 1976).

The DC's occupation of the centre of the party system makes the centrifugal drive towards the extreme ends of the political spectrum predominant over the centripetal drive:

> In other terms, the very existence of a centre party (or parties) discourages 'centrality', i.e., the centripetal drives of the political system. And the centripetal drives are precisely the moderating drives. This is why this type is centre-fleeing, or centrifugal, and thereby conducive to immoderate or extremist politics.
>
> (Sartori 1976: 135)

According to Sartori (1976), the long-term consequence for the DC of the centrifugal drive is the erosion of its voting base, as voters move away from the centre towards the extremes. However, major factors which could minimise the effect of the centrifugal drives are the turn to 'clientelistic politics' (Pasquino 1985), and the colonisation of the state apparatus, public economic and social agencies by the party (Leonardi 1981). These trends, together with the intensive competition derived from the nature of the party system, opened the way to what is called the *partitocrazia*.

Specifically, *partitocrazia* is distinguished by two different, but related, factors. First, the 'penetration' of political parties to state organs, bureaucracy, judiciary system, public firms, and other crucial sectors of social life, such as mass media. Second, the absence of clear lines of separation between majority and opposition, namely, the invisible and visible levels of co-operation, which is called in Italy *trasformismo* for historical reasons. No traditional party, of course, could deal with the *partitocrazia* issues because all the traditional actors were involved in this system. As a result, the governmental parties, especially the DC, expanded their own sphere of influence within the state, contributing to the 'degeneration' of a party-based democratic regime where parties are no longer responsible for their actions before the citizens (Paci 1978).

The Italian case focuses on intraparty conflicts which have emerged within the DC and the PCI in the run-up and during the 'historic compromise'. In simplest terms, it was a long-term strategy put forward by the PCI which argued that profound changes in Italian society would only be possible if serious political polarisation were avoided. And the only way to guarantee against such polarisation was an alliance between the major political forces in the country, that is, the DC, PCI and the PSI. From the very beginning, however, this proposal was framed with reference to very pressing short-term problems. The large-scale political terrorism and scandals combined with adverse economic conditions have challenged traditional patterns of interparty co-operation during the mid-1970s.[3] The effect of the PCI's initiative on the internal arena of the main parties and the ways it influenced patterns of coalition bargaining are addressed in the analysis of the DC and the PCI cases.

Britain

For much of the post-war period Britain has been described as having a two-party system because the existence of third parties 'did not prevent the two major parties from governing alone' (Sartori 1976: 186, 188). Electorally, the Conservatives and the Labour party gained around 87 per cent of the vote in 1945, and around 97 per cent in 1951. In the 1960s, the two parties' shares fluctuated and tended to fall. But, at the three elections between 1964 and 1970 the two parties received between seven-eighths and nine-tenths of the total vote (see Appendix 2.7).[4] Between 1945 and 1970, the decline in one party's share was matched in the main part by an increase in the vote for the other; the Labour share of the vote fell by around 5 per cent, while the Conservative share rose by 6.8 per cent (Rose and McAllister 1986).

It was in this context of two-party dominance that four minority governments were formed. Whereas from 1910 to 1915 a minority

Liberal government was dependent upon the support of Labour and the Irish Nationalists for its parliamentary majority, two Labour governments were in a minority position in 1924 and 1929. A partial explanation for the prevalence of these minority governments rather than coalition in Britain lies in the conventions associated with the processes of government formation and dissolution. For government formation, after a general election in which no party has been able to gain an overall majority, the Sovereign is not required to nominate a Prime Minister who can secure a majority in the Commons, but rather one who can survive as leader of the largest (or in 1924 the second largest) minority party. For the dissolution, if defeated on the Address, the prevailing assumption is that the Prime Minister of the minority government can secure a dissolution of Parliament. Both conventions, therefore, make it likely that minority government rather than coalition will be the result of a hung parliament (Bogdanor 1983).

By the 1970s, however, both the Conservative and Labour parties' share of the vote declined. The decline in dominance by both parties was reflected by their falling combined share of the total vote: from 80 per cent in 1951, through 74 per cent in 1959, to 56 per cent in October 1974 (Crewe *et al.* 1977). Yet, this decline in the two-parties combined vote was hardly reflected in their parliamentary representation – the total seats of Liberals at Westminster during the period 1951–75 ranged from six, during the three elections in the 1950s, to fourteen in February 1974 (see Appendix 2.7). It was, however, the total parliamentary representation for all parties other than the major two that rose from the range of zero to six during 1951–70, to twenty-three and twenty-six in the elections of February and October 1974, respectively. Looking more closely at this development, it becomes apparent that the two-party system strictly existed, if at all, only at the parliamentary level, with the electoral system as the remaining key determinant, and even the parliamentary two-party system has come under great challenge.[5]

To understand the context in which the Lib–Lab pact was formulated it is necessary to appreciate the parliamentary situation prior to March 1977. In October 1974 Labour succeeded in gaining a small overall majority, but this was gradually eroded through by-election defeats and defections, so that by April 1976 the party found itself in a minority again. The immediate consequences were twenty-nine government defeats in the House of Commons between June 1974 and March 1977, during which time the Lib–Lab Pact was formulated (Norton 1980). Moreover, the Parliament witnessed the first 'mass' use of the guillotine which has been described as 'the most drastic method of curtailing debate known to procedure' and 'the extreme limit to which procedure goes in affirming the rights of the majority at the expense of the minorities of the House' (Erskine May 1976: 448). On 20 July, 1976, for example, the government carried three guillotine motions on five Bills; one motion for the Aircraft and Shipbuilding Industries Bill, a second for the Rent (Agriculture) Bill and the Education Bill, and a third for the Health Services Bill and the Dock Regulation Bill.[6] Clearly, from the viewpoint of the government, it achieved the orderly dispatch of their business, but this was not without cost. To be forced to rely on the naked force of the guillotine gave an advantage to the opposition in terms of their prestige.

Difficulties to the minority Labour administration also emerged at the internal level. In February 1977, the Labour government achieved the distinction of being the first government to be defeated on a guillotine motion, mainly due to dissent by vote or abstention of the government backbenchers. The government struggled with the Scotland and Wales Bill through ten Committee days but it finally decided that the question could not be postponed. As The *Guardian* reported:

> what Mr Foot and his more timid colleagues in the Cabinet have decided to take a gamble on is that enough of the rebels will back down on the night when they are brought face to face with the disastrous consequences of an effective backbench rebellion. . . . The Cabinet decision follows weeks of intense activity by the Labour whips as they sought to assess the scale of any possible backbench revolt and to identify the possible weak links among the rebels. They appear to have confirmed Mr Foot's view that the earlier the motion was tabled the better in terms of the number of rebels. For ministers recognise that the longer the timetable is delayed the more stringent it will have to be, and therefore, the greater the indignation among its opponents.[7]

When the decision was made, the government was defeated by twenty-nine votes; twenty-two Labour MPs voted against the government and fifteen abstained.[8] Such government defeats due to Labour's rebels, which had occurred over eight divisions between January 1975 and March 1977, emphasised the weak position of the Labour government.

Added to the minority situation in which the Labour Party found itself in April 1976 and its weak parliamentary position, were the influences of the economic crisis. By 1976, the financial and economic crisis was such that the IMF could dictate terms to the Labour

Government in return for international support for Britain.[9] The starting point of the analysis is March 1977, when the Lib–Lab Pact was formed. Modes of conflict manifestation and resolution and their impact on legislative bargaining are investigated in light of the rich material which was furnished by the experiences of the Labour and Liberal parties during the Lib–Lab Pact.

France

The most significant changes in the French party system between 1981 and 1988 were the transformation of the Socialist Party into a mainstream social-democratic government party, the continuing and accelerating decline of the Communist Party, the weakening of the Socialist–Communist alliance, and, finally, the emergence of the National Front as an important force.

The major constraint on the Socialist Party during the 1970s was the need for an alliance with the Communist Party. Moreover, the existence of a large pro-Moscow Communist Party loyal to the dogmas of Marxism and Leninism served to hinder the Socialist Party from developing into a 'catch-all' party able to rally the centre and middle-class vote which is essential to any election victory and successful government (Bell and Criddle 1988). Since 1981, however, the French Communist Party has been subjected to a process of degradation in all aspects: a series of electoral failures; loss of positions of local power; fall in membership and drop in militant activity, and unfavourable development of its image in public opinion (Ranger 1986). In the 1978 national legislative election the Communists won around 21 per cent of the poll, 16 per cent in 1981 and around 10 per cent in 1986 (see Appendix 2.8). Clearly, the main beneficiaries of the Communist collapse were the Socialists, since the steady decline of the Communist vote eliminated the Communist Party as a major force on the left. In 1978, this process contributed to the actual break-up of the alliance with the Socialists. Strategically, the political game changed from being one of trying to maintain an alliance with the Communists to that of wooing voters away from the right with an appeal to the traditional virtues of patriotism, administrative efficiency and change within continuity, packaged as 'modernising' socialism (Bell and Criddle 1988).

It was from the larger structural changes taking place within the French party system, particularly the slow but steady decline of the Communist Party, that the National Front emerged as a political force. Capitalising on social tension and anti-immigration attitudes, the

National Front had attracted 8–11 per cent support during the period 1983–86 in four very different elections: local elections in 1983, European elections in 1984, departmental elections in 1985 and legislative elections in March 1986. Added to the exploitation of the immigration issue, the electoral breakthrough of the extreme right in France since 1983 was enhanced by the political situation of a left which has proved disappointing in power, and the capacity of the party leader, Le Pen, for turning the hostility of the media to its advantage (Charlot 1986). However, the political strength of the National Front, namely, issue voting, was also its political weakness. Following the gap between Le Pen's commitments to traditional values of the past, and the basically non-traditional commitments of the largest group of its supporters, the leadership of the National Front failed to augment the latter group (Schain 1987). This failure was manifested by the poor 1988 election results.[10]

To explain the context in which Rocard's 1988 minority government operated, it is also necessary to appreciate how a particular French legislative institution, called Article 49–3, shapes bargaining between the Government and the National Assembly. This Article is perhaps the most potent of many Fifth Republic legislative institutions designed to restrict the legislative role of the parliament (Wright 1989). According to the Article, when the government engages its own responsibility on a text, the Bill in question is considered to be passed unless a motion of censure is lodged and voted by an overall majority. In other words, in the vote of censure, both votes in favour and abstentions are considered favourable to the government. If the government fails to reach an absolute majority of the 577 deputies, under Article 49–3 the government is brought down. The Article, then, forces the National Assembly to choose between accepting the government's version of a Bill and throwing the government out of office.

In the June 1988 legislative elections no party obtained a majority in the National Assembly. The PS, who obtained 275 of the 577 seats, formed the first minority government in the history of the Fifth Republic. Theoretically, potential partners were the Gaullists (RPR, 130 seats), the UDF (90 seats), and the Centre (UDC, 41 seats) – as well as the Communists with 25 seats. This parliamentary situation provides a starting point for the analysis of the PS and the PCF cases.

SUMMARY AND CONCLUSION

The description of intraparty contexts in the first section was guided by a set of dimensions over which the distribution of effective decision-making authority within the party has been assessed. At first sight the approach employed to classify parties may appear primitive compared to Janda's (1980) methodology which is based on a variable-specific scale upon which each of eight basic variables are scored. The scales encompass the number of individuals participating in decisions and some of them go further by tapping the structural position and functional composition of party organs. Thus, Janda is able to tap the number and location in the organisational hierarchy of party organs and individuals.

However, underlying Janda's (1980) methodology for tapping the locus of power – that is, 'who is in control?' – is the presumption that, indeed, there is some individual or party organ in control. Put differently, it is assumed that in each party there are actors which dominate decisions critical to party structure and activity. This is a reasonable assumption when the period under investigation is a long one – as indeed Janda's coverage is. However, if one views a party in transition during a short period (i.e. one to three years) or a party in turmoil, intraparty politics is more complex; there may be cases where it is not at all clear whether any individual or party organ is in control. A classic example may be a party during a leadership transition where those party organs led by the 'old guard' are in fact subordinated to preferences and priorities set by an emerging leadership. Another example is a party which is divided into two factions, with each internal process being subject to a power struggle – the result of which is 'shifting locus of power' over time periods and over decisions. This is precisely the reason that the analysis of centralisation/decentralisation of each of the parties observed is restricted to a given (and limited) period.

Overall, this chapter has shown that there exists a large variation in the intraparty and parliamentary contexts (e.g. electoral system, the frequency of minority governments and government formation rules) within which party elites operate.

The questions which arise at this stage are as follows: 'Do variations in intraparty attributes create variations in the strategies adopted by internal opposition as well as by those who attempt to pacify it?', and, 'Do variations in constitutional attributes create variations in parties' considerations during coalition bargaining under conditions of severe internal conflicts? The empirical analysis which follows attempts to answer these questions.

3 Modes of conflict manifestation in centralised parties

How can 'claims' be made by actors operating within centralised parties on the party elites? An affirmative answer begins with an analysis of patterns of internal opposition within four centralised parties, namely, the Danish Social Democratic Party (1978–79), the Norwegian Centre Party (1989–90), the Italian Communist Party (1976–79) and the French Communist Party (1988–91). The analysis of each case begins with a brief discussion of the position of the party leader within the party and organisational trend which affected the leadership position during the period under investigation,[1] the background for the coalition agreement and the decisive preferences underlying it. I hope to show that, in the cases observed, whereas intra-elite opposition adopted the 'exit' option as well as the 'voice' mode *within* party bodies, followers' hostility tends to adopt the 'voice' mode *outside* the party. Attention now turns to the case of the Danish Social Democratic Party.

THE DANISH SOCIAL DEMOCRATIC PARTY (SD), 1978–79

The position of Anker Jørgensen within the SD and the decisive preferences of his alliance strategy are critical factors in the development of the party's coalition strategy during 1975–82. At the outset, Jørgensen's position during 1972–77 seemed relatively restricted as he was elected in a way more reminiscent of a 'coup'. According to his memoirs, he was hand picked mainly by Jens Otto Krag, Erling Dinesen and K.B. Andersen (Jørgensen 1989). The 1975 and 1977 elections, however, gradually strengthened his position. In addition, his experience as the former President of Denmark's largest trade union federation (the National Union of General workers) combined with ten years' parliamentary experience and two years as a prime minister contributed to the dominant position he enjoyed during 1977–82. A substantial reason for the overall support Jørgensen enjoyed at the level of the party organisation is suggested by a former minister and the editor of the SD's newspaper *Aktuelt*, Bent Hansen:

> He became Prime Minister at a time when the Danish Social Democratic Party needed [a] popular leader with social engagement and reared in the type of environment that the Social Democratic Party represents politically. His two immediate predecessors had an academic background, and notwithstanding their great qualifications there was a political–psychological need for a leader who had his origin in the midst of the Social Democratic Party's electorate. On top of that, Anker Jørgensen was given the difficult task of uniting the Danish labour movement after the question of Danish membership of the EC had divided the movement. . . . Both in his capacity as trade union president and prime minister he was authoritative and reserved. These were however qualities that were closely bound up with these taxing functions, and they were offset by both a humane and personal openness in all other relations, whether on a high intellectual level or down to earth.[2]

An additional factor that contributed to Jørgensen's position within the party was the formation of *ad hoc* minority governments during 1975–78. Because the SD and the parties to its left lacked a majority, the SD entered into informal alliances with the CPP, KrF, CD and the RV during that period. A classic example was the agreement between the SD and these parties over the passage of the 1976 budget which provided for the introduction of heavier penalties for breaches of current collective wage agreements and a complete wage and price freeze. Although Jørgensen went back on the first part of this agreement, following the strong opposition from the LO, the four parties mentioned above voted with the SD on December 1975 over wage and price freeze proposals.[3]

Given the *ad hoc* nature of informal minority governments, the SD elites could select the least 'expensive' partner available. Two examples concerning the inclusion of the RV in some of the 1977 alliances and its exclusion from others spring to mind. In April, co-operation between the SD, RV, V and the CPP resulted in the adoption of an emergency Bill giving legislative effect to the collective agreement for a two-year period.[4] Similarly, on 6 September, 1977, the government which was supported by these parties secured parliamentary approval for a package of increases in indirect taxes on petrol, tobacco and spirits.[5] On the other hand, the RV was excluded from the agreement among the SD, V, KrF, CPP, and the CD over a four-year extension of

Table 3.1 List of events in Denmark, 1975–90

9.1.75	General elections
13.2.75	Formation of Jørgensen's II minority government
11.3.75	A statutory two-year income policy passed
22.1.77	Dissolution of the *Folketing*
15.2.77	General elections
25.2.77	Formation of Jørgensen's III minority government
15.4.77	Collective agreement for two-year period passed
28.8.78	The formation of Jørgensen's IV minority SD–V government
28.9.79	The SD–V minority government collapses
23.10.79	General elections
26.10.79	The formation of Jørgensen's V minority government
12.11.81	The rejection of the government's economic programme
8.12.81	General elections
30.12.81	The formation of Jørgensen's VI minority government
3.9.82	Resignation of Jørgensen's VI minority government
10.9.82	Formation of Poul Schlüter's I minority government
7.12.82	The government defeated over defence issue
16.10.82	The main provisions of the 1983 Budget passed
5.1.83	The government defeated over defence issue
2.6.83	The government survives a vote of no-confidence
3.11.83	SD proposal enjoining the government to work 'actively' to halt the arms race was passed
1.12.83	SD proposal instructing the government to refuse to take any responsibility for deployment was passed
15.12.83	Resignation of Schlüter's I minority government after being defeated over the 1984 Budget
10.1.84	General elections, formation of Schlüter's II government
23.2.84	The 1984 Budget passed by 79 votes to 27
5.84	The government defeated over defence issues
29.6.84	An agreement on defence budget for 1986–89
29.3.85	The government's energy plan defeated
14.11.85	The government defeated over defence issue
12.85	The 1986 Budget passed in the *Folketing*
21.1.86	Schlüter's government unable to sign the 'Single European Act' following lack of *Folketing's* support
27.2.86	A referendum over the 'Single European Act', 56.2% in favour and 43.8% against
20.5.86	The government defeated over defence issues
12.86	Adoption of the 1987 Budget
8.9.87	General elections, formation of Schlüter's III government
14.4.88	Government defeat over nuclear weapon policy
10.5.88	General election
3.6.88	Formation of Schlüter's IV minority government
22.11.90	Poul Schlüter calls an early general election for December.

Source: Keesing's Contemporary Archives, 1975–90.

the defence Budget in March 1977.[6] Obviously, as there were many feasible partners, the SD elites could oppose the demands of the RV and the extreme left-wing parties without risking its legislation over this issue. This factor also contributed to the strong position enjoyed by Jørgensen in the party organisation.

The above pattern of ongoing and relatively successful SD informal alliances was modified during 1978–79 towards a formal minority government with the Liberal Party which was based on the decisive preferences of 'economic recovery' and 'economic democracy'. The serious economic problems, triggered off by the first oil price increase, and the political difficulties created by the 1973 'electoral earthquake' led to the shift in SD strategy. Anker Jørgensen signed an accord which provided for the implementation of an economic stabilisation plan designed to consolidate the limited progress made by the 1977 minority government. Consequently, in November 1979 few Bills which were described in a *Financial Times* report as Denmark's 'toughest price and wage freeze since wartime emergency measures', were adopted by large *ad hoc* majorities while narrow majorities were recorded for other Bills.[7] Underlying the SD-V alliance was the desire to form a stable government which could adhere to a long-term economic policy which could bring about economic recovery.[8] The idea of using an economic umbrella as the central energiser of the SD-V coalition was suppose to generate the widest possible support within both parties. The accord reached between the parties involved an understanding that three economic policy proposals strongly supported by the trade unions would not be pursued. These proposals were: (1) a tax reform, (2) housing reform and (3) the introduction of wage-earner co-ownership of industry ('economic democracy').[9]

During the period in which informal minority governments were formed, that is from 1975 to 1978, no intraparty conflicts were recorded. It would be somewhat misleading, however, to contend that SD elites shared Jørgensen's views with regard to preferable parliamentary partners. On the contrary, while Jørgensen preferred to co-operate with *Venstre*, elite members found it much easier to co-operate with the Conservatives. As Svend Jakobsen, the Minister of Inland Revenue at that time, recalled:

> The Prime Minister, Anker Jørgensen, was more in favour of co-operation with *Venstre* than the Conservatives. He saw the Conservatives as the party to the right. . . . Some of us were discussing the situation already in the middle of the 1970s because

in concrete discussions it was much easier to negotiate with the Conservatives than with *Venstre*.[10]

The reasoning by certain members of the SD's elite to prefer the CPP rather than the Liberal Party as a partner for parliamentary co-operation, probably lay in their perception of the CPP profile as closer to the SD line. Bent Hansen, who was at that time a chief editor of the Social Democratic's newspaper, *Aktuelt*, explained:

> In a way, I think that the Conservative Party compared with the *Venstre*, is more close to us. . . . We have more interests in common because we want full employment and we want the industry and the economic life to have good conditions. First of all employment and, second, to enhance the possibilities of increased standards of living and making social reforms. And I think that the Conservative Party which has its roots in the urban Bourgeoisie circle, has some idea in common with us, they also want standards of living to increase . . . the *Venstre* is a very reactionary party.[11]

The importance of this difference between Anker Jørgensen and some elite members can hardly be overemphasised. After all, the SD alliance strategy involved mainly informal alliances with the CPP together with other centre-right parties. Moreover, the participation of the Liberal Party in some of the SD legislative alliances during 1977 was only on an informal, *ad hoc*, basis which did not antagonise centre-left elements within the party elites.

However, it was due to the shift in party strategy from informal co-operation to a formal one during 1978–79 that differences within the party elites (which also reflected the difference between the party line and the trade union's approach) resulted in intraparty conflicts. At the outset, the fact that the LO is strongly involved in SD politics and there is reciprocal representation on the executive committees of LO and the SD meant that any conflict between the two would be reflected within both elites. Furthermore, it was from the beginning of the negotiations between the SD and the V that Anker Jørgensen could have expected a conflict to evolve within the SD elites, as well as between the party and the LO. As Karl Hjortnæs, a former minister, recalled:

> There have been very important negotiations over the weekend between the leaders of the Liberal Party and the leadership of the Social Democratic Party. By the end of the negotiations there was a very important meeting between Mr Anker Jørgensen, the chairman of the Labour movement, Thomas Nielsen and Jens

Risgaard Knudsen, the chairman of the Social Democratic parliamentary group. Thomas Nielsen and Risgaard Knudsen told Anker Jørgensen that they were against the majority government between the two political parties. They advised him that he should not go inside and form such a majority government.... For Thomas Nielsen it was very important to have a deal about 'economic democracy'. He knew that it was impossible to have economic democratisation in our firms so long as the Liberal Party was inside the government. I think this was the reason why he was against it.[12]

In the months following the coalition agreement strong opposition was evident within the party. At the SD Congress in December 1978, an open dispute took place between Anker Jørgensen and Thomas Nielsen (Jørgensen 1990). While the Prime Minister thought that there was no alternative to the SD-V government, the LO chairman hoped that the government would not survive the next 100 days. Thomas Nielsen, furthermore, criticised the way the government formation process had taken place by calling it a 'coup'. He demanded a 'public apology' from Anker Jørgensen. The latter, on the contrary, did not think he owed an apology, only an explanation (Jørgensen 1990). In the following days:

the strifes continue both internally and externally.... [The] previous Minister of Finance, Henry Grunbaum, and George Poulsen, the new chairman of the Metal Workers Federation, urged a change of [party] chairman. But other leading figures within the party and the trade unions went the opposite way and called for calm and ending the strife.

(Jørgensen 1990: 153)

Yet, whatever the reason for the strife between the SD and the LO (i.e. matters of principle or the personal relationships between the two leaders), it was the conflict within the SD parliamentary group which was characterised by an unprecedented form of vociferous internal dissension. According to Svend Jakobsen, the Fisheries Minister in the SD-V government:

I don't think we can say there was a leader, it was not organised inside the party.... Inside the party group, I think Mr Jens Risgaard Knudsen was the major opponent. Maybe there was a relation . . . he was former Secretary in LO, he was very strongly against.... When ministers came to the group it was many times very difficult for [them] to have the support from the group because [members of the group] often said [the item] was influenced by the

Liberals. I would say [that] if ministers, as members of a Social Democratic minority government, had come with the same position, it would have been much easier to get the support from the group than when they come from the coalition government. At that way you saw opposition in the parliamentary group.[13]

In addition, the leader of the SD parliamentary group, Jens Risgaard Knudsen, resigned during the first meeting of the SD parliamentary group subsequent to the conclusion of the SD-V accord. Knudsen, however, made no formal effort to organise those MPs who opposed the SD-V accord. On the contrary:

I have not heard about Risgaard Knudsen's position and his advice [before the meeting of the parliamentary group]. He could have phoned me or other persons in the Social Democratic parliamentary group but he made the choice that he would not contact any person.[14]

Given the discipline record of the SD parliamentary group, it was clear to Knudsen that any formal attempt to mobilise support for its cause was doomed to failure. Besides, differences of opinion also emerged within the LO. While the chairman, Thomas Nielsen, opposed the SD-V government, Poul Christensen, the SID chairman, favoured it.[15] As a result, a cohesive internal opposition could not have been formed.

Regarding the internal disagreement within the Liberal Party, only Iver Hansen was against the formation of the SD-V accord 'because he was more ideological, liberal and tended to be against socialism'.[16] However, the importance of his opposition can hardly be overemphasised because after the coalition agreement was signed Hansen's dissatisfaction was neutralised by allocating him the portfolio of Public Works. It must be conceded, moreover, that neither patterns of 'voice' or 'exit' were evident within the Liberal Party. Hence, intraparty conflict did not evolve within this party.

THE NORWEGIAN CENTRE PARTY (SP), 1989–90

Turning to the changes within the SP elites during the late 1980s, our first concern is to demonstrate just what Hirschman (1970: 71–2) claims, that, 'for voice to function properly it is necessary that individuals possess reserves of political influence which they can bring into play when they are sufficiently aroused'. This involves a discussion not only of 'attitudes', as disembodied sets of ideas and values, but also of the position of the party leader within the party.

Most notably, Anne Enger Lahnstein, who served as deputy leader of the SP parliamentary group during 1983–89, was elected the group leader in 1989. Lahnstein led the internal opposition in the SP during 1985–86 which demanded the participation of the parliamentary group in decisions taken by the SP–KrF–CP government. As elected representatives, SP members of the parliamentary group refused to serve as a 'rubber stamp' for government decisions. Consequently, the SP parliamentary group militantly opposed numerous items. Eight days after the coalition was formed, for example, a proposal was made by the SV, SP and Liberal MPs that the *Storting* should again debate the question of the deployment of nuclear missiles in Europe before their deployment went into effect. The proposal was only defeated by one vote, with only a handful of Centre Party MPs voting with the government.

Lahnstein was relatively successful in mobilising MPs' support against SP cabinet members. As Käre Willoch, the Prime Minister, described:

> In reality, members of government would consult with members of parliament when government was discussing controversial issues and sometimes the government postponed decisions in order that members [of government] might consult with their members in parliament. What should have been respected to a greater degree was that members of government should have authority to negotiate compromise which members of parliament should accept. Their signs should be given in advance so that there might be negotiations leading to a result. But what gradually developed was a system through which compromises should be adjusted and always in the same direction, that means always in the direction of great expenditure. Because the two smallest parties [i.e. the SP and KrF] are, what I called, 'expenditure parties'. Their basis is the ability to get more government revenue for the . . . particular interests of their voters.[17]

The SP parliamentary group which was led by Lahnstein during 1985–86 has established itself as necessary, not merely relevant actor, in the government decision-making process. This, in turn, undermined the effectiveness of the process; much more time had to be spent on discussions between the government and the SP parliamentary group producing results which meant increasing government expenditure. Lahnstein's views on the party's coalition strategy effectively represented these of the parliamentary group: 'We are a little bit special party. . . . We are always seeking power, and, we are always taking responsibility.'[18]

Table 3.2 List of events in Norway, 1975–90

21.1.76	The Formation of Nordli's minority government
11–12.7.77	General elections
4.2.81	Gro Harlem Brundtland took office as PM following Nordli's resignation for health reasons
4.81	Gro Harlem Brundtland elected chairwoman of the DNA
13–14.9.81	General Elections
14.10.81	Kåre Willoch took office as PM
8.5.83	Formation of CP–KrF–SP coalition led by Willoch
16.6.83	A proposal in the *Storting* to debate the question of the deployment of nuclear missiles in Europe was defeated by a margin of one vote
12.9.83	Local elections
8–9.9.85	General elections
6–25.4.86	Industrial disputes over wage increases
7–15.4.86	Industrial disputes over wage increases
2.5.86	Kåre Willoch resigns following his government's defeat of no-confidence motion by 79 to 78
2.5.86	Gro Harlem Brundtland formed a Labour minority government
22.5–5.6.86	Selective strikes of local government workers
17.6.86	Austerity measures approved by *Storting* after an agreement with the KrF and SP
8–9.86	Willoch resigned as the Conservative's candidate for PM and was replaced by Rolf Presthus
16.12.86	The 1987 Budget was approved after the government secured the support of the SP and KrF
12.6.87	Two motions of no-confidence presented by right-wing and centre parties had failed to unseat the government
13–14.9.87	Local elections
18.12.87	The 1988 Budget approved with the support of SP and KrF
23–24.1.88	J.P. Syse was elected unopposed as leader of the Conservative Party in succession to Presthus who died in January.
12.4.88	The *Storting* passed legislation effectively freezing wages which was supported by the SP
6.6.88	*Storting* approved a new law regulating the Oslo stock exchange supported by the SP and KrF
11.9.89	General elections
16.10.89	J.P. Syse formed a CP–SP–KrF minority government
9.90	J.P. Syse resigned as PM

Source: Keesing's Contemporary Archives, 1975–90.

After becoming party leader in 1989 Lahnstein incorporated her 'reserves of political influence' into the SP bargaining plane by collaborating with the Party Secretary, John Dale. The political influence of John Dale grew out of two sources: (i) the control over party members, and, (ii) the divergence between the cabinet members and the party organisation. Dale managed political activities which involved 49,000 members in 1989. Although a gradual decline in the SP membership was evident throughout the 1970s and 1980s – for example, 63,000 members in 1969, 52,000 members in 1981, and 49,000 members in 1989 (Heidar 1990a: 7) – one could not blame the party secretary. Almost all Norwegian parties faced similar trends throughout this period (Heidar 1990a: 7,11). According to Hirschman (1970):

> When a uniform decline hits simultaneously all firms of an industry, each firm would garner in some of the disgruntled customers to its competitors. In these circumstances the exit option is ineffective in alerting management to its failings.
>
> (Hirschman 1970: 26)

The decline in the SP membership, therefore, did not undermine Dale's position within the party. Heidar's (1990b) study, furthermore, suggests that the political influence of the Party Secretary during the period under investigation was considered 'strong' by 47 per cent of both top and middle-level party elites.

The divergence between the cabinet members and the party organisation, which was evident throughout the 1989–90 formal alliance with the CP and the KrF, was both organisational and ideological. Being in the government, cabinet members were exposed to a different set of political interactions which made solidarity at the governmental level inevitable. A widening ideological difference between SP cabinet members and SP activists further enhanced the co-operation of the latter with the parliamentary group.

Consequently, the SP cabinet members faced a trade-off between government solidarity and parliamentary group hostility during 1989–90. According to John Dale:

> This is a classical conflict because you have negotiations in the government and you have negotiation here. . . . [Yet] the question you posed is surprising. You asked what is the parliamentary group allowed to do. This is not the question. The question is what are the cabinet ministers allowed to do, because, in our system the parliamentary group has got a 'say'. They are the people that must take responsibility here in the *Storting* by their voting. . . . They [cabinet members] cannot come to the parliamentary group and say 'listen, we demand from you', its more the other way around.[19]

Because of the intensity of the intra-elite conflict, the SP cabinet members were unable to embrace policy fully without offending the leader of the parliamentary group and the party secretary. A classic example is the interparty negotiation over the 1990 budget. The SP acted inconsistently during these negotiations, breaking up the negotiations following the FrP participation but, in the end, signing the agreement. Given the FrP's strategy shift in 1989, seeking co-operation with the non-socialist government,[20] it is hardly surprising that the party was considered a relevant partner for an informal alliance over the Budget. However, while the KrF and the CP agreed to form such an alliance with the FrP, the SP parliamentary group were bitterly opposed.

Two days after the pre-negotiations over the 1990 budget had started, that is the negotiations whether to negotiate, the SP parliamentary group refused to co-operate with the FrP and broke up the discussions. According to FrP member in the Finance Committee, Tor Mikkel Wara:

> For two days, nights and days, we negotiated with the three parties whether we are going to negotiate about the Budget. The result was that we were going to do it. The Centre Party did not like to have this budget co-operation with us. . . . So, when we were going to . . . get it through, to have a balance, they said that they would like to negotiate both with the Labour Party and the Progress Party. We said 'no chance, you have to make a decision, either the Labour Party or the Progress Party'. . . . The result was that all the media and press wrote that the Progress Party won these negotiations because the Centre Party had to chose the Progress Party as their co-operation partner to get the budget through.[21]

An additional cause of dissatisfaction for the SP parliamentary group were the direct negotiations between the Prime Minister, Jan P. Syse, and the FrP leader, Carl Hagen. According to the latter:

> The Prime Minister and I settled the 1990 budget in a meeting in his office. It was following the negotiations we already had and we made some minor adjustments to bridge the gap from the meetings between the parliamentary leaders. . . . We made a binding agreement that we will cut expenditure during the revised Budget in May [1990], 450 million Krones.[22]

Following the governmental co-operation with the FrP, the conflict between the SP parliamentary group and Cabinet members intensified to an overt hostility – the consequences of which will be explored later.

THE ITALIAN COMMUNIST PARTY (PCI), 1976–79

To understand the logic beyond the development of the PCI alliance strategy it is necessary to appreciate the organisational trends during the 1970s. During the mid-1970s the PCI elites faced a new phase in relation to the Italian community (Barbagli and Corbetta 1982b). First, a 20.2 per cent increase in party membership was recorded during 1968–76. Additionally, the adherence rate (i.e. the percentage of party members as a ratio of the total electorate) rose from 4.2 per cent to 6.7 per cent during 1968–77 (see Appendix 3.1). Second, after 1968, the territorial differences in membership distribution diminished across voter categories, i.e. men, women and young people. Third, the percentage of new recruits has increased, attaining in 1972, 1975 and 1976 a higher level than before, while a decline in the percentage of non-renewals was recorded. Fourth, the number of sections increased, suggesting there was an improvement in the stability of the organisational base. Fifth, the tendency among communist members to support their party financially was distinctly strengthened between 1974 and 1977. Finally, a decline in the age of the party leadership was recorded from the beginning of the 1970s. Consequently, the links between the PCI and the community were strengthened and the general instability of the party organisation – led by a seven-member secretariat under the leadership of Berlinguer – was reduced considerably (Barbagli and Corbetta 1982b).

Undoubtedly, the main issue on the PCI's agenda from September 1972 was the 'historic compromise'. According to Chiaromonte (1986: 182–3), 'the reasoning of the secretary of the PCI moved within the ambits of the great political ideas of Palmiro Togliatti'. Thus, the 'historic compromise' was presented as a continuation of the immediate post-war strategy of broad co-operation between political forces including those representing the middle strata. Such presentation throughout the exploration of the compromise was aimed at preparing the party base for the actual co-operation.

Added to this pattern of presentation was the step-by-step evolution of the PCI strategy through the course of events. Clarification of the PCI's strategy occurred after the following events:

1 the disturbing swing to the right following the MSI gains in 1970, 1971 and 1972;
2 the Chilean 1973 experience;
3 the erosion of the Catholic subculture as evident in the 1974 referendum;

Table 3.3 List of events in Italy, 1972–79

17.2.72	Formation of Andreotti's I government
26.2.72	Government collapse after a vote of no-confidence
24.6.72	Formation of Andreotti's II government
9–10.72	Publication of three articles by Berlinguer in *Rinascita*: The emergence of the Historic Compromise
12.6.73	Resignation of Andreotti's II government
7.7.73	Formation of Rumor IV government
2.3.74	Resignation of Rumor IV government
15.3.74	Formation of Rumor V government
3.10.74	Resignation of Rumor V government
11.11.74	Formation of Moro IV government
15–16.6.75	Regional, provincial and municipal elections
16.7.75	B. Zaccagnini elected as DC's party secretary
10.75	Right and left wing incidents, kidnappings
7.1.76	Resignation of Moro IV government
2.2.76	Formation of Moro V government
3–7.3.76	PSI's 14th Congress – the endorsment of 'the alternative of the left'
17–18.3.76	DC's 13th Congress – B. Zaccagnini re-elected as party secretary
14.4.76	A. Fanfani elected chairman of the DC's National Council
20–21.6.76	General election
13.7.76	F. De Martino, PSI's party secretary, resigned
16.7.76	B. Craxi becomes PSI's party secretary
30.7.76	Formation of Andreotti's III government
1.10.76	Moro elected as DC's President
8.10.76	First austerity package
10–12.11.76	Second austerity package
2.77	Student disturbance
4.77	Political terrorism, kidnappings
6.4.77	Third austerity package
25.4.77	Approval of IMF loan
13–15.7.77	Formal policy agreement between the DC, PCI, PSI, PRI, PLI, PSDI
16.1.78	Collapse of Andreotti's III government
13.3.78	Formation of Andreotti IV government
16.3.78	Moro's kidnapping by the Red Brigades
9.5.78	Moro's death
14–15.5.78	Partial municipal and provincial elections
31.1.79	Resignation of Andreotti IV government
1.4.79	President Pertini dissolved Parliament and called an election for June 3–4

Source: Keesing's Contemporary Archives, 1972–79.

4 the movement to the left of important sectors of the middle strata in the administrative election of 1975; and
5 the impressive PCI's gains in the 1976 general election.

During these events, to mention only one example, the PCI position concerning NATO and its existing bases on Italian territory was modified.

However conclusive the above-mentioned trends may have been, it was the PCI decisive preferences of 'obtaining full legitimation as a governing partner' (i.e. breaking up the 'convention of exclusion') and 'the defence of democracy' which shadowed any short-term aims. As Berlinguer explained:

> The struggle to democratise the State is an essential condition in order to fulfil a revolutionary policy, which, to be revolutionary, must always aim at destroying the class limits which are so strong in our country, in spite of the importance of the struggles and strength of the popular and worker's movement. Without this struggle it is impossible to get closer to our historical target, which is to fulfil a complete democracy and the coming of the working class and of its allies to the direction of the State.
>
> (Berlinguer, E. cited in Vacca 1987: 60)

The decisive preference of overcoming the *conventio ad excludendum* did not preclude the possibility of revolutionary policy nor did it mean changes to the existing constitutional framework. It actually meant that the various patterns of government were to be considered as intermediate targets, during a process aimed at deeply changing the Italian legitimate political spectrum. Such a strategy should take place by bringing the PCI inside a 'government of democratic change' and, consequently, preventing a shift of the middle strata towards the right (Berlinguer E., cited in Vacca 1987).

Perhaps, most important of all, was the economic and institutional crisis (*La crisi Italiana*) which provided the issue upon which a visible convergence between the DC, PCI, PRI, PLI, PSDI, and PSI was reached.[23] For the PCI, the crisis, which worsened dramatically in the mid-1970s, was considered an element aiding the historic compromise. The fact that major economic decisions of national necessity were agreed upon by a large part of the bourgeoisie could justify co-operation among the working class and the socialist movement in order to widen their action to a national level.

The PCI's decision in 1976 to enter into bargaining with the DC was taken by the elite collectively and unanimously, thus significantly reducing potential dissatisfaction at the elite level (Chiaromonte 1986: 39). According to the chairman of the PCI's parliamentary group, Alessandro Natta:

> I have spoken about doubts in the body of the party. The choices [that] were made in that period were accepted by all the leadership of the party, by all the Central Committee of the party. There was no contrast, no division within the leadership at the top of the party . . . I can add that the comrade Longo expressed some *riserva* about the idea of historic compromise. Sometimes he said; I don't like this term 'historic compromise'. I would prefer that people will use the term which was used by Gramsci 'new social political bloc' which means that he had some doubts not only about this strategy but also about solution like the government of abstention.[24]

However, at the organisational level, the PCI elites faced potential opposition to their strategy. At the outset, the PCI elites had to implement its strategy in light of two instability sources:

1 the 20.2 per cent rise in the party membership which was recorded during 1968–76 (Barbagli and Corbetta 1982b: 81), and
2 the fact that the most important decision-making bodies within the party were afterwards informed of and duly ratified the decision to launch the policy (Pasquino 1988: 36).

For a time it appeared that the internal conflicts aggravated by heterogeneity and the negative aspect of 'democratic centralism' were costs the leadership was willing to pay. Surprisingly, the 'doubts' in the body of the party were perceived by PCI elites as only concerning with the economic and institutional crisis. As the PCI economic spokesman, Giorgio Napolitano, put it:

> I want to emphasise the awareness which was represented in our rank-and-file people on the serious[ness] of the national situation from two fundamental aspects; inflation and terrorism. So, the idea that it was necessary to put together all democratic forces in our country to fight these two threats was accepted . . . at that moment we had to decide without delay. We could not engage our party and other parties in months of discussion in a possible common programme. A government had to be formed also because those two threats were really urgent.[25]

In order to cope with the potential follower's opposition following the decision of the party elite to enter into coalition bargaining with the DC, the PCI elites decided to initiate 'explanatory pedagogy' through public meetings (see Chapter 5), and to enter a transitional period of no no-confidence (i.e. from August 1976 to July 1977). The transitional period has created an image of long, difficult and complex PCI–DC negotiations. This, in turn, was intended to satisfy elite members and party followers whose orientations were still largely attuned to the ideological aspect of co-operation. This view confirms Luebbert's (1986: 52) argument that it is wrong to assume that because interparty negotiations take a long time much is being negotiated among the parties. Rather, most negotiations are actually taking place between leaders and their followers and among rival factions within parties.

The bilateral discussions, informal interparty meetings, telephone calls and private conversations during the transitional period is crucial to explain both the November proposals concerning the government economic strategy and the formation of a formal alliance later in the early 1977. It was in this transitional period that the PCI had produced, and brought up to date, alternative policies to those followed by successive governments throughout its period in opposition. Furthermore, in the months following the informal alliance, Napolitano, who led the PCI's economic team, co-operated both with Stammati, who was a DC technical expert brought in to strengthen the quality of economic advice, and the Prime Minister (Roscue 1982: 95). The PCI's strategic line was also dependent on a more or less contemporaneous convergence between the strategies of several different parties. Since no formal agreement was signed during the transitional period, one could not expect to find intensive internal disagreement within the different parties. Within the DC, for example, it was mainly Fanfanians who argued against deepening the co-operation with the PCI. They stated that although the DC was open to 'dialogue' with the PCI there must be no confusion of roles between government and opposition. For the small parties, whereas the vast majority of the PRI favoured the 'no no-confidence' formula,[26] the PSI elites seemed to have no other option than to support it.

It is important to note that the PSI, at that time, faced a period of transition, from the dominance of the centre faction led by De Martino towards the succession of the Craxi–Signorile group to win a majority in the Central Committee (Hine 1979: 135). The resignation of the PSI's secretary following the 1976 election results, furthermore, reflected the uncertainty within the PSI. As Silvano Labriola, a PSI member of Parliament, put it:

> I'll be very honest. After the general election in 1976 there was a sort of shock in the PSI because at that time we reached our historical

minimum, the lowest level of the party. Hence, in the leadership of the party emerged the wish to find out new ways, new paths, so as to enhance a little bit the people's feeling *vis-à-vis* our party.[27]

Not surprisingly, Craxi was left with no possibility other than to participate in the six-parties alliance.

The formal minority government, formed in July 1977, started a new stage of interparty co-operation in the Italian party system. Marradi (1982: 60) claims that 'the DC is aware that it can accede to many of its partners' requests in the program drafting stage, since it retains an almost absolute control upon which policy measures to take, to block, and which to subvert'. Consequently, a substantial reason for the formation of the formal alliance was due to the DC acceptance of some PCI's elements of planning in the agreement. According to Giorgio Napolitano, the head of the PCI's economic team:

We tried to agree on some elements of planning in order to correct some traditional imbalances in our economy and our society. Particularly, we focused on some Bills to be adopted in Parliament. First, for industrial policy, industrial planning. The idea, approved by other parties, including the DC, was that all incentives should be given on the basis of sector plans . . . [according to] some goals, such as the reduction of the imbalances between north and south or as the reduction of structural weaknesses in our industrial system. Second, a similar mold for agriculture. Third, a plan for public housing. These three Bills put together could represent a new framework for public intervention in economic development.[28]

These three conditions did not embarrass the Government because its monocolour position implied no real possibility for the PCI to control the implementation of these reforms. The fact that one finds almost exactly the same items in the official programme of past DC's governments (Marradi 1982), reveals Andreotti's tactics to form a formal alliance while paying much less in return.

The agreement was, in that case, presented in the Chamber of Deputies as a motion signed by the six parties and approved section by section by a large majority.[29] The vote on the final motion was 442 in favour, 87 against, 16 abstaining and 85 absent. Although the total strength of the parties officially opposing the programmatic accord was only 45, possibly more than 100 out of DC's 263 deputies either voted against it, abstained, or were intentionally absent, as a sign of their disapproval of the new commitment (Wertman 1981). The evolution of intra-elite conflicts within the DC, which were first evident in the above-mentioned vote, and the followers' dissatisfaction within the PCI, which was worsened following the formation of the formal alliance, are our next business.

To explain the way in which the internal dissatisfaction within the PCI was manifested following the formation of the formal minority government, requires specification of the party's strategic model to mediate between their internal life and their political behaviour (Tarrow 1983: 141). For the PCI, the internal difficulties faced by the party elites during the implementation of the historic compromise had two dimensions which were mutually reinforcing. The first lay in the lengthy lack of the membership and militants' support for the party line. The second dimension lay in the absence of a mediator role in the PCI structure.

From its beginning, the PCI strategy displayed open hostility at the grass-roots level. Those hostile attitudes were recorded when the 'explanatory pedagogy' was implemented; over 11,000 public meetings took place in the first three months of 1977 (Cervetti 1977). Even within the highly centralised context of the PCI one confronts striking intraparty variation over the issue of supporting the party line. According to Barbagli and Corbetta's (1982a) research, dissent from the party line was greater among the members than among the section secretaries, at least during the period 1976–78. Based on data from members of the Bologna federation at the beginning of 1978 and from section secretaries collected in the second half of the same year, 20 per cent of PCI members were explicitly against the party policy and almost all the section secretaries were in favour of collaboration with the DC under the political circumstances at that time (Barbagli and Corbetta 1982a: 218). During this period, it could be said that the positions of the elites and that of the followers moved steadily apart after the formation of each government, diminishing clearly when the latter entered into crisis.

The PCI followers militantly opposed the official party's line. The climax of the militants' activities took place late in 1977, when the militant metalworkers' union (FLM) precipitated a governmental crisis against the PCI's wishes. As Napolitano noted:

> There was an alarm with some partial election already in spring 1978. . . . But another very dramatic moment was a general strike of metal workers at the end of 1977. I think that this was the reason for the Cabinet crisis of January 1978 because we felt that there was dissatisfaction among the workers with the economic policy of the government we were supporting.[30]

Violent demonstrations by approximately 200,000 workers in the streets forced the PCI to modify its alliance strategy. Additionally, the party elites were forced to initiate an 'articulation of ends' in order to pacify the follower's dissatisfaction, which was facilitated by the government economic policy of 'austerity'.

Of equal relevance was the organisational decline of the party. A 1.3 per cent loss of party membership, a 2.3 per cent decrease in the adherence rate, a 21.2 per cent decrease in the new recruits, and a 3.2 per cent decline in the non renewals, were recorded during 1977–78 (see Appendix 3.1). These trends implied that the PCI elite was not able to embrace its strategy fully without offending the members' ideological heritage. The limitations of the PCI's strategy are well described in the draft theses for the Fifteenth PCI Congress, in December 1978:

> There has been a disparity between the efforts devoted to work in the institutions and relations among the political forces, on the one hand, and initiative to promote united movements involving broad masses around concrete goals and problems, on the other hand. This has led to difficulties in maintaining and strengthening the party's relations with various strata of the working population at all times and in all phases of the struggle, in organically linking our presence and action in society with our activity in the institutions and in exercising our government functions in the most effective manner.[31]

A clear change in the position of the section secretaries was recorded following the experience of the Andreotti governments from 1978 onwards. Almost all those interviewed in Barbagli and Corbetta's (1982a) research still thought that 'the most possible, most realistic government' would be based on an alliance between their party and the DC. However, the preference of the relative majority of those interviewed was in favour of a government of the left (Barbagli and Corbetta 1982a: 222).

Overall, the worsening of the followers' dissatisfaction was facilitated by the absence of 'mediators' (e.g. groupings) within the party. At a time when the elite-follower conflicts evolved, the PCI structure, in which a strong apparatus confronted the party's intermediate and peripheral associations, risks the control over the intermediate position between the members and the apparatus (i.e. the militants). The rank and file hostility, on the one side, and the apparatus's efforts to get them to accept the party line, on the other side, resulted in the increased tension and political fatigue within the militants.

THE FRENCH COMMUNIST PARTY (PCF), 1988–91

La France Unie was the essential spirit of Mitterrand's campaign strategy in the May 1988 Presidential election. He called for an opening of the new presidential majority to the centre and centre-right politicians, implicitly refusing the old Fifth Republic pattern of bipolarisation between the left and the right. Additionally, he had rejected any parliamentary pact which might reduce his image as a candidate who could offer a synthesis of the various policies that had been adopted, under left and right, during his first seven-year presidency.

Throughout the campaign Mitterrand was careful not to call for a formal alliance. He promised implicitly that his election would be followed by a political realignment, and that a new presidential majority backing Mitterrand would have to comprise those centre and centre-right politicians who were willing to support the new President.

Table 3.4 List of events in France, 1988–90

4–5.88	F. Mitterrand elected as France's President
12.5.88	M. Rocard announced his minority Cabinet list
14.5.88	F. Mitterrand dissolved the National Assembly and announced the first round of legislative election
14.5.88	P. Mauroy elected as PS secretary by 63 votes to 54 votes for M. Fabius, who was supported by Mitterrand
6.88	Legislative election
15.6.88	P. Méhaignerie announced the formation of the UDC
23.6.88	M. Fabius elected as President of the Parliament
28.6.88	M. Rocard announced his enlarged Cabinet list
20.8.88	Signing of the New Caledonian Agreement
10–11.88	Public sector strikes
6.11.88	National referendum on New Caledonian
9.12.88	A motion of censure against the government failed to win the necessary support
22.12.88	The 1989 budget aimed at reducing the budgetary deficit was adopted
12.88	First attempt by senior PCF members to circulate a dissident publication inside the party
3.89	Local elections, the PS won control over an increased number of large towns
4.89	Threat to opposition leadership led by P. Seguin and M. Noir
6.89	Election to the European Parliament with separate UDC list
25.9.89	C. Millon elected as parliamentary UDF leader
11.2.90	RPR National Congress in which J. Chirac was re-elected unanimously as the RPR leader while leadership challenge continues
3.90	PS party congress at *Rennes*

Source: Keesing's Contemporary Archives, 1988–90.

Mitterrand's view, however, did not preclude an alliance with the PCF. The PS gesture of reducing the number of seats required to form a parliamentary group, from thirty to twenty-five, in order to institutionalise the PCF's position within parliament as a potential partner, exemplifies this point.

After the election, an informal alliance, comprised of the PCF, the UDC and individual MPs, was indeed formed on the basis of 'unity' in light of the 1991 EC's single economic market. Following PS–PCF co-operation, elite-follower conflicts emerged within the latter. The ex-Ministers, Anicet Le Pors and Andre Lajoinie, were notably more favourable to co-operation with the government, while militants from the Communist-led CGT wished the party to oppose the government's economic policy. This conflict was recorded especially during the public strikes in October–November 1988 (Elgie and Maor 1992). According to The *Times*, the strike on 20 October was the first since 1968 that saw the leaders of the CGT marching in the same protest with those of the moderate *Force Ouvière*.[32] Moreover, violent demonstrations were conducted outside the *Hotel Matignon*, on 23 November, by 200,000 miners from the impoverished regions.[33]

Whereas all the union federations accepted the government's offer of two catch-up pay raises, militant workers from the CGT did not want to follow the calls for a compromise from the PCF elites. Such a compromise was considered necessary in order to form a pact with the reluctant Socialist elites for the local elections which were due in the spring of 1989. Unless they did compromise, they risked losing some of their few remaining sources of power and patronage in France's big towns. Additionally, the PCF elites assumed they had tacit support from left-wing Socialists unhappy with Rocard's government. This was especially significant in light of the latter's fear of losing touch with the party base in the public sector and teachers' unions because, of 275 Socialist deputies, 115 had a background in teaching.[34]

Dissenting voices were also recorded inside the party. In the first attempt by senior party members in more than 60 years to circulate a dissident publication inside the PCF, a new magazine – *Reconstruction Communiste* – published in December 1988, attacked the secretary-general, George Marchais.[35] This is not to say that those attacks were simply the result of co-operation with Rocard's government. Rather, it is to stress that the events in Eastern Europe and the public sector unrest in France throughout the winter and spring of 1988–89 – a sector where the CGT is particularly strong – were equally if not more important. Altogether, these manifestations of elite-follower conflicts have resulted in the break-up of the PS–PCF co-operation.

SUMMARY AND CONCLUSION

A centralised party leaves intra-elite opposition with two alternatives; resignation and attempts to disturb the day-to-day operation of the alliance. For the former, top elite members may believe that their resignation would disrupt or terminate the coalition bargaining and the process of government formation. A classic example of such an attempt is the resignation of the leader of the SD parliamentary group, Jens Risgaard Knudsen, during the first meeting of the group subsequent to the conclusion of the SD–Liberal accord. For the protest option, party elites may assume that constant attempts to disturb the day-to-day operation of the alliance would terminate the coalition bargaining. During the 1989–90 co-operation among the Norwegian Centre Party, Conservative and the Christian People's Party, for instance, members of the former parliamentary group had expressed their dissatisfaction (following the direct policy negotiations between the Prime Minister, Jan P. Syse, and the leader of the Progress Party, Carl Hagen) by trying to delay the conclusion of the 1990 budget negotiation. Consequently, the SP acted inconsistently: it first broke up the negotiations following the participation of the Progress Party in the discussions, but in the end, signed the agreement.

In cases of elite-follower conflict within centralised parties a different picture emerges. In the case of the PCF, the ex-Ministers, Anicet Le Pors and Andre Lajoinie, were notably more favourable to co-operation with the government, while militants from the Communist-led trade union (CGT) wished the party to oppose the government's economic policy. This conflict was recorded especially during the public strikes in October–November 1988. Furthermore, violent demonstrations were conducted outside the Prime Minister's office by approximately 200,000 miners from the impoverished regions. Similarly, in the case of the PCI, the climax of the militants' activities took place late in 1977, when the militant metalworkers' union (FLM) precipitated a government crisis against the PCI's wishes. A general strike of metal workers at the end of 1977 which was accompanied by a violent demonstration of approximately 200,000 activists, reflected the dissatisfactions among party followers.

In the beginning of the chapter I posed the question 'How can 'claims' be made by actors operating within centralised parties on the party elites?' The analysis has provided an affirmative answer to this question by studying patterns of internal opposition in four centralised parties. As shown in Table 3.5, it demonstrates that, in the cases observed, whereas intra-elite opposition adopted the 'exit' option and

Table 3.5 Modes of conflict manifestation in centralised parties

Party	Period	Alliance partners	Decisive preference underlying the alliance*	Decisive preference underlying party strategy**	Pattern of organisational decline	Dominant mode of conflict manifestation
(i)	*Centralised parties which face intra-elite conflicts*					
SD	1978–9	Liberal Party	Stable cooperation which could adhere to long-term economic recovery		Exit	Resignation of the leader of the parliamentary group, Jens Risgaard Knudsen
SP	1989–90	Con. KrF	Fighting inflation		Voice	Calls within the parliamentary group against the party's alliance strategy and an attempt to delay the conclusion of the Finance Bill
(ii)	*Centralised parties which face elite-follower conflicts*					
PCI	1976–9	DC, PSI, PRI, PSDI	Restoring public order/economic recovery	Obtaining PCI's full legitimacy	Voice (outside the party)	Violent demonstrations of approx. 200,000 activists
PCF	1988–90	PS	Unity		Voice (outside the party)	Violent demonstrations of approx. 200,000 activists

* As evident from the coalition/pact's agreement or 'understanding'.
** As evident from political statements and elite interviews.
Source: Maor (1995a: 77).

the 'voice' mode *within* party bodies, followers' hostility tends to adopt the 'voice' mode *outside* the party.

Existing accounts of coalition bargaining make central mistakes in dealing with the interplay between intra- and interparty politics. First, they ignore party organisation attributes when attempting to explain strategies of party sub-groups. Second, they ignore the potential effect some modes of conflict manifestations may have on the ability of centralised parties to commit themselves to a co-operative relationship. This chapter and the next show that variations in the distribution of effective decision-making authority within the party create variation in dissent strategies by party members and subgroups. Although leaders of party sub-groups are only one set of actors in quite a complex internal picture, they confront a relatively limited range of decision choices in so far as the manifestation of internal dissatisfaction is concerned. Centralised organisations indeed drastically reduce this range.

4 Modes of conflict manifestation in decentralised parties

Conventional accounts of coalition bargaining have failed to grasp the advantages in allowing party elites and sub-groups to challenge party's policy and strategy. They have failed to comprehend that precisely this flexibility offsets any attempt for dissatisfaction to emerge outside the party, that is, outside the leadership's 'zone of control'. Moreover, conventional accounts have paid too little attention to the functions of factions in maintaining party stability during periods of political turmoil. To bridge this gap this chapter aims to explore factional activities as a key means of helping party elites to pacify and neutralise internal dissatisfaction. Allowing members of the party elites and sub-groups to express dissatisfaction within the party assures the party leadership that its coalition strategy would remain unaltered and their own position secured.

The chapter analyses the manifestation of intra-elite and elite-follower conflicts within four decentralised parties, namely, the Italian Christian Democratic Party (1976–79), the British Labour Party and Liberal Party (1977–78), and the French Socialist Party (1988–91). The analysis of each case begins with a brief discussion of the position of party leaders within the party, the background for the coalition agreement and the decisive preferences underlying the agreement. I show that, in the cases observed, intraparty opposition within decentralised parties pursued only the voice option within the party and the parliamentary arenas. Attention now turns to the emergence of intra-elite conflicts within the Italian Christian Democratic Party during the 'historic compromise'.

THE ITALIAN CHRISTIAN DEMOCRATIC PARTY (DC), 1976–79

To understand the logic underlying the development of the DC alliance strategies it is necessary to appreciate some organisational trends during the 1970s and the elite structure within the party. Perhaps the most important trend that evolved within the DC was a fall in party membership of almost 580,000 during 1973–77; the bulk of this fall occurred in 1976 (see Appendix 4.1). This decline in party membership led to a significant deterioration in the DC's image and raised calls to end the regime of the *correnti* which had resulted in the removal of Fanfani from the DC Secretaryship and his replacement by the 'reformer', Zaccagnini. Zaccagnini's approach was to mobilise a strong movement within the DC for the reorganisation process against an opposition of the party's centre and right. Consequently, the major issue within the DC, prior to the historic compromise, was the revitalisation (*rifondazione*) of the party. The saliency of the *rifondazione* lies, naturally, on the view that DC could no longer base its political fortunes on the anti-communist issues or the links to the Catholic church.

Regarding the elite structure, the DC leadership included seven factions under the leadership of Moro, namely, *Forze Nuove* (13 per cent), *Base* (10 per cent), *Morotei* (10 per cent), *Rumor-Gullotti* (9 per cent), *Colombo* (7 per cent), *Dorotei* (23 per cent) and *Fanfani* (12 per cent) (Leonardi and Wertman 1989). However the distribution of posts within the DC (mentioned above in brackets) did not accurately reflect the internal balance of power. At the outset, whereas Moro was elected as DC's President by a 165 majority of the 183 votes cast in the party's national council, the more powerful post of party secretary was held by Zaccagnini, who had been re-elected, in the 1976 party congress, by 51.6 per cent against 48.4 per cent.[1] Further limitations to Zaccagnini role, beyond the narrow majority he won in the Congress, was the election of Senator Fanfani as the chairman of the party's national council and twenty-one of his supporters as executive committee members. Additionally, the prime ministership was given to Giulio Andreotti, the most right-wing leader with governmental experience.

However mutable Zaccagnini and Fanfani strengths may have been, it was Moro who possessed the major influence within DC. According to the leader of the DC's parliamentary group, Flaminio Piccoli:

> Moro was the leader of the left within the DC after being the leader of the centre in the DC, and in that moment, the position between

Mr Moro and Fanfani began to [be] diversified. Even if Mr Zaccagnini was the Secretary General of the party, at that moment, the real leader was Moro. Thus, from this reason I saw Moro and Fanfani and not Zaccagnini and Fanfani [as opponents] even if Zaccagnini was a real cultural and sensitive man. But the real leader of the party was Moro. So, if we can speak about discussions between two persons we should speak about those between Moro and Fanfani. Zaccagnini interpreted Moro, and I say this not as to be offensive against Zaccagnini. Moro was intellectually superior and he had a really high prestige among all parties.[2]

Thus, it was Moro who enjoyed a dominant position within the DC in the mid-1970s.

Perhaps most important of all was the economic and institutional crisis (*La crisi Italiana*) which provided the issue upon which a visible convergence between the DC, PCI, PRI, PLI, PSDI, and PSI was reached. As noted earlier, for the PCI, the fact that major economic decisions of national necessity were agreed upon by a large part of the bourgeoisie, could justify co-operation among the working class and the socialist movement in order to widen their action to a national level. For the DC, on the other hand, the economic and institutional crisis was a matter of government and party survival. Pridham's (1988: 216) finding, that 'the DC emerges as 'a power-motivated party prepared at almost all costs to preserve its role in the state', emphasises choosing a consensus-based aim as DC's decisive preference. Beyond the notion of *emergenza*, lies the preferences that derived from the most widely-shared values within a party and directly engage the party's most basic sense of purpose. In other words, the preference which above all minimises party disunity. This observation is undeniably appropriate to the cases of DC, PSI, PRI, PLI, and PSDI.

The nuances of Andreotti's bargaining tactics are of equal relevance. A classic example was the decision that the PCI's member Pietro Ingrao, who was considered a potential rival to Berlinguer, would be elected President of the Chamber while Amitore Fanfani, who was considered an opponent to any DC co-operation with the Communists, would be re-elected President of the Senate. Beyond the fact that this decision had been taken at a joint session of six parties lies a clear indication that Andreotti aimed at minimising the DC's disunity as well as the PC's disunity. Moreover, in order to minimise DC's disunity, a total of forty-seven under-secretaries, adherents of the main *correnti*, were appointed. This was an increase of eight on the number in the outgoing Government.

Added to these tactics was Andreotti's attempt to cover his exposed right flank following the PCI's hope to shift the balance within the DC to a degree sufficient to permit the formation of a coalition (Lange 1975). Perhaps following external pressures from the right-wing factions within the DC, a break-up within the MSI–DN parliamentary group occurred in December 1976. The reason was, according to MSI's MP Raffaele Valensise:

> because in 1976 there were those who left the MSI who thought it was possible to cover the manoeuvre of Signor Andreotti who had already obtained the abstention of the Communist Party, and thus, it would have been possible to obtain also the abstention of at least some members of the MSI. . . . I think this was the main cause of the break, a sort of temptation into which some of our members fell to cover the manoeuvre of Andreotti with the assistance of the Communist Party.[3]

Given that almost half the deputies in the MSI–DN parliamentary group left the party over the issue of abstention in parliament, it is hardly surprising that the DC obtained a 'sleeping partner'. The MSI–DC informal co-operation, aimed at voting out the Abortion Bill in early 1977 in the Senate, suffices to underline this point (Roscue 1982).

The formal minority government, formed in July 1977, started a new stage of interparty co-operation in the Italian party system. The DC was able to satisfy many of PCI requests in the coalition agreement, since it retains an almost absolute control upon which policy measures to take, to block, and which to subvert. Indeed, the DC accepted some elements of planning in the agreement, such as industrial, agriculture and public housing planning. These concessions did not embarrass the Government because its monocolour position implied no real possibilities for the PCI to control the implementation of these reforms. The agreement was, in that case, presented in the Chamber of Deputies as a motion signed by the six parties and approved section by section by a large majority.[4] As noted already, the vote on the final motion was 442 in favour, 87 against, 16 abstaining and 85 absent.

Attention now turns to the evolution of intra-elite conflicts within the DC. It was from the PCI's call for 'a government of unity and national solidarity', following the FLM activities, that intra-elite conflict evolved within the DC. Debate as to whether to include Communist support for the new government on the vote of confidence was evident along ideological and factional lines. A classic example was the 'group of 100', consisted especially of the *Dorotei* and

Fanfanian's deputies, which opposed any new steps in the co-operation with the PCI. Moreover, survey results indicated that 64 per cent of DC's 205 deputies asked were against the entrance of the PCI into the majority (Malatesta 1978). Yet, it is misleading to contend that the party's decision-making bodies shared the approach of the 'group of 100'. On the contrary, the DC National Executive Committee, for example, had accepted a policy statement which favoured the inclusion of all the six parties in a 'parliamentary convergence'. This would involve a government programme, worked out in detail with the opposition, which would enjoy the active support of the Communists in Parliament.[5]

The assassination of Moro by the Red Brigades opened a new era in the relationship between the DC and the PCI elites. However, the intra-elite conflicts within the DC, following the introduction of the PCI into the majority, evolved before the kidnapping. Gerardo Bianco, a DC MP, recalled that:

> Tensions had already appeared during the formation of [the new] Andreotti government. As it is known, difficulties were overcome only after the speech of Aldo Moro to the parliamentary group. But the speech did not give immediate results as some historians have written. . . . Some signatures were gathered with which he was asked not to accept the vote of the Communists. There were long negotiations during the whole night, then, a document was drafted and presented to the Communist Party which approved it. This was the passage with many many resistance ranged from the centre to the so-called *Sinistra Sociale* by Donat Cattin who were against this kind of alliance.[6]

It was during the long crisis of January–March 1978 (i.e. following the introduction of the PCI into the majority) that a new dividing line emerged. This cleavage cut across various factions, especially *Forze Nuove*, *Base* and *Dorotei*. It separated those who were apparently inclined to work in the long-term direction of an agreement with the PCI and those who worked in the direction of re-establishing a privileged relationship with the PSI while isolating the Communists. Zaccagnini, Andreotti's supporters and Piccoli represented the former tendency. A less homogeneous group including Mario Segni, Mazzotta, De Carolis, the *Dorotei* led by Bisaglia and his supporters together with Donat Cattin, represented the latter direction (Pasquino 1980).

As noted earlier, at the heart of DC's strategy lay Moro's position within his party and, thus, his ability to win the support of the party's parliamentary group. However, it was after Moro was murdered that factional activities reached a new climax. In spite of Zaccagnini's effort towards the revitalisation of the party, new forces were institution-alised within the DC during 1978–79. Whereas two new factions, namely, *Iniziativa Democratica* and *Proposta*, grew out of the anti-communist subculture, a technocratically-oriented group associated with Umberto Agnelli has emerged. Furthermore, a student movement of approximately 100,000 members, namely *Communion and Liberation*, grew out of the Catholic subculture and concentrated its activities in that direction (Wertman 1981: 81–2).

To sum up, the main manifestations of the intra-elite conflicts within the DC during the historic compromise were 'voices' in the parliamentary party and the formation of three new factions. Intra-elite conflicts which occurred within the DC were manifested within the party. Since the DC elites accepted the formation of new factions, it became clear that as long as dissatisfaction would be expressed through the diffused mechanisms within the party no change in the elites' strategy would be required.

THE BRITISH LABOUR PARTY AND LIBERAL PARTY, 1977–78

To understand the tactics which were implemented by David Steel, the Liberal Party leader, and James Callaghan, the Labour Party leader, it is necessary to appreciate the positions of both leaders within their respective parties. Prior to the Pact, both the Labour and the Liberal parties had elected new party leaders. Under the multi-ballot system in which the successful candidate would have to obtain an overall majority of the total electorate of 317 Labour MPs, Callaghan was elected leader of the PLP on the third ballot by a majority of 39 MPs.[7] David Steel, on the other hand, contested his election under new rules which provided for an electoral college composed of constituency representatives, and was elected by a majority of 5,509 out of 19,573 voters.[8] These results eliminated any further challenges to the leader-ship within those parties. Whereas, in the Labour Party, 'Michael Foot accepted the result without any difficulties and worked as deputy leader with James Callaghan and gave him a hundred and fifty per cent support',[9] in the Liberal Party, John Pardoe told Steel that 'the party could have only one leader and one strategy' (Steel 1980: 23). Both leaders, therefore, enjoyed a dominant position within their respective parties.

Since the leader is at the centre of a range of internal forces which he must seek to pacify or neutralise, the style of leadership assumes

Table 4.1 List of events in the UK, 1974–79

10.10.74	General election (Lab. 319, Con. 277, Lib. 13)
11.2.75	Margaret Thatcher elected as Con. leader
26.6.75	Labour lose Woolwich West by-election
18.1.76	Formation of the Scottish Labour Party (2 MPs)
16.3.76	Harold Wilson announces resignation
5.4.76	James Callaghan becomes Prime Minister
10.5.76	Jeremy Thorpe resigns as Liberal leader
7.7.78	David Steel elected Liberal leader
9.9.76	Unemployment reaches 1,588,000
28.9.76	James Callaghan speech demanding financial prudence
21.10.76	Michael Foot elected Deputy Leader of the Labour Party
27.10.76	Pound reaches its lowest level ($1.56)
4.11.76	Labour lose Workington and Walsall North by-elections
15.12.76	Healey announces letter of intent for IMF loan and drastic cuts
21.2.77	David Owen becomes Foreign Secretary
22.2.77	Government defeated on devolution guillotine
17.3.77	Aircraft and Shipbuiding Act finally passed
23.3.77	Lib–Lab Pact saves government in confidence motion
31.3.77	Labour lose Stechford by-election
28.4.77	Labour lose Ashfield by-election and hold Grimsby
5.5.77	Labour lose Greater London Council and other local election contests
15.7.77	Healey outlines Phase III of incomes policy
8.77	Unemployment peaks at 1,636,000
13.12.77	PR for European Elections rejected by the House of Commons
26.1.78	Special Liberal Assembly conditionally endorses Pact
23.1.78	Government defeat on Green Pound devaluation
2.3.78	Labour lose Ilford by-election
25.5.78	Announcement of forthcoming termination of the Pact
31.5.78	Labour wins Hamilton by-election
7.9.78	Prime Minister announced 'No election'
21.9.78	Ford Strike against 5% offer begins
2.10.78	Labour conference rejects 5% wage limit
26.10.78	Swing to Labour in Berwick and East Lothian by-elections
13.12.78	Commons vote 285–283 against government sanctions on employers breaking the 5% pay policy
1.3.79	Devolution referendum in Scotland and Wales
28.3.79	Government loses confidence vote 311–310
29.3.79	Election announced for 3 May

Source: Keesing's Contemporary Archives, 1974–79.

particular importance. Style of leadership, which commonsense suggests is influenced heavily by past experience, provides us with the nuances of leader-elite communications within the parties. According to Tom MacNally, the private secretary of the Prime Minister, James Callaghan was considered to be:

Very relaxed, very much as chairman of the board, head of a team. I think he brought to the prime-ministership a lot of his experience of his early youth as a trade union negotiator and also by the time he became PM almost a decade as a senior colleague of Harold Wilson, so, he had seen the advantages and the disadvantages of Harold Wilson's style. I think he consciously tried to have a more open relationship with his colleagues and because he was at the autumn of his political career, I think, he had a more relaxed and philosophical attitude about Cabinet government. He saw it as an opportunity to allow individual Ministers to develop their ideas rather than trying to be the head of every initiative and the final arbitrator of every decision.[10]

That David Steel had a completely different leadership style and political background is undoubted, as described by John Pardoe, his competitor in the leadership election and the informal deputy leader during the Pact:

David Steel . . . is passionately interested . . . in the mechanics of politics. It is politics that interested him, not political ideas. . . . And the game of politics was not communication with people, it wasn't even creating power, it was just being there. He loved every minute of it, he loved manipulating politicians, he loved manipulating beyond the scene. And he had never done anything else; he had gone out of University's student union, student's politics, straight from that into what was a research or organisation job with the Liberal Party in Scotland and then he joined the Parliament in an early by-election.[11]

At face value these statements are not incorrect. However, in our concern to explain the main variables operating during the formation of the Pact, it is more relevant to consider the interaction of these two party leaders during the actual bargaining rather than limit our discussion to their position within the confines of their respective parties.

Undoubtedly, it was the preference of 'economic recovery' which serves as a visible point of departure in the bargaining between Callaghan and Steel (see Appendix 4.2). The idea of using an economic umbrella as the central energiser of the Pact was sufficiently focused that it generated the widest possible support within both parties. Furthermore, since no policy concessions over this issue were explicitly mentioned in the Pact, it was sufficiently vague and opaque that it did not initiate intraparty disagreement. It was seen as a decisive point that the Liberals, by forming the Pact, obligate themselves to support a broad target, namely, 'work with the government in the pursuit of economic recovery', that is convergent with their party program.

As potential coalitional partners, both parties could limit themselves to one visible decisive preference as a basis for all government activity. This was especially relevant to the Liberal MPs who insisted on PR for the European elections as a precondition to any formal alliance with the Labour Party. In order to capture the actual bargaining between Steel and Callaghan over this issue we must examine the bargaining position of both actors.

The Labour Cabinet had, prior to the loss of the government's majority and any discussion of a Pact, already accepted a version of the Finnish regional system of PR, which the Secretary of State for Foreign and Commonwealth Affairs, David Owen, had suggested for the election to the European Parliament (Owen 1986: 38). As David Owen recalled:

> It was a cabinet decision. It was discussed twice in Cabinet. The first time I raised it as a possibility and then we took it away and came back with a paper on it, so that it was a formal majority decision. . . . It was a clear majority in the Cabinet, I mean, we didn't vote. Callaghan summed up and said that we agree. . . . When I knew that these discussions [over the Pact] were going on . . . Jeremy Thorpe was then shadowing the Foreign Affairs. . . . I did actually tell him that the Cabinet had decided that there would be PR. . . . The attempt was to stiffen his arm on the issue.[12]

Given that there was a cabinet decision over PR to the European Election which was known to a key Liberal MP, it was very surprising that Steel did not insist that the Liberals' support could not possibly continue if the Cabinet's advocacy of this issue was not carried on to the statute book. During the final interparty negotiations, the issue which worried the Liberal MPs most was the European Elections and PR for those elections; 'they insisted that the Government should be bound to legislate for the election in the present session of Parliament, and that they should be pledged to introduce PR' (Michie and Hoggart 1978: 51).

Debate in the Labour Party as to whether PR for the European Election should be introduced was due mainly to the fear that it might be the harbinger of a similar system for the British elections. The observation of Lord Donoughue, the head of the Labour think-tank, that 'It was not an issue that Mr Callaghan ever wished to raise to a high profile because it would have divided the party just as the EC divided the party',[13] gave rise to Callaghan's proposal in which he agreed to offer a choice of electoral systems, between the regional list system of PR and the 'first past the post' system and promised to take account of the Liberals' views on the subject while giving a private assurance that he himself would vote for PR (Callaghan 1987: 456–7). By forming the Pact, therefore, Callaghan did not obligate his party to support a policy that was at variance with the preference of some of its MPs. Since both leaders preferred a formal alliance, they formulated the Pact in such way that no commitment was formalised over an issue which was at variance with any of the party's preferences.

There is, nevertheless, general agreement that for David Steel, 'obtaining governmental experience' was a decisive preference. According to his political adviser, Richard Holme:

> For Steel, the main price was not the condition of the arrangement but the arrangement itself. For Steel, the price, the victory . . . was the arrangement that a marginal party had become part of the process of public policy determination, become more governmental. . . . [For him], it seemed almost the ideal compromise that he could both get involved in government but not commit his party which [would] not have been willing to form a coalition.[14]

Given such a view, it is hardly surprising that the major part of the Pact dealt with the institutionalisation of regular contacts between the two parties. A joint consultative committee which met regularly under the chairmanship of Michael Foot, the leader of the House of Commons, was set up. Yet, in order to minimise disunity within both parties it was stated that 'the existence of this committee will not commit the Government to accepting views of the Liberal Party, or the Liberal Party to supporting the Government on any issue' (see Appendix 4.2).

Additionally, there would have to be an immediate meeting between the Chancellor of the Exchequer and the Liberal Party's economic spokesman before the Pact was finalised, to confirm that there was agreement upon an economic strategy based on a prices and income policy and reductions in personal taxation. Furthermore, a regular consultation was suppose to take place between Labour's minister and the appropriate Liberal spokesmen along with meetings between the Prime Minister and the Liberal leader as necessary. Finally, the terms of the agreement were to be published as a formal exchange of letters (see Appendix 4.2).

Attention now turns to the immediate response of the Liberal party to the Pact. At the outset, the major part of the negotiations over the

Pact took place between Callaghan and Steel. However, whereas Liberal MPs were aware of the nature of the discussions, most people within the PLP were not informed about the negotiations. Not surprisingly, no conflicts within the Liberal Party were recorded immediately after the formation of the Pact. The very few Liberals MPs who argued against the Pact (namely, Jo Grimond and David Penhaligon) had agreed to act upon the majority decision (Steel 1980: 39).

A basic question still remains unanswered: how did Steel manage to sign a Pact which had no commitment by Labour to legislate the issue of PR to the European Election? In other words, how did Steel act contrary to his MPs' overwhelming concern? The answer lies in Steel's idea of 'realignment of the left' which was demonstrated by him on at least three public occasions: at the end of June 1974 as a Chief Whip, in May 1975 as a candidate to the party leadership, and finally, in September 1975 as party leader (Steel 1980: 17, 22–5). In the latter occasion, televised live, Steel (1980) argued:

> We must be bold enough to deploy the coalition case positively. We must go all out to attack the other parties for wanting power exclusively to themselves no matter on how small a percentage of public support. If people want a more broadly based government they must vote Liberal to get it. And if they vote Liberal we must be ready to help provide it.
>
> (Steel 1980: 25)

Logically, the fact that the leadership election took place under a more representative system then the previous election (the new rules included an electoral college composed of constituency representatives), provided Steel with wider support for his ideas of 'realignment of the left'. The long process of preparing the Liberal party for the idea of 'realignment of the left' clearly served to minimise disunity within the party. Consequently, the issue of PR for the European elections and the views of the opponents to the 'realignment of the left' were altogether subordinated to Steel's decisive preference of 'obtaining governmental experience'. It must be conceded that, however influential were the opponents to the Pact, it was the preference of 'economic recovery' which generated the widest support of Liberal MPs, rank-and-file and voters.

Attention now turns to the immediate response of the Labour Party to the Pact. At the outset, 'the mood of the majority of the PLP was of course to accept it because it would at least make certain that we would remain in command of the Commons for another year'.[15] Yet, it is somewhat misleading to contend that total harmony existed within the Cabinet and the PLP. A motion by forty-eight left-wing Labour backbenchers suggested that they did not regard themselves as bound to implement the Pact (Callaghan 1987: 458). Moreover, in the Cabinet, four members – namely, Stanley Orme, Albert Booth, Tony Benn and Bruce Millan – argued against the Pact (Bogdanor 1983: 154). Most of the members, both in Cabinet and in the PLP, who expressed their objection to the Pact were organised in the left-wing faction the Tribune Group. It was only after the Prime Minister reaffirmed that neither he nor Michael Foot would have recommended the Pact if it in any way damaged the integrity of the Labour Party that the left-wing cabinet members, who objected to the idea of the Pact, agreed to continue in office.

However mutable the left-wing strength may have been in the mid-1970s, it did not prompt determined action from Callaghan because he assumed that Labour MPs would support the party over no-confidence motions and, perhaps, over other critical divisions in the House. Moreover, Callaghan assumed that the TUC leaders would prefer to keep Labour in power despite the Pact with the Liberal Party rather than having an anti-TUC Conservative government. Based on these assumptions, the Pact was presented to Parliament on 23 March 1977 and helped Labour overcome a no-confidence motion by 322 votes to 298, the government being supported by the thirteen Liberals and assisted by three Ulster Unionist abstentions.[16]

Attention now turns to the internal dissatisfaction within the Labour and the Liberal parties during the Pact. Rather than support for the Lib–Lab Pact, the orientation of large sectors of the Labour elite and the Liberal base was most expressed by dissenting voices, challenging the alliance strategy of the respective party elites. These developments were stimulated and reinforced by the ability of the opposition within both parties to demonstrate their attitudes in the party arena as well as the parliamentary one.

For the Labour Party, a significant increase of intraparty dissent was demonstrated by votes in the House of Commons' division lobbies during the Pact. Whereas around 15 and 17 per cent of divisions (expressed as a proportion of non-free divisions in each session) witnessed one or more dissenting votes by Labour members during 1974–75 and 1975–76 respectively, dissent by Labour backbenchers during 1976–77, 1977–78 and 1978–79 were 30, 36 and 45 per cent respectively (Norton 1980). Not only did Labour members vote against their own party in more divisions than before, there was also greater willingness to enter the Conservative lobby, thus, government backbenchers were prepared to vote in the opposition lobby on some occasions in which the government had no overall majority.

The result was twenty-two government defeats in the lobbies during the Pact, most of which it accepted. Of the twenty-two, nine were attributable to opposition parties combining against a minority government (or to confusion in the lobbies or miscalculation by the whips), and thirteen to Labour members combining with Opposition members to defeat their own side. However, whereas several of the defeats took place on important items of government legislation or policy it was not until defeated on a vote of confidence that Callaghan requested a dissolution.

Perhaps most important of all was the activity of the Tribune Group within the Labour Party. As the source of the separation within the Labour Party was both ideological and organisational, cross-voting or abstention by members of the Group resulted in numerous governmental defeats. The defeat of the government on the Expenditure White Paper in March 1976, the loss of clause 40 of the Scotland Bill, the defeat on an amendment to the Nurses, Midwives and Health Visitors Bill in February 1979, and finally, the number of defeats suffered by the government in Standing Committee suffices to underline this point. Undoubtedly, the issue which caused the most serious intra-elite conflict within the Labour Party was the devolution of certain powers to elected assemblies in Scotland and Wales. The assertion of one author that 'The issue of devolution was one which could not be seen in terms of left or right-wing attitude, at least not solely so' (Norton 1980: 443), represents the difficulties faced by Labour elites. According to the Liberal chief whip, Alan Beith:

> People had talked about the devolution debate as a revolving door; as soon as you [Labour government] improved the Bill someway so that we [the Liberals] were happier and the SNP were happier, more of Labour's own supporters are going out at the same door because they were opponents of devolution.[17]

The existence of a 'revolving door' combined with incremental improvements in the Bills are crucial in explaining the tactics of the Conservatives. At the outset, it is worth mentioning that whereas cross-voting and abstention by the Tribune members caused the loss of clause 40 of the Scotland Bill, votes by other political wings and groupings within the PLP caused various defeats on the Scotland Bill, three of the four defeats on the Wales Bill and the loss of the guillotine motion for the original Scotland and Wales Bill (Norton 1980).

The intra-elite conflicts over the devolution issue did not evolve only at the visible sphere of Labour's party politics. Given that various political wings and groupings within the PLP were divided, it is hardly surprising that co-operation between Labour and Conservative MPs evolved. George Gardiner, the organising secretary of a Conservative group, the Union Flag, confirmed this direction:

> I had a regular liaison with Tam Dalyell and George Cunningham ... and also with Enoch Powell and the Ulster Unionists because we often needed them to help us with some filibustering. And there was coordination too in the drafting of certain amendments ... and there was a lot of consultation, of course, over the amendment, that in the end, on the first Bill, enforced a referendum anyway, and certainly discussions and contacts over the second Bill beyond George Cunningham's amendment which brought the 40 per cent threshold.[18]

Additionally, at the level of the Conservative's shadow cabinet, Mr Teddy Taylor, the Scottish spokesman, had 'total and complete co-operation'[19] with Tam Dalyell, George Cunningham, Betty Harvie Anderson and Tom Galbraith.

The above tendencies emphasise that strife over the devolution issue evolved within the Conservative Party. This rift was extremely visible because the pro-devolutionists were an important minority, and included Edward Heath and the Shadow Scottish Secretary, Alec Buchanan-Smith (Norton 1980: 454). In the division on the Second Reading of the Scotland and Wales Bill, for example, five Conservatives cross-voted to support the measure and an additional twenty-nine, including Mr Heath, abstained from voting.[20] Furthermore, the standing within the Party of some of the Conservative dissidents, the resignation of Mr Buchanan-Smith, and the refusal of the Conservative Front Bench speakers to offer any alternatives to the Government proposals in the debate reflected the serious division within the Conservative ranks. To sum up, it was a fact that the issue of devolution was generally one which did not split into clear-cut left or right-wing that enhanced internal conflicts within the major British parties.

The nuances of the elite-follower conflicts within the Liberal Party are of equal relevance. If, as Healey (1989: 403) claims, 'it was never easy working with the Liberals, since David Steel was unable to control his tiny flock', one should expect to see numerous Liberal dissents. Surprisingly, the Liberal parliamentary group did not succeed in concerted opposition to the Pact although there was a gap between Steel and most of the group as the latter wanted tangible achievement whereas Steel was more interested in the agreement itself.

A substantial reason for the lack of intra-elite conflicts within the Liberal Party lies in the inability of Liberal MPs to organise their opposition to the Pact. According to John Pardoe, a substantial reason for this lay in the fact that:

> We did not agree on the reasons why we didn't like the Pact. And, frankly, it was some doubt in Penhaligon's phrase about 'turkeys voting for Christmas' because, basically, most of my parliamentary colleagues were scared stiff of fighting an election at that time. They thought they were going to lose their seats.[21]

The arguments presented by a large number of Liberal MPs suggest another reason. As Lord Hooson put it:

> I also took the view that for one member to resign would undermine the whole object of it [the Pact]. The Liberals have always been accused on never being able to agree on anything, and if one individual, which I did consider doing, resigned half way through the Pact, [he will] probably, be followed by two or three more. If I would have resigned, Cyril Smith would have resigned and David Penhaligon would have done, and Richard Wainwright would have done.[22]

Given that the Liberals were so concerned with electoral performance, it is hardly surprising that Steel's view of the Pact as an opportunity to bring the Liberals into association with government for the first time, served to eliminate internal dissatisfaction within the parliamentary group.

At the opposing extreme, however, were the party followers who called a Special Assembly to discuss the renewal of the Pact. Despite the Liberal MPs' insistence on the importance of PR to the European Parliament, Steel refused to make it a point at which he was prepared to bring down the government. A party council which met in mid-November 1977 passed a resolution demanding a special assembly if Labour failed to deliver PR to the European Elections (Steel 1980: 106). The assembly was suppose to consider the future of the Pact and to discuss questions of electoral strategy.

Additionally, in a meeting of the standing committee prior to the gathering of the assembly, a direct challenge to Steel's alliance strategy was recorded. According to Steel, it was his worst meeting with the Party Executive ever. He wrote in his diary:

An appalling meeting with the Executive which at one point is a shouting match. Several say the party is disintegrated, and I listen to worthy verbal essays about 'participating democracy', etc. Towards the end one member actually mentioned inflation. I leave angry and depressed.

(Steel 1989: 139–40)

Similar elite-follower conflicts were not evident in the Scottish Liberal Party or in the Welsh Party Council. A substantial reason for this lies, of course, in the favourable position of the party over the devolution issue.

To sum up, during the Lib–Lab Pact intra-elite conflicts were evident within the Labour Party whereas elite-follower conflicts were evident within the Liberal Party. In both cases internal opposition opted for the 'voice' option rather than 'exit'. Manifestations of internal dissatisfaction in both cases were also restricted to the party and the parliamentary arenas.

THE FRENCH SOCIALIST PARTY (PS), 1988–91

To understand Rocard's alliance strategy during 1988–90, it is necessary to appreciate his position within the PS, as well as Mitterrand's strategy in the 1988 Presidential elections. For the former, the contrast between, for example, Chirac and Rocard was great. Chirac was the founder of the RPR and its undisputed leader in 1986. Not surprisingly, all RPR ministers were subordinate to him. By contrast, Rocard was Mitterrand's choice as Prime Minister, rather than that of the PS. Although Rocard enjoyed a relatively high level of popular support, he lacked the immediate support of his own party. His relatively small faction suffices to underline this argument. As Cole (1989b: 17) noted about Rocard's position in the post-1988 period:

He is distrusted not only by the new PS leadership under the control of Mauroy, but also by a majority of Anti-Rocardian PS deputies.

The Economist, furthermore, concludes that:

As a rebel of the most irritating sort (one whom time, in certain respects, has proved right), Mr Rocard was never going to become a party darling just by becoming prime minister. Though popular with the public, his following among Socialists is small. His harping on politicians' failure to represent 'civil society', his insistence on giving opposition parties their due, his courtship of centre-right politicians – none of this is calculated to win the hearts of party workhorses.[23]

Since Rocard was at the centre of a range of internal forces which had to be pacified or neutralised, his style of leadership becomes of particular importance. According to Machin (1990: 109), a shared leadership pattern had evolved between Rocard and Mitterrand, replacing the previous pattern of 'imperial presidency'. The solution of the crisis in New Caledonia, for example, was clearly Rocard's work and most domestic policy choices appeared to have been worked out with little presidential intervention. The President did not publicly weigh in on the dispute between the Prime Minister and the Finance Minister about the rates for a re-imposed wealth tax. Additionally, Mitterrand did not intervene when Rocard overruled his Justice Minister over a proposal to house those convicted of political violence with other prisoners.[24]

Undoubtedly, Rocard's style of leadership was a critical factor which contributed to the shift towards a shared leadership. According to Dominique Strauss-Kahn, PS member of the National Assembly and the President of the Finance Committee:

> Rocard tries to manage a form of consensus. I am not quite sure this is linked to the minority situation of the government. I think even if the Socialists had a huge majority, Rocard, for personal reasons, would have this kind of leadership. He is more a man of consensus than a man of a conflict. Of course, in the situation today, when the Socialists have no majority in the parliament, it is not only a question of taste, it is also a question of necessity.[25]

Given Rocard's relatively weak position within the PS, it is hardly surprising that a consensus-oriented strategy was implemented in the party arena. Yet, in order to have a complete picture of PS politics in late 1990 it is also necessary to appreciate Mitterrand's strategy in the 1988 presidential elections.

As noted earlier in the PCF case, *La France Unie* was the essential spirit of Mitterrand's campaign strategy in the May 1988 Presidential election. He called for an opening of the new presidential majority to the centre and centre-right politicians, implicitly refusing the old Fifth Republic pattern of bipolarisation between the left and the right. Throughout the campaign Mitterrand was careful not to call for a formal alliance. He promised implicitly that his election would be followed by a political realignment, and that a new presidential majority backing Mitterrand would have to be comprised of those centre and centre-right politicians who were willing to support the new President.

As a partial explanation for the above strategy, reference to Mitterrand's *Letter to all the French People*, provides a starting point.[26] National unity was needed, Mitterrand claimed, due to the importance of the completion of the 1992 EC internal market. Special issues concerning France's preparation for this step, such as educational training and poverty problems, were needed to be tackled peacefully by 'a sort of dialogue'. However, a different explanation to the implementation of Mitterrand's strategy suggests that the importance of the above-mentioned economic challenges can hardly be overemphasised. According to Cole (1988), the 'national unity' slogan can be considered as an attempt to respond to the large consensus in French society on most aspects of policy prevailing among two-thirds of French voters after the contrasting experience of the 1981–86 Socialists and 1986–88 Conservative governments.

The preferences that embody contested principles of policy or programme direction (i.e. the decisive preference in alliance formation), Luebbert (1986) argues, were due to their impact in minimising party disunity. Given Mitterrand's 1988 campaign slogan, *La France Unie*, and the relatively weak position of Rocard within the PS, it is hardly surprising that 'unity' was adopted as the decisive preference in the bargaining over the formation of the 1988 alliance. Such a preference implied that the PS would not form a formal alliance, as such a commitment opposes the essence of 'solidarity'. Clearly, this broad aim would not have alienated any group within the PS and was sufficiently focused to generate the widest possible support within the PS, as well as within its partners.

To understand why Rocard seriously took into account a potential emergence of dissatisfaction within the PS, it is necessary to appreciate the attitudes of large sections in the party to any co-operation with the PCF or the Centrists. The reluctance of these sections resulted from the alliance strategy implemented by both the PCF and the centre throughout the 1970s. At the heart of the PCF alliance strategy throughout the 1970s lay a certain ideological affinity shared with the PS. After all, during this period the two parties have, to a greater or lesser extent, co-operated in the opposition as well as in government (1981–84). Clearly this does not mean that no conflict emerged between the two parties. It does mean, however, that relationships were easily manageable, not only as a result of the ideological affinity, but also due to the PCF's dependence on Socialist support for the election of its deputies and municipal councillors. The ideological affinity, however, gave rise to a fear within the PS elite when intraparty implications were examined. As Jean-Pierre Worms, PS member of the National Assembly, argues:

> From 1988 onward, the fear of a lot of Socialist rank-and-file members or leaders is that the Communist Party may cultivate a certain amount of discontent within the salaried classes and could gain a new strength. This is a sort of ideological blackmail or pressure which the Communist Party can [exert] on the French Socialist Party, especially on the rank-and-file members. So, there is a pressure not to go far away from the Communist Party. [Yet], the fact that the Communist Party apparatus now is very much old-style Stalinist position makes co-operation with the Communist Party very difficult. . . . Officially, the very strong opposition to certain type of Communist thinking is the Rocard group, but very deeply I would say that most of the leaders of the Socialist Party today are conscious of the necessity to separate [the party] clearly from the old-style [Communist] party but most of them do not dare to say it publicly.[27]

This is not to say that the PCF would unconditionally support the government nor did it mean that the PS government would be likely to have such type of PCF support. It is rather to stress that, beyond the Presidential constraints upon Rocard's alliance strategy, there was a reluctance within the PS to engage in formal co-operation with the PCF.

The UDC represented the other possible partner for the government. As members of the CDS the centrists could not dissociate themselves from the UDF. Yet, the very nature of Pierre Méhaignerie's skill enable them to disassociate themselves, at least temporarily, from their traditional right-wing allies. This was done by the establishment of a separate centrist group in the National Assembly, namely, the UDC, whose stated aim was to form a constructive opposition to the government. The formation of the UDC was strongly opposed by UDF leaders, such as Giscard d'Estaing and Francois Léotard. However, in spite of the criticism, the group consisted of thirty-four deputies with seven others allied to it, including Raymond Barre. The latter, in turn, stated that he would support the Socialist government whenever it was necessary in the interests of the country.

The group's position was partly inspired by the presence of a small number of centrist and right-wing ministers in Rocard's government. These figures included the Labour Minister, Jean-Pierre Soisson (ex-UDF), the Minister of Overseas Trade, Jean-Marie Rausch (CDS), the Minister for Tourism, Olivier Stirn (ex-UDF), and the Secretary of State responsible for economic planning, Lionel Stoleru (ex-UDF). Their presence in the government meant that if the UDC censured the government, then it would also be censuring members of its own party and former colleagues. Moreover, the centrists possessed a certain affinity for Michel Rocard. Thus, Rocard was the person in the PS with whom the centrists felt that they were most able to do business.[28]

However conclusive such affinity has been, there were still attitudes which opposed co-operation with the Centrists, shared by the majority of the PS elite and the grass-roots. As Jean-Pierre Worms explains:

> There is a strong ideological reticence towards any form of agreement with the Centrist group or with politicians who come originally from the Centrist group.... Even a man like the present Minister of Work and Employment, Jean-Pierre Soison, who comes from the Barrists – Raymond Barre supporters – is still considered by a large fraction of the Socialist party members as somebody rather suspicious who cannot be trusted in spite of the fact that he is one of the best ministers in this government.[29]

These factors indicated that Rocard's tactical moves, such as the 'opening' of his government to the centre-right politicians, have cleared the way to PS–UDC co-operation on grounds other than the formal one.

Given the internal constraints upon Rocard's strategy, it is hardly surprising that he 'took great care in not being prisoner of any configuration'.[30] An informal alliance, comprised of the PCF, the UDC and individual MPs, was therefore formed on the basis of 'unity' in light of the 1991 EC single economic market. By negotiating each issue separately and on an *ad hoc* basis, the PS elites could pick the least 'expensive' alliance partners available, i.e. the one which does not pose a threat to the PS stability. This direction was confirmed by Rocard's legislative adviser, Guy Carcassone:

> Among the 19 independents, 12 have already joined the 'presidential majority' and will never vote against Rocard. Thus, we just need to find 6 or 7 abstentions in the opposition if ever the Communists voted the dismissal. This may be quite easy as far more than 6 or 7 deputies would refuse to join their vote with those of the Communists, in an artificial majority without any future. We naturally know who can easily be convinced.[31]

In addition to the above-mentioned informal alliance, Rocard could rely on Article 49–3. Two advantages of the Article were evident:

1 the government's dismissal would need a common vote of right and left-wing oppositions (129 RPR, 91 UDF, 41 UDC, 26 PCF at least 2 of the 18 independents) in order to reach the absolute majority (289); and
2 the government does not need a positive majority vote, i.e. it just needs 16 of the 305 'non-socialists' deputies to refrain from voting against it.

Thus, not surprisingly, the government position in mid-1988 could be considered relatively secured.

To describe the extent of the internal dissatisfaction within the PS, requires specification of the voices which were recorded during 1989–90. For the PS, intra-elite conflicts were particularly apparent between the parliamentary group and the government. The PS group saw itself as being relegated in importance behind the PCF and the UDC, with the government taking its support for granted. Additionally, there was a division between centrist factions, led by Rocard, and more leftist factions, due primarily to the negative reaction of many Socialist deputies to the government's effort to co-operate with the UDC in 1988. A partial explanation of this division is provided by Jean-Pierre Worms:

> In my opinion, within the party, the only organised group which publicly opposed any sort of co-operation with the Centrist would be the ex-Trotskyist, Julian Dray group. I would explain that, very cynically, by the fact that it is the only tendency within the PS which is not represented in the government. [However], this is a very popular angle of attack on the government within the Socialist Party which was widely manifested during the preparation of the last Congress.[32]

In the months following the passage of the 1989 Budget, the PS parliamentary group featured a militant disposition. The votes in March and December 1989, where the government had to use Article 49–3 in order to force dissident PS deputies into line, exemplifies this argument. As Elgie (1993) noted about the passage of the 1989 budget:

> Despite the opposition of these two groups [i.e. PCF and UDC], the Prime Minister's parliamentary advisers were still confident that Article 49–3 could be avoided. They had received assurances from a sufficient number of individual UDC and independent deputies, so that they believed they would not have to resort to a no-confidence vote. However, the leader of the PS parliamentary group, Louis Mermaz, refused to accept this strategy and insisted that Article

49–3 be used. He felt that it would be better for the PS's image to resort to this article, rather than relying on a few cobbled-together centrist votes. The preparation of the PS's party congress a few months later was certainly the main inspiration behind Mermaz's decision. As a result, Rocard was obliged to use 49–3 twice in order to pass the Bill. After a referral to the Constitutional Council the Bill became law on 30 December 1989.

(Elgie 1993: 91)

The events during the PS's party congress in *Rennes* – where delegates, elected by the local federations, were supposed to debate policy and to elect the *Comite Directeur*, which determines the composition of the Executive Bureau – are indeed critical to our analysis. Whereas for much of the 1970s and 1980s the party consensus on Mitterrand's leadership enabled the party to escape internal divisions, in 1989 the various groups that formerly supported Mitterrand began to oppose each other as the party searched for a new First Secretary. Before, as well as during the party Congress at *Rennes* in March 1990, numerous Socialists kept criticising Rocard's government either because they did not accept his legislative strategy or because they wanted to enhance their visibility. The division was marked primarily by a conflict between three individuals, namely, Lionel Jospin (Minister of Education), Laurent Fabious (President of the National Assembly), and Louis Mermaz (President of the PS parliamentary group). According to *The Times*, the conflict reached a climax in the Party Congress:

> For the first time since President Mitterrand took over the leadership of the Socialists in 1971, a party congress has ended in disarray. Hundreds of delegates at the congress in *Rennes* hissed and yelled at M. Louis Mermaz, a senior official, as he stood on the platform yesterday to announce that their leaders had failed to reach a consensus. . . . Rivalry has consistently been a feature of these party congresses, but, amid much brinkmanship those concerned have previously managed to produce a late compromise. This year's failure to do the same puts the Socialists in the same boat as the deeply divided right-wing opposition and the Communists.[33]

The battle in the party congress at *Rennes* was fuelled by Laurent Fabius and Lionel Jospin's personal ambition to be the best placed to step into President Mitterrand's shoes if and when, in the middle distance, he should step down. Thus, division surfaced between the two which resulted in the break-up of the Mitterrand faction into two clear factions. First, Mermaz, Jospin and Mauroy colluded in order to form the MJM faction. Second, the Fabius's grouping which enjoyed Mitterand's support throughout the party Congress, and the Poperen's grouping, remained within Mitterrand's faction but were operating independently. All the new and established factions were still operating alongside the other factions, namely, Rocard, Chevènement and Julian Dray's factions. After the factional split, a new list of deputies was drawn up in which each grouping had a fair share of the jobs (Elgie and Maor 1992).[34]

Perhaps of equal importance is the evolution of intra-elite conflicts within the right-wing opposition parties. At the outset, given that numerous right-wing members (such as, Raymond Barre, Valery Giscard d'Estaing, Francois Léotard and Jacques Chirac) who considered themselves candidates for the Presidency, it was hardly surprising that a division within the right-wing had evolved. The source of this division, organisational as well as ideological, manifested itself in a break-away group from the centre right, namely, the UDC, and a split in the UDF between Valery Giscard d'Estaing who aimed at leading the centre-right in 'constructive opposition' to Rocard, and Francois Léotard who favoured alliance with the neo-Gaullist Jacques Chirac.

During 1988–90, therefore, new and existing factions within the right-wing opposition parties had featured a militant disposition. First, in April 1989 a group of young deputies, namely, the *Renovateurs*, emerged to challenge the established leadership of the right-wing elites by calling upon Giscard d'Estaing to relinquish his position at the head of a joint UDF/RPR list for the June 1989 election to the European Parliament. The faction failed to achieve its goal but support for the renovators had grown to include 42 deputies and three senators.[35] Second, in February 1990 a faction in the RPR, led by Charles Pasqua, and the Renovator faction, led by Philip Seguin, challenged the RPR leadership by putting forward their own joint motion which obtained 31.4 per cent of the national congress vote.[36] This motion advocated a revival of nationalist Gaullist tradition to distinguish the RPR electorally from other right-wing parties and called for more party independence. Additionally, these dissenting RPR factions opposed the creation of the so-called *Union Pour la France* in November 1990, which was an umbrella organisation for the RPR, UDF, and UDC designed to organise the opposition's electoral strategy for the regional elections in 1992 and the legislative elections in 1993.

It is reasonable to argue that the PS case illustrates – as all other cases of decentralised parties examined here – that internal opposition tends to opt for the 'voice' option rather than 'exit', and that manifestations of internal dissatisfaction is restricted to the party arena. In other words, a decentralised organisation is characterised by the existence of mechanisms for the diffusion of dissent. Such mechanisms enable members of the parliamentary and extra-parliamentary party members to express their dissatisfaction in many ways, but within clearly-defined arenas.

SUMMARY AND CONCLUSION

The analysis so far indicates that a decentralised party organisation permits party members as well as members of the party elite to express dissatisfaction in many ways, such as, formation of new factions, 'voices' against the party leadership in party organs, dissensions in cabinet and parliament, and so on. As shown in Table 4.2, it demonstrates that, in the cases observed, intra-elite and follower opposition adopted the 'voice' mode *within* party organs, parliament and cabinet.

In the case of the decentralised DC it was shown that the evolution of intra-elite conflicts during the 'historic compromise' was especially evident after the assassination of Moro by the Red Brigades. New forces have emerged within the DC as follows: *Iniziativa, Democratica, Proposta* and *Communion* and *Liberation*. A similar mode of conflict manifestation was recorded during 1988–89 within the decentralised PS. During the 1990 PS Congress, division between Laurent Fabius and Lionel Jospin had resulted in the break-up of the Mitterrand faction into two clear factions. First, Mermaz, Jospin and Mauroy colluded in order to form the MJM faction. Second, the Fabius's grouping which enjoyed Mitterrand's support throughout the party Congress, and the Poperen's grouping, remained within Mitterrand's faction but were operating independently. The analysis also examined the worsening of the intra-elite conflicts within the Labour Party and the evolution of elite-follower conflicts within the Liberal Party. The former were mainly manifested by a massive dissension in parliament; twenty-two government defeats in the lobbies during the Pact, most of which it accepted. The conflicts in the Liberal Party were evident after the Liberal executive called a special assembly of the party in order to discuss the Pact's renewal.

These illustrations of the ways 'claims' can be made by actors operating within decentralised parties on the party elites lead to the conclusion that the first key step in understanding intraparty politics is to shift away from the variables proposed by public choice scholars,

Table 4.2 Modes of conflict manifestation in decentralised parties

Party	Period	Alliance partners	Decisive preference underlying the alliance*	Decisive preference underlying party strategy**	Pattern of organisational decline	Dominant mode of conflict manifestation
(i)	Decentralised parties which face intra-elite conflicts					
DC	1976–9	PCI, PRI, PSDI, PSI	Restoring public order/economic recovery	The continuation in power of the DC and the wearing out of the PCI	Voice	Formation of new factions: *Iniziativa Democratica, Proposta, Communion and Liberation*
Labour Party	1977–8	Liberal Party	Economic recovery		Voice	Dissension in Parliament: dissent Labour MPs during 1976–7, 1977–8 and 1978–9 were 30, 36 and 45%, respectively. The result was 22 government defeats during the pact
PS	1988–90	PCF, UDC	Unity		Voice	Break-up of the Mitterand faction into two factions; the formation of a new faction, MJM; break-up of the Party Congress at *Rennes*
(ii)	Decentralised parties which face elite-follower conflicts					
Liberal Party	1977–8	Labour Party	Economic recovery	Obtaining governmental experience	Voice	A Special Assembly following calls against the party's alliance strategy

* As evident from the coalition/pact's agreement or 'understanding'.
** As evident from political statements and elite interviews.
Source: Maor (1995a: 76).

and to focus on parties' organisational attributes. Doing so would enable students of politics to grasp the advantages in allowing party elites and sub-groups to challenge party's policy and strategy because it is precisely this organisational flexibility which offsets any attempt for dissatisfaction to emerge outside the leadership's 'zone of control'. Factions and factional activities are functional to the stability of parties; they are the channels through which internal dissatisfaction is mobilised, pacified and neutralised without serious consequences for the party's coalition strategy. When intraparty conflict emerges the absence of factions significantly contribute to the decline of party stability especially during periods of political turmoil. Factions are a key means of helping party elites to pacify and neutralise internal dissatisfaction. Allowing members of the party elites and sub-groups to express dissatisfaction within the party assures the party leadership that its coalition strategy would remain unaltered and their own position secured.

In the next two chapters I hope to show that the reason opposition within decentralised parties tend to limit their activities to 'voices' within party organs lies in the assumption that party elites would tolerate internal dissatisfaction. Formation of new factions, 'voices' against party strategy in party bodies and dissensions in parliament, to mention only few, are used to pacify dissent within the party. These mechanisms allow the party to handle internal dissent in a variety of manageable ways without forcing members to leave the party or express dissatisfaction outside the party. Thus, a decentralised organisation possesses more defences with respect to internal challenges, as their instruments of control over such uncertainties are dispersed among party sub-groups. By contrast, centralised parties lack the internal fluidity necessary to adjust to dissent among its members, forcing them to resign, leave the party or express dissatisfaction *outside* the party. The lack of similar mechanisms for the diffusion of dissent implies that party elites are less able to pacify party members, and less equipped to neutralise violent demonstrations of militants and activists. The next chapter explores strategies of conflict resolution employed by party elites who operate in a centralised organisations.

5 Modes of conflict resolution in centralised parties

This chapter analyses the responses of party elites operating in centralised organisations to internal opposition. It focuses on the strategies employed by party leaders to pacify and neutralise internal dissatisfaction. This chapter complements the analysis in Chapter 3 of the manifestations of intraparty conflicts where it was shown that, in the centralised organisations observed, intra-elite opposition adopted the 'exit' option as well as the 'voice' mode *within* party bodies, whereas followers' hostility tends to adopt the 'voice' mode *outside* the party. The analysis covers four centralised parties, namely, the Danish Social Democratic Party (1978–79), the Norwegian Centre Party (1989–90), the Italian Communist Party (1976–79) and the French Communist Party (1988–91).

I hope to show that, in the cases observed, centralised parties attempted to resolve internal conflicts by emphasising the alliance's decisive preferences, and imposing structural constraints on the coalition bargaining and the day-to-day operation of the government. In cases of elite-follower conflicts, the party elites initiated an 'articulation of ends' (Lowi 1971) and imposed a transition period before a formal accord was concluded. In all cases observed these measures failed to neutralise internal dissatisfaction, forcing the party elites to modify their coalitional strategy and break up the alliance.

THE DANISH SOCIAL DEMOCRATIC PARTY (SD), 1978–79

However mutable the strength of the opposition within the SD may have been during 1978–79, it prompted determined action from Anker Jørgensen to deal with the internal dissatisfaction. A three-fold strategy was implemented: first, Jørgensen insisted on the decisive preference of 'economic recovery'; second, structural constraints were imposed on the day-to-day operation of the coalition government, and third, the SD alliance strategy has been modified. As the former strategy has already been dealt with in Chapter 3 attention is focused on the latter two.

At the heart of Jørgensen's strategy to cope with the intra-elite conflict lay the notion that imposing structural constraints on the day-to-day operation of the coalition government might ensure SD control over most government decisions, thus, pacifying opposition within the SD parliamentary group. Beyond maintaining the prime ministership and key ministerial portfolios (such as Finance and Education) with the SD,[1] a coordination committee (i.e. inner cabinet) was formed and the principle of 'mutual veto' in the governmental decision-making process was established. The coordination committee, which was comprised of four Social Democrats and three Liberal ministers, discussed issues before the ministers were allowed to publicise their opinion.[2] The principle of 'mutual veto' was operatated by establishing a system of 'contact ministers'. SD ministers had to contact Liberal ministers in order to get approval for proposals they wished to promote, and *vice versa*.

The constraints on the day-to-day operation of the government had an immediate impact on the process of governmental decision-making. According to Svend Jakobsen, SD Minister of Fisheries:

> It was near disaster because the government was not well prepared. There were so many differences between the two parties. Also, the major issues where written partly on a paper . . . and all new items, all new cases, all new proposals were difficult to agree upon. The internal meetings in the government were very, very long. We discussed in the group of ministers [and] we discussed between the contact ministers. In the last part of the government's life the coordination committee discussed everything [including] smallest things to place on the agenda.[3]

Added to these difficulties in the day-to-day operation of the government, inherent in its structure, was the failure of the two parties to agree on how to implement a prices and incomes policy. Thus, not surprisingly, neither the SD nor the Liberal Party were able to embrace their views fully without offending one another.

The structural constraints on the day-to-day operation of the government failed to neutralise the dissatisfaction within the SD parliamentary group. Consequently, Jørgensen had to break up the formal alliance with the Liberal Party in order to maintain SD stability. In 1979, a shift in the SD strategy from a formal to informal alliances was recorded.

THE NORWEGIAN CENTRE PARTY (SP), 1989–91

As noted earlier, the conflict between the SP parliamentary group and Cabinet members intensified to an overt hostility following the governmental co-operation with the FrP. The interesting question that the analysis now turns to is: how did the SP cabinet ministers resolve the conflict? A two-fold strategy was implemented by Johan J. Jakobsen, the SP leader and Minister of Local Government and Labour. First, a decision-making 'troika', responsible for shaping party strategy, was established. It was comprised of Johan Jakobsen, Anne Enger Lahnstein, the leader of the parliamentary party, and John Dale, the party secretary. Second, the SP alliance strategy was modified, that is, the SP–CP–KrF formal alliance had collapsed following the refusal of the SP to support the government policy over the issue of EEA. To understand how the modification of the SP alliance strategy was an inevitable consequence of the establishment of the 'troika' requires a more detailed examination.

The analysis begins with the fall of Gro Harlem Brundtland's minority government in 1989. A partial explanation for this fall is provided by a newspaper interview with John Dale. In the interview, Dale expressed the view that Labour's EC policy was one of the main reasons why the SP wanted a change of government.[4] While the SP tried to start a debate on Norway's and EFTA's adaptation to the single market of the EC during the 1989 electoral campaign, Gro Harlem Brundtland did not want to divulge to the public the government strategy in the EFTA negotiations on EC adaptation. Immediately after the election, Gro Harlem Brundtland drafted a series of memos on adaptation substantiating the SP arguments that the final aim of the DNA was to make the question of EC membership a mere formality (Rommetvedt 1990: 21).

In 1990, the SP's bargaining position over a similar issue contributed to a government collapse. As the SP was strongly opposed to membership of the EC or even a full customs union of the EC and the EFTA for all products, a commitment to a 'broader trade agreement' with the EC was a necessary part of the 1989 coalition agreement.[5] The government crisis surfaced over the question of forming a free internal market in Western Europe (i.e. the EEA), between EFTA, of which Norway is a member, and the European Community. While the SP insisted that Norway would refuse to abandon its concessionary laws which impede foreign ownership of property, financial institutions and industrial enterprises in the country, the CP adopted a more conciliatory position. To understand how the SP position over the above-mentioned issue was formulated, it is necessary to appreciate the role of Lahnstein and Dale in the 'troika'.

From its beginning, the SP strategy over this issue grew out of the views held by both Dale and Lahnstein, According to Ole Gabriel Ueland, SP member of *Storting*:

> Our tough leaders are represented in the parliament, in the government and in the administration. You have a 'troika' there of Jakobsen, Lahnstein and Dale, they are all in the centre of the discussions. . . . But the person that without any doubt had used most time and has had most interest for this question during the last year was John Dale.[6]

As party secretary, Dale could not initiate a government crisis without the firm backing of party members, nor could he and Lahnstien act without the approval of the parliamentary group. Their political skill, however, enabled them to establish an informal support base within the party organisation and the group in parliament. Within the party organisation, Dale met SP leaders at the local level and probably won their support. Discussions in the parliamentary group had taken place approximately 2–3 weeks before the actual crisis. In both cases, Dale and Lahnstien did not seek the formal approval of the various party bodies for his strategy. The 'troika', dominated by Lahnstein and Dale, had acted independently with respect to the issue in question.

The above-mentioned process and the disapproval of almost half of the parliamentary group of the 'troika' strategy were confirmed by SP member of *Storting*, Ole Gabriel Ueland:

> I think that after we have been discussing it now for 2–3 weeks, really every day, there are more differences in the group still. But, we had a meeting 2–3 weeks ago with the members of the party from all parts of the country, such as the leaders of every county, and then, I guess, our party leaders got the backing they needed to go on with the process. . . . It is not possible to speak about stable party relations. . . . John Dale has been travelling around the whole country and told the people about this. And they are only a small part of it [i.e. the party]. But it is easy to tell people, who don't know too much about the question, what's wrong. . . . [Besides] we are doing more in directing the policy as a member of the government even if we are not a part of the majority [over the EEA issue] . . . I think more than half [share my view]. Normally, perhaps

one or two of the parliamentary group would prefer to be free and out of the government. [Another problem] is to be in the parliament and don't always know what's going on at the top.[7]

Clearly, the decision taken by the 'troika' to bring down the government over the issue of a 'European Economic Area', was taken without any approval, in voting terms, of the parliamentary group and the party organisation. Neither was it taken after the parliamentary group had been informed about the negotiations with the government.

THE ITALIAN COMMUNIST PARTY (PCI), 1976–79

As noted in Chapter 3, the PCI elites faced potential internal opposition after the decision to enter into coalition bargaining with the DC, as well as militants' hostility during 1977, and especially following the government's economic policy of 'austerity' in 1978. To cope with potential opposition following the elite's decision to enter into negotiation with the DC, the party decided to initiate 'explanatory pedagogy' through public meetings, and to enter a transitional period of no no-confidence (i.e. from August 1976 to July 1977). Beyond the former tactic lay the assumption that the party strategy is meaningful only in so far as it can be implemented at the grass roots. This required the establishment of certain norms, that is, the belief that the strategy chosen by the party elites is good for the followers, the application of sanctions against deviations from the norms, and the use of a specific pedagogy related to the transmission and justification of the strategy. Hence, through the public meetings and the lengthening of the process of forming a formal alliance, the PCI elites translated the abstract strategy into concrete action at the grass-roots level. Further elements which served to minimise potential disunity were the fairly general government programme over the decisive preference of 'economic recovery' and the absence of joint consultation among the parties. The transitional period has created an image of long, difficult and complex PCI–DC negotiations. This, in turn, was intended to satisfy elites' members and party followers whose orientations were still largely attuned to the ideological aspect of the co-operation.

The co-operation between the PCI and the DC led in 1977 to violent demonstrations of PCI militants. The presence of approximately 200,000 workers on the streets immediately forced the party elites to modify their alliance strategy. This change caused the collapse of Andreotti's third government. Further hostility following the formation of Andreotti's fourth government in March 1978 and the implementation of an austerity policy forced the PCI elites to initiate an 'articulation of ends' (Lowi 1971).

Debate as to whether to accept the government policy of austerity, which called for sacrifices by the workers, continues within the PCI and between the PCI and the union throughout the period of formal co-operation with the DC. Both the PCI elites and the followers recognised that increasing conflict over the austerity issue would result in a disastrous outcome. The assertion of Rose and Mackie (1988: 552) that 'the greater the importance of ideology within a party, the greater the risk that ideological discussion will lead to ideological disputes, and then to splits', suffices to underline this point. At the same time, the pragmatic co-operation with the DC and the support of the austerity policy did not coincide with the official aim. Thus, the collective identity of the PCI followers was at stake as the official goal of revolution as the basis of the movement's collective identity was constantly evoked.

In order to cope with the above-mentioned gap, the CGIL leader, Luciano Lama, suggested the immediate target of reducing unemployment as a justification to the workers' sacrifices (LaPalombara 1981). The PCI elites, on the other hand, decided to take an initiative designed to demonstrate that the party's long-range goals had not been abandoned. In a speech to the PCI Conference of Intellectuals, in January 1977, Berlinguer specified that:

> A policy of austerity is not a policy that tends to level everyone towards indigence, nor can it be pursued with the aim of enabling an economic and social system now in crisis to survive. A policy of austerity must instead have as its aim the establishment of justice, efficiency, order and, I would add, a new morality; and it is precisely for this reason that it can and must be adopted by the workers' movement. Seen in this way, while it does involve giving up certain things and making certain sacrifices, a policy of austerity acquires meaning as renewal and becomes, in effect, a liberating act for broad masses long kept in a position of subjection and pushed to the sidelines of society: it creates new forms of solidarity and, thus, rallying growing consensus becomes a broad democratic movement, at the service of social transformation.[8]

In Theodore Lowi's (1971: 49) terms, a process of 'articulation of ends' was initiated by the PCI elites. The official party aim of 'social transformation' was not abandoned, nor did it become a mere 'facade'. Rather, the party official aim was adapted to the organisational need.

As a result of the articulation of ends a solid part of the section secretaries in 1978 accepted the position of the party elites on wage restriction and argued for it in line with the elites' view. After 1978, however, when the section secretaries abandoned the line of the historic compromise, they inevitably ended by rejecting the 'austerity' policy. This was manifested by the 51 per cent rise in the share of section secretaries opposed to the limitation on wage demands between 1978 and 1980 (Barbagli and Corbetta 1982a, 1982b). The 'articulation of ends' failed to pacify the party's followers in a way which enables the continuation of the party's alliance strategy. The PCI elites failed to safeguard the believers' identity with constant and ritual references to the ideological goals, and with caution in their choice of alliances. As followers' dissatisfaction continued, the party was forced to change again its legislative behaviour. This modification led to the collapse of Andreotti's fourth government.

THE FRENCH COMMUNIST PARTY (PCF), 1988–91

As noted earlier, the elite-follower conflict in the PCF was recorded especially during the public strikes of October–November 1988. According to *The Times*, the 20 October strike was the first since 1968 that saw the leaders of the CGT marching in the same protest with those of the moderate *Force Ouvière*.[9] Moreover, violent demonstrations were conducted outside the *Hotel Matignon*, on 23 November, by 200,000 miners from the impoverished eastern region of Lorraine.[10] The strikes at *Finance*, a strong movement at the PTT, the dissatisfaction among the teachers and the strike at *Peugeot* indicated an increase in popular discontent.

A few weeks after the strikes and the violent demonstrations, the PCF elites were forced to modify the party's alliance strategy, i.e. to break up the informal alliance with the PS. In early 1989, the PCF elites announced that they would not support the government's Finance Bill. They furthermore made numerous 'non-credible' policy proposals, such as, an insistence on a hugh increase in the wealth tax and a demand that the formula for distributing federal money to local government institutions will continue to be determined by the VAT revenues (Huber 1991: 25). Consequently, no PS–PCF co-operation was recorded over the 1990 Finance Bill.

SUMMARY AND CONCLUSION

This chapter illustrates the failure of party elites operating in a centralised context to mobilise, pacify and neutralise internal opposition in a way which would enable the parties to continue their alliance strategy. It demonstrates that considerations of such parties during coalition bargaining are not grounded simply in the parties' response to external forces and stimuli which are numerous and powerful, but in the organisational limits of the parties. In the SD case it was shown that in order to pacify intra-elite opposition, the Prime Minister, Anker Jørgensen, imposed constraints on the day-to-day operation of the coalition government. A coordination committee (i.e. an inner cabinet) was formed and a principle of 'mutual veto' in the governmental decision-making process was established. The latter principle was established by creating a system of 'contact ministers'. SD ministers had to contact ministers from the Liberal Party and obtain approval for proposals which they wished to promote, and *vice versa*. Because of the continued internal dissatisfaction within the SD, however, Jørgensen was ultimately forced to break the SD–Liberal government coalition in order to maintain party stability. In the SP case it was shown that a two-fold strategy was implemented by Johan J. Jakobsen, the party leader. First, a decision-making 'troika', responsible for shaping party strategy, was established. After this measure failed to pacify the internal opposition, the SP broke up the co-operation with the CP and the government collapsed over the issue of 'European Economic Area'.

Regarding centralised parties which face elite-followers hostility, it was shown that in the case of the centralised PCI, the presence of approximately 200,000 workers on the streets immediately forced the party elites to modify their alliance strategy. This change caused the collapse of Andreotti's third government. Further hostility following the formation of Andreotti's fourth government in March 1978 and the implementation of an austerity policy forced the PCI elites to initiate an 'articulation of ends'. The PCI official aim of 'social transformation' was not abandoned, nor did it become a mere 'facade'. Rather, the party's official aim was adapted to organisational need. However, as followers' dissatisfaction continued, the party was forced to change again its legislative behaviour. This modification led to the collapse of Andreotti's fourth government. Similarly, in the case of the PCF, violent demonstrations which were conducted outside the *Hotel Matignon* by 200,000 militants, and strikes led by party activists, forced the party elites to modify their alliance strategy.

This chapter has revolved around the question: how can the party elites who operate in a centralised context pacify internal dissent? The analysis of the four cases suggests that the ways party elites tend to resolve internal conflicts may be affected by the distribution of power

Table 5.1 Modes of conflict resolution in centralised parties

Party	Period	Modes of conflict resolution
(i)	*Centralised parties which face intra-elite conflicts*	
SD	1978–79	• Emphasising decisive preferences • Establishing the principle of 'mutual veto' in the government's decision-making process • Establishing an inner cabinet in order to resolve internal disputes among the alliance partners before they reach the public
SP	1989–90	• Emphasising decisive preferences • Establishing a decision-making 'troika' responsible for shaping party strategy which included the key dissenting MPs
(ii)	*Centralised parties which face elite-follower conflicts*	
PCI	1976–79	• Emphasising decisive preferences • Imposing a transitional period before a formal alliance was concluded • Undertaking an 'articulation of ends'
PCF	1988–90	• Emphasising decisive preference

Source: Maor (1995a: 79).

between the different levels of the party's leadership as well as the nature of the conflict. As demonstrated in Table 5.1, once intraparty conflict occurred, centralised parties examined have attempted to emphasise the alliance's decisive preferences, and impose structural constraints on the coalition bargaining and the processes of government formation and maintenance. In cases of elite-follower conflicts, the party elites initiated an 'articulation of ends' and imposed a transition period before a formal accord was concluded. Overall, the lack of mechanisms for the diffusion of dissent within the party seems to be the most significant factor explaining the failure of party elites to mobilise, pacify and neutralise internal opposition in a way which would enable the parties to continue their coalition bargaining.

This argument suggests some useful, if necessarily interim, conclusion. A centralised party is at a disadvantage when it enters conflict-inducing coalition negotiations with other parties. When inter-party negotiations induce intra-elite or elite-follower conflicts, members may be forced to leave the party, or air their dissatisfaction outside the party, as their primary mechanisms for the expression of dissent. A centralised, rigid organisation – especially when confronted with the latter conflict mode – can lead to party disintegration when such a party enters serious coalition negotiations with other parties.

Finally, many aspects of the interaction between intra- and inter-party politics are still cloaked in appalling ignorance. We know very little about the extent to which party elites are able, or even forced, to change party policy and strategy in response to pressures derived from party sub-groups. Existing public choice accounts claim to offer an empirical, non-normative account of the central dynamics of coalition politics. But by focusing exclusively upon policy promises of prospective government partners as the core of the coalition bargaining process and upon portfolio allocation as the mechanism of government formation – as Laver and Shepsle (1990a, b) do – this literature risks being contaminated by policy thinking. It ignores organisational attributes which promote or inhibit the ability of party elites to pacify and neutralise internal dissatisfaction. These organisational imperatives bear upon the credibility of policy promises of prospective government partners.

6 Modes of conflict resolution in decentralised parties

This chapter focuses on the strategies employed by party leaders who operate in a decentralised context to pacify and neutralise the dissatisfaction of elite and party members. It complements the analysis in Chapter 4 of the manifestations of intraparty conflicts where it was shown that in the cases observed intra-elite and follower's opposition adopted the 'voice' mode *within* party organs and parliament. The analysis covers four decentralised parties, namely, the Italian Christian Democratic Party (1976–79), The British Labour Party and Liberal Party (1977–78), and the French Socialist Party (1988–91). I hope to show that, in the cases observed, decentralised parties have tended to resolve internal conflicts by emphasising the alliance's decisive preferences and by tolerating factional activities as well as the formation of new factions.

THE ITALIAN CHRISTIAN DEMOCRATIC PARTY (DC), 1976–79

Perhaps the most important strategy to cope with potential opposition within the DC once it decided to enter into coalition bargaining with the PCI was the focus on the decisive preference of the economic and institutional crisis (*La crisi Italiana*). This crisis was a matter of government and party survival, thus facilitating an emphasis of a consensus-based aim as DC's decisive preference. Beyond the notion of *emergenza* lies the preferences that derived from the most widely shared values within a party and directly engage the party's most basic sense of purpose. Additional measures included the re-election of Amitore Fanfani, as President of the Senate, who was considered an opponent to any DC's co-operation with the Communists, and the appointment of forty-seven under-secretaries, adherents of the main *correnti*. This was an increase of eight on the number in the outgoing Government.[1]

However mutable the intra-elite opposition may have been during 1978, it prompted determined action from Piccoli, the president of the DC's parliamentary group, and Aldo Moro. As the former indicated:

> Moro proposed to introduce the PCI into the majority. . . . There were a lot of problems [and] questions on the centre and right of the party, a lot of perplexities. . . . I was leading the parliamentary group of the DC, [and] at that moment I decided to stop that and to support what the party was doing . . . because Moro himself, in a very famous speech, explained his position [to us] and raised a lot of questions. First, he told us the positive things, but he then told us of all the risks. He called for the parliamentary group and the party to be united because, he said, only by working together could we continue to go forward. This was the feeling, the tone, of what really happened. The step he took was very hard. First, we were all waiting to see what would happen and then we all supported everything he said. So, if his aims could be achieved we would all have become characters in this country's history.[2]

Thus, The DC elites neutralised the dissatisfaction during the decision to enter into co-operation with the PCI by relying on Moro's dominant position within the party as a 'buffer' and his ability to win the support of the party's parliamentary group. After Moro was murdered factional activities reached a new climax and three new factions were institutionalised within the DC during 1978–79, namely, *Iniziativa Democratica*, *Proposta*, and the student movement – *Communion and Liberation*. No disciplinary measures were taken against the leaders of these factions.

'It is necessary to deepen the internal crisis of the Christian Democratic Party', writes Berlinguer, 'in order to determine a change in its position . . . ' (Berlinguer, E. cited in Vacca 1987: 61). At face value this statement is not incorrect. However, in its concern to choose between factions with respect to their attitude towards DC–PCI co-operation rather than to consider seriously the interaction between the factions, it is misleading. Beyond Berlinguer's attitude towards a deep change in the internal equilibrium within the DC lies the assumption that the DC's internal inequalities tend to be at least in part exogenous, i.e. externally imposed. Alliance with the PCI could, therefore, destabilise the DC by putting additional de-institutionalising pressures on it, thus increasing its internal tension. Yet, when intra-elite conflicts occurred within the DC they were manifested within the party. Since the DC elites accepted the formation of new factions, it became clear that as long as dissatisfaction would be expressed through the diffused mechanisms no change in the elites' strategy would be required.

THE BRITISH LABOUR AND LIBERAL PARTIES, 1977–78

Given that internal conflicts have evolved within the Pact's partners, the respective elites had to respond in order to maintain stability and cohesion. In both cases the intra-elite conflicts were resolved internally, yet, even within the decentralised context one confronts striking variations in the strategy adopted to cope with the conflicts.

Elected as a leader while Labour was in power, Callaghan faced two alternatives; whether to follow the guiding principle of the PLP's organisation, namely, intraparty democracy, or to modify this line of behaviour in response to other principles. Undoubtedly, the former alternative was chosen by Callaghan, and was implemented both at the level of Cabinet and the PLP. Within the Cabinet, dissidents over the Pact's agreement were Tony Benn, Peter Shore, Albert Booth, Stanley Orme and Bruce Millan. The reason for the modest political significance of this intra-cabinet opposition had two dimensions. The first lay in the 'The harmlessness of the Pact'.[3] According to Tom MacNally:

> The individual MPs and Peers designated to deal with ministers on particular areas were no more than lobbies with good access because they didn't have the back-up. . . . So, it was a most unequal relationship, anyway, and on top, as I said, there was no sign that the Liberal Party has thought its way through, it had no shopping list, it had no clear objectives, and this meant that as far as Callaghan was concerned it was a relatively comfortable one because, on the one hand, it cushioned him from the pressure of his left . . . because he could say I can't do this because the Liberals won't let me, and on the other hand, there was no great shopping list of Liberal demands that he had to sell to his own party.[4]

Yet, even within the 'harmlessness' context of the Pact, Callaghan confronted some variation within the members of his Cabinet; most notably, Tony Benn. David Owen summarised this problem:

> Even with Benn, he [Callaghan] clearly had a very difficult relationship. He tried to lean over backwards to give him a hearing in Cabinet, to let him feel he had an opportunity to express his views and to isolate Benn by being seen effectively to have let him display

the fact that he was in a minority, so, not to shut him up. . . . He wanted to give people like Albert Booth, Stanley Orme . . . Michael Foot . . . a forum. . . . And again, he would give Michael his hand, let him listen, let him feel he had a case to argue, but he was always able to mobilise a majority of the Cabinet to his point of view.[5]

Added to these intra-cabinet difficulties which were successfully managed by Callaghan, was the factional nature of much of the PLP dissent. As previously stressed, what constituted significant difficulties were the large number of divisions witnessing dissenting votes, the size of the dissenting lobbies, and finally, the willingness of MPs to enter a whipped opposition lobby and deprive the government of a majority. For the government, it was both politically and managerially a difficult parliament. Assuming in each case that the views of the dissenters coincided roughly with those of the opposition, or sufficient opposition members to mould a majority in the lobby, there was always the danger of a motion or legislative provision being defeated if it ran into opposition from left-wing MPs, or its right-wing, or from a cross-section of the parliamentary party. Furthermore, there was always the danger of a defeat by a combination of the official opposition and the minor parties in the House.

A substantial part of Callaghan's and the Whips' strategy lay in their perception of the nature of the internal conflicts and its derived consequences. According to William Rodgers, the Secretary of State for Transport:

The question [is] what do they do at a crucial time; do they bring down the government? Now, the assumption which Mr Callaghan would have made was that in the end my people are not going to bring down the government. But equally, the rebels have to consider how far can we get this change or amendment without bringing down the government. It's a very delicate relationship.[6]

Indirectly, dissensions by Labour MPs resulted in the government's final defeat. On 28 March 1979, the House debated a motion of no-confidence which had been tabled in the wake of the March referendum in Scotland and Wales in neither of which was the 40 per cent threshold requirement achieved. This requirement existed because Labour backbenchers had voted with opposition members to impose it upon an unwilling government. Indeed, had it not been for the threat of dissent, there would not have been the decision to hold a referendum. Consequently, the government was defeated by 311 votes to 310, after which Callaghan had requested a dissolution.[7]

At the opposite extreme was Steel's strategy to cope with the followers' dissatisfaction which evolved in late 1977. By threatening his own resignation, he had managed to persuade the Party Executive to hold the assembly as late as possible after the PR vote in the Commons, so that tempers had cooled. But most important of all, according to Michie and Hoggart (1978), was the fact that the Liberal activists were still a minority in the party. Hence, when the assembly met, the silent majority wanted to reaffirm their loyalty by voting for Steel. In the end, Steel won by 1,727 votes to 520, and the Pact had been renewed again (Steel 1989).

THE FRENCH SOCIALIST PARTY (PS), 1988–91

To cope with the intra-elite conflicts which emerged within the PS during the period under investigation, Rocard has implemented a twofold strategy. First, dissenting voices which were raised within the parliamentary group did not trigger off a reaction from Rocard. Second, new factions formed in 1990 were tolerated by the party organisation.

It was during the period that factional activities reached a climax that Rocard's leadership of negotiated consensus became of the utmost importance in the resolution of the intra-elite conflict. Guy Carcassone, Rocard's legislative adviser, highlighted the first aspect of Rocard's strategy:

> Naturally, some Socialists hardly accepted this new situation. But from time to time we let them present their own propositions without interfering. Generally they discover their inability to obtain a majority and call the government in rescue. This is certainly the best evidence of the fact that if we deal with other groups, it is not for pleasure or strategy but by mathematical necessity. However, it is true that Rocard has always been suspected of preferring a coalition with the Centrists to a coalition with the Communists (in fact, he would prefer no coalition at all if the PS were strong enough). The reasonably good relations we have with the first ones feed the suspicious. Yet, the PS cannot but see that we also have reasonably good relations with the Communists and that we keep the balance. . . . And to any Socialist who would attack us on that matter, we would just ask for a better solution.[8]

Clearly, Rocard assumed that the different factions would prefer to keep the Socialist Party in power despite the informal alliance with the Communists and the Centrists, rather than have a right-wing government.

The second aspect of Rocard's strategy was the acceptance of the activities of new factions. As noted earlier, intraparty conflicts during the congress at *Rennes* resulted in a break-up of the Mitterrand faction into two, namely: the MJM faction and the Fabius groupings. The latter remained within Mitterrand's faction but were operating independently. The formation and activities of these new factions were tolerated by the party organisation and by Rocard himself. No disciplinary measures were taken against the leaders of these factions.

SUMMARY AND CONCLUSION

In this chapter the task has been to try to analyse the ways party elites who operate in a decentralised organisation can pacify internal dissent. Conventional accounts of coalition bargaining have been heavily scep-tical in orientation. Factions and factional activities have been largely treated as a constraint on coalition bargaining and the process of government formation. In other words, discussions of the topic have concentrated almost exclusively on the negative influences of party disunity and the strategies of party elites to cope with these (for instance, through the allocation of portfolios). Little attention has been devoted to the strategic advantages in a diversity of policy orien-tations among senior ministers, as well as among party sub-groups. Most scholars have operated without a clear conception of how party elites can take advantage of the structural context in which they operate in order to neutralise internal dissent.

This chapter illustrates the ability of party elites operating in a decentralised context to mobilise, pacify and neutralise internal opposition in ways which enable the parties to continue their coali-tion bargaining. It demonstrates that the presence of mechanisms for the diffusion of dissent in decentralised organisations allows the party to handle intra-elite and elite-follower conflicts in a variety of manageable ways without forcing members to leave the party. As a result, the party can enter into conflict-inducing coalition negoti-ations with other parties without risking its hold on its own members.

In the DC case it was shown that Aldo Moro emphasised the economic and institutional crisis as the party's decisive preference. In addition, both Moro and Piccoli had tolerated dissenting 'voices' which were raised when the DC decided to enter into co-operation with the PCI. After Moro was murdered, it was shown that factional activities reached a new climax and three new factions were institutionalised within the DC during 1978–79, namely, *Iniziativa Democratica, Proposta,* and *Communion and Liberation.* No disciplinary measures were taken against the leaders and members of these factions.

In the case of the British Labour Party, James Callaghan (the Prime Minister and Party Leader) emphasised 'economic recovery' as the decisive preference of the Labour Party during the bargaining over the Pact. Once the Pact was approved, Callaghan confronted five dissenting Cabinet members as well as a large number of divisions witnessing dissenting votes by Labour MPs which led to twenty-two government defeats during the Pact. A substantial part of Callaghan's and the Whips' strategy to tolerate dissent from MPs and Cabinet members lay in their assumption that in the end these MPs were not going to bring down the government.

Similarly, in the case of the elite-follower conflicts within the British Liberal Party, David Steel, the party leader, allowed dissenting voices to be manifested within the party. The primary impetus for the dissatisfaction of the Liberal followers has been the lack of tangible achievements throughout the Pact, primarily over the issue of proportional representation (PR) to the European elections. A party council which met in mid-November 1977 passed a resolution demanding a special assembly if Labour failed to deliver. By threatening his own resignation, Steel had persuaded the Party Executive to hold the Special Assembly as late as possible after the PR vote in the House of Commons, so that tempers had cooled. When the Assembly met, Steel won and the Pact had been renewed.

In the PS case, Rocard tolerated 'voices' against the party strategy of co-operation with the PCF and the UDC as he assumed that the different factions would prefer to keep the Socialist Party in power despite the informal alliance with the Communists and the Centrists, rather than have a right-wing government. In addition, no disciplinary measures were implemented following the rise of factional activities and the break-up of the Mitterrand faction.

This chapter has revolved around the question: 'how can the party elites who operate in a decentralised context pacify internal dissent?' As demonstrated in Table 6.1, decentralised parties which were examined have tended to resolve internal conflicts by emphasising the alliance's decisive preferences and accommodating factional activities as well as the formation of new factions. These strategies are in stark contrast to what was shown in Chapter 5 where centralised parties tended to emphasise the alliance's decisive preferences, impose structural

Table 6.1 Modes of conflict resolution in decentralised parties

Party	Period	Modes of conflict resolution
(i)	*Decentralised parties which face intra-elite conflicts*	
DC	1976–79	• Emphasising decisive preferences • Tolerating factional activities and the formation of new factions
Labour Party	1977–78	• Emphasising decisive preferences • Allowing Cabinet members to air their dissatisfaction • Tolerating massive dissension in division lobbies as well as numerous governmental defeats
PS	1988–90	• Emphasising decisive preferences • Tolerating factional activities and the formation of new factions
(iii)	*Decentralised parties which face elite-follower conflicts*	
Liberal Party	1977–78	• Emphasising decisive preference • Allowing party executives and members to air their dissatisfaction at a Special Assembly

Source: Maor (1995a: 79).

constraints on the decision-making process, and, in cases of elite-follower conflicts, initiate an 'articulation of ends' and impose a transition period before a formal accord was concluded. Thus, the ways party elites tend to resolve internal conflicts vary remarkably in line with the distribution of power among the different levels of the party's leadership as well as the nature of the conflict.

7 Modes of coalition bargaining

Intraparty disharmony and conflicts are often thought inimical to the effectiveness of parties in coalition bargaining. Consensus within the party is commonly viewed as a prerequisite for the effectiveness of parties entering into conflict-inducing coalition negotiations. This view has commanded many distinguished advocates among political scientists. None of them, however, offered the slightest sustenance for the theory that under some circumstances what looks like intraparty consensus is incompatible with a party's effectiveness in coalition bargaining. Indeed, in the previous chapters we observed that there are many parties whose coalition strategies – formulated on the basis of the consensual principle of democratic centralism – are easily disturbed by internal conflicts, forcing them to modify their coalition strategies. But, at the same time, there are many parties that maintain their coalition strategies under conditions of intense internal conflicts. Our inquiry into the internal dynamics of party politics has, thus, pinpointed the unique character of decentralised parties and their ability to diffuse internal dissatisfaction. This thread now draws us deep into the bargaining arena. Our focus is now shifting towards the consequence of the successful and unsuccessful resolution of internal conflicts in terms of parties' bargaining power.

At the outset, party elites which face intraparty conflicts function largely as a negotiation organ for the various members or groups even before the party declares its bargaining position. Each bargaining position, however, reflects the trade-off between party cohesion and legislative strategy. Each position is thus a product of internal compromise which might affect the party's bargaining power. In the parliamentary arena, both voice and exit are costly in terms of a party's bargaining power. The cost of devoting even a modicum of elites' time and resources to resolve internal conflict may undermine their bargaining power in the parliamentary arena. In addition, the credibility of such a compromise may be significantly affected by the ability of the party elites to neutralise internal opposition. A failure to resolve such conflicts seems, therefore, most likely to undermine the credibility of elites' proposals and threats.

This chapter brings out very clearly the consequences of the modes of conflict resolution with respect to the party's bargaining power and legislative strategy. These consequences are explored in relative terms since a party's bargaining power can be judged relative to its coalition partners. I therefore bring to the fore, among others, attitudes of members of the party's coalition partners in addition to members of the party under investigation. I hope to show that a party's bargaining power over its decisive preferences (i.e. the preferences which underline the party's strategy) relates to the mode of conflict resolution. A successful resolution of internal conflicts seems more likely to have no effect, or a positive one, on a party's bargaining power. This contributes to the continuation of coalition bargaining. The failure of elites to neutralise internal opposition undermines their bargaining power which, in turn, leads to the termination of coalition bargaining and the process of government formation. Thus, when intraparty conflicts occur, a decentralised party is most likely to sustain its bargaining power over its decisive preference, and thus, to continue the coalition bargaining and the process of government formation. A centralised party which faces internal conflicts is most likely to face a decline in its bargaining power over its decisive preference, leading to the break up of the coalition bargaining and the process of government formation.

THE SD–V COALITION BARGAINING IN DENMARK, 1978–79

The structural constraints on the day-to-day operation of the government which have been introduced by Jørgensen failed to neutralise the dissatisfaction within the SD parliamentary group. This was immediately translated to an inferior position in the coalition bargaining plane. As a former minister, Svend Jakobsen, explained:

> The major price was that we could not start economic democratisation in Denmark. We had it as an important part of the package and also, in relation to the Labour unions, it was a very important thing. . . . Therefore, there was a clash between Anker Jørgensen and Thomas Nielsen after the package. Only because of this we

could not make a majority for establishing the first step on a way to economic democratisation.[1]

Added to these influences was the fact that since only seven portfolios were allocated to the Liberal Party, each minister from that party controlled two SD ministers. This, in turn, contributed to the superior position of the Liberal Party in the bargaining arena. This was confirmed by Knud Engaard (Liberal), the Minister of Interior:

> We had double the task and double the influence. We could stop everything that we did not like. . . . That is a problem with a coalition government between two parties of very different principles, that is, you cannot always have a compromise between principles and if you do not reach a compromise . . . then such a government would have to stay away from legislation in such areas.[2]

Thus, the bargaining power of the coalition partners in this context was manifested by the ability of one party to block the initiative of its counterpart. In this respect, the Liberal Party had succeeded in blocking the SD's main proposals of 'economic democratisation', tax and housing reform which were strongly supported by the LO.

THE SP–CP COALITION BARGAINING IN NORWAY, 1989–91

The emergence of the SP parliamentary group's leader, Anne Enger Lahnstein, as the prominent figure in the party, and her co-operation with the party secretary, John Dale, were critical factors in the worsening of intra-elite conflicts within the SP during 1989–90. In order to neutralise the internal opposition, the SP leader, Johan J. Jakobsen, established a decision-making 'troika', comprised of Lahnstein, Dale and himself, which was responsible for the formulation of the party strategy. However, the failure to pacify the internal opposition was translated to an inferior position in the bargaining arena. During the period under investigation the Conservatives made relatively minor concessions to its partners. For the KrF, during the negotiations over the 1990 budget it was decided that 10,000 Krones would be given to every child under five years old, and a government commitment given to formulate a plan aimed at reducing the number of abortions. Additionally, the CP had promised the KrF that the issues of gene technology and the opening hours of shops during religious holidays would not be dealt with by the government.[3] Concessions to the SP were made during the negotiations over the 1990 budget when it was decided to lower Value Added Tax on milk, and to increase the amount of money towards environmental protection.[4] These minor concessions were a source of irritation for the SP. In an interview with John Dale, conducted two hours before the CP-led government collapsed, he confirmed the relatively low level of the SP bargaining power:

> The Conservatives do not respect our attitudes. They have thought that this is a small party and, [therefore], they could be the bosses. And we, as a small party, we should only obey them. It was wrong. Their mistake was that they thought they could more or less force us to obey them instead of respecting us and respecting our programme, our own right to decide our policy.... [They] try to use all kind of force, threats, year by year; [for example, they said] 'if you do not obey us we shall crush you'. This is their big mistake.[5]

Based on the SP experience during 1989–90, it is indeed hardly surprising that in the crisis over the 'European Economic Area' the SP militantly opposed Syse's position, forcing the resignation of his government.

THE DC–PCI COALITION BARGAINING IN ITALY, 1976–79

The successful resolution of the intra-elite conflicts within the DC was translated immediately into a superior position in the parliamentary bargaining arena. In contrast, the inability of the PCI elites to control the follower's dissatisfaction was translated into a relatively low level of bargaining power. This observation is undeniably appropriate to the periods of the informal alliance, from August 1976 to July 1977, and the formal alliance, from July 1977 to January 1979. Consequently, the DC elites had implemented a strategy of confrontation towards the PCI in the bargaining arena, which was sometimes diffused to the electoral arena.

For a time it appeared that the PCI had gained extensive policy influence due to the formal consultation with the government over major issues following the 'programmatic agreement' (*accordo programmatico*). Furthermore, the 'institutional agreement' (*accordo istituzionale*) in 1976 provided the PCI with the Presidency of the Chamber and also four committee chairmanships. It is somewhat misleading to insinuate, as Hellman (1988) does, that in the period of 'National Unity' during 1976–79, the Communists were granted extensive influence and eventually everything short of cabinet positions in the government. There is, nevertheless, conclusive evidence that the

DC's government controlled the interparty relationships within the alliance.

First, the DC dominance during the historic compromise was demonstrated by its control of all ministerial portfolios compared with its 39 per cent strength in the Chamber of Deputies. A single-party (*monocolore*) cabinet provided the DC with total influence over policy implementation. Thus, consultations with the other parties appeared to be a 'visible price' that was not translated to actual policy concessions. This direction was confirmed by the PCI economic spokesman, Giorgio Napolitano:

> The main difficulty was not to be inside the Cabinet, to have an all-DC government without the possibility of controlling day by day the implementation of the common programme and the Bills which had been adopted by Parliament.[6]

The DC elites, for example, did not take into consideration the views of the PCI and the Trade Union in drafting their three-year economic plan, nor did it initiate changes in the agrarian policy, pension policy and university reform.[7] Furthermore, Andreotti's refusal in September 1977 to dismiss Signor Vito Lattanzio, the Minister of Defence, together with the Prime Minister, ignoring the Communist view on the nomination of new chairmen to various state bodies,[8] exemplify this argument. This does not mean that the PCI had no impact on the policy process and its outcomes. On the contrary, Lindblom's (1965: 229) observation, that all affected interests can have at least some influence in the policy-making process, is valid. However, the PCI bargaining power did not lie in the ability to affect the outcome. But rather some outcomes were designed with consideration of the position or objection of the Communists. The delegation of powers and functions to the new regional governments, the implementation of a major reform in the tax system, and the complicated *equo cenone* (fair rent) law which was passed by Parliament in 1977, suffice to underline this point.

Not surprisingly, the introduction of the PCI in the majority (*nella maggioranza*) did not constitute a change in the party's position. According to the leader of the PCI's parliamentary group, Alessandro Natta:

> The most relevant political concession was the fact that in 1978, following the proposal of the Andreotti's government, we moved from an ambiguous and even equivocal formula ... towards a constitution of a true and proper parliamentary majority in which

the PCI took part. I don't know if you can call this a concession, but certainly it was the acknowledgement that the PCI was a legitimate governing force in our country.[9]

The distinction which was drawn between 'political majority', i.e. formal coalition majority, and 'parliamentary (programme) majority' (Andreotti 1981: 181), created a bridge between the different ideologies. But, at the same time, it committed the Communists to the discipline of the majority. This raises an inevitable question concerning the PCI insistence on maintaining the formal alliance.

As a partial explanation for the PCI insistence to maintain the formal alliance, reference to the visible decisive preference of 'economic and institutional recovery' provides a starting point. The PCI's room for manoeuvre was heavily restricted when its elites decided to form an informal alliance in 1976 over the preference of 'recovery'. According to Gerardo Chiaromonte:

> We did not have other choices besides those which we had to actually choose. Once we had started a certain path with the abstention in August 1976, we were in a certain sense obliged to continue towards that unitary government of emergency that we thought was necessary for the country and for the democratic regime.[10]

Following the visible DC–PCI convergence over the preference of 'economic and institutional recovery', an ordinary voter would expect the coalition bargaining and the process of coalition maintenance to last at least until some improvement in the Italian economy and institutions occurs.

For the PCI, furthermore, the preference of economic recovery coincided with the period of time suffices to obtain full legitimacy as a governing partner. However, although both preferences were crucial to the formation of the formal alliance, the visible preference of 'recovery' was the only issue over which the alliance could be broken up. A break-up of the alliance, determined by PCI obstinacy, over issues other than the visible decisive preference, could 'promote confusion in the conduct of the election campaign' (Chiaromonte 1986: 160).

Given that the PCI was subordinate to the DC and clearly received an unfair rate of exchange, one would ordinarily expect interparty conflict to be endemic, or at least that the dominant patterns would require the repeated application of naked power. However, the assertion of the leader of the DC parliamentary group that until Moro was kidnapped 'there were no dramatic problems and questions' suggested a much more relaxed interparty atmosphere.[11] A substantial reason for this evaluation lies in the PCI's search for legitimacy which served to maintain the formal alliance. This preference made the commitment enforceable because it provided the PCI with the recognition of future opportunities for governmental co-operation that will be eliminated if the commitment is not maintained.

It can be concluded that whereas the decisive preferences of 'legitimacy' and 'recovery' preceded demands to break up the commitment, the elite-follower conflicts (and especially the militants) dictated the evolution of the PCI–DC co-operation. In other words, the organisational inadequacies which forced the PCI's elite to create governmental crisis in 1977 and 1978 emphasised the loss of the PCI elites' initiative.

The nuances of the intra-coalition politics which involved other partners, besides the DC and the PCI, are of equal relevance. For the PSI, the disappointing 1976 electoral results undermined its position as a third party. The fact the the PSI elites felt squeezed following the DC–PCI co-operation is often used to infer the inconsistent tactics during the historic compromise (Merkel 1985: 45). The PSI surprising break with the other parties' solidarity during the Moro kidnapping and its reluctance in 1977 to sign the 'programmatic agreement' spring immediately to mind. Added to the PSI's marginal strategic position during 1976–79 was the reluctance of the new leadership to implement incisive changes. This direction is confirmed by Hine (1980: 140), who argues that Craxi needed a period in which the main centre of power in the party would remain the party organisation and not the ministries and para state agencies. This was mainly because the ministers and the para state agencies offered a reservoir of patronage through which individual leaders could obtain members' support independently of the apparatus.

Given the PCI orientation towards co-operation with the DC and the weak PSI position, it is hardly surprising that difficulties in the PSI–PCI relationships developed. As Labriola, a PSI member of Parliament, put it:

> There were very bad relations because in that framework we have always blamed the PCI for a couple of things. First, there was a certain trend to establish a kind of regime together with the DC, and second, they [the PCI] had also the attitude to act as a fireman, a saver, in solving existing social tension. . . . The Communists had always preferred the DC rather than the Socialist side and I think this was a sort of historical mistake by Mr Berlinguer. They had not developed, during the period of the National Unity, any real

contacts, Communists and Socialists. Berlinguer had rather preferred to establish a sort of direct link between *Botteghe Oscure* and *Piazza del Gesu*.[12]

Consequently, the PSI ran a campaign in 1979 that was evasive and disturbing to the PCI. Craxi announced that his major obligation was to ensure that the vote led to a 'governable' Italy. In other words, the PSI edged back toward direct co-operation with the DC, emphasising the political isolation of the PCI.

If, as Napolitano claims, 'we had good relations in almost all fields with the Republican Party and with Ugo La Malfa',[13] a substantial reason for this lies in the 'bad' relationships between PCI and PSI during the historic compromise. It was mainly at the Congress of Turin in 1978, where the *Socialist Plan for a Left Alternative* was accepted (thus, consecrating Craxi's leadership), that the Socialists became engaged in bitter controversy with the PCI. The reason was that the former opposed the historic compromise and tried to create a left-wing alliance. The PRI, therefore, could act effectively as a third party while taking advantage of the past experience of co-operation with the DC.

Beyond its 3 per cent parliamentary strength, the PRI took advantage of few factors which mostly characterised the party. As Giorgio La Malfa, the party leader, argues:

> The Republican Party is considered to be, first, an extremely steady organisation in terms of the stability of views. . . . Second, it is considered to be extremely loyal, [i.e.] people know that we keep the agreements. And third, the quality of the people is considered to be higher than generally speaking. . . . If we suggest a solution to a problem they tend to think that we are right and they are wrong. . . . [Furthermore] my father was the leader of the party and he commanded a great respect.[14]

The PRI acted as a mediator between the PCI and the DC, limiting the use of extreme bargaining tactics and regulating the nature and intensity of the bargaining. Other parties, such as the PSI, PSDI and the PLI (in the earlier period), with interests somewhat different from those of the main coalition parties may have been drawn into the bargaining frays at varying points in time. Still, there were mainly three parties whose strategic considerations formed the relevant bargaining arena during the historic compromise, namely, the DC, PCI and the PRI.

Beyond the PCI's loss of the initiative following the elite-follower conflicts and its inability to control policy implementation, was the negative DC attitude towards the PCI in the electoral arena. According to Giorgio Napolitano:

> There were some Ministers who had a negative attitude to us, for example, Donat Cattin who was in charge on Industry and who was supposed to implement that important Bill on industrial policy. According to us, he was more or less openly sabotaging it. But independently from some ministers, the question was the attitude of the DC as a whole. For instance, while we were so much committed to the struggle against terrorism during the period of Moro's imprisonment, there was a partial local election campaign in Spring 1978 . . . and we were really struck by the behaviour of so many DC candidates, national leaders who were campaigning against us. So, we thought that there were double standards in the DC, particularly, after Moro's death because he had been able to put in evidence the necessity of loyal relationships with our party.[15]

Whether DC's attitude towards the PCI were disembodied sets of hostile ideas and values or the consequences of intraparty conflicts within the DC, Napolitano's perception of the DC's negative attitude provides us with a convenient point of departure in discussing the collapse of the historic compromise.

It was after the alliance successfully re-established the international stability of the Italian currency, reduced inflation and induced employment-creating investment (Tarrow 1981), that the break up of the commitment was initiated over the issue of Italy's membership in the EMS. Following the PRI threat that it would withdraw its support unless Italy joined the EMS, a resolution in favour of membership was carried in the Chamber with the Communists voting against and the Socialists abstaining. Further cause for the government victory over this issue, was the crucial MSI vote in favour of membership. This is not to say that tacit co-operation developed between the DC and the MSI elites. According to members of the MSI elite, namely, Raffaele Valensise and Francesco Baghino, the party's approach towards supporting Andreotti's government was not a result of a formal or tacit request from the DC.[16] Valensise adds that:

> I did the speech explaining why we were going to vote in favour of Italy joining the EMS because there were some national reasons for us. And I remember Signor Andreotti turning towards me and really gazing at me with very open eyes.[17]

It was, rather, the voting of DC, PRI and the MSI in favour of membership which provided the PCI with an argument salient enough to be labelled as decisive to the break-up of the historic compromise. Besides, the timing of the alliance break-up coincided with the PCI's decisive preferences of 'economic and institutional recovery' and 'obtaining full legitimacy as a governing partner'.

To sum up, the failure of the PCI elites to pacify their followers significantly undermined the bargaining power of the party. Although the PCI elites were far more concerned with breaking up the *conventio ad excludendum* than it was in any policies which the alliance might bring about, no major concessions were achieved by the PCI through the actual bargaining. Chiaromonte's evaluation that the historic compromise was a 'losing experience' (Chiaromonte 1986: 195), together with Paggi and D'Angelillo's (1986: 6) assertion that it 'opened a crisis in the political programmatic identity of the PCI', summarised the PCI's experience.

THE LABOUR PARTY–LIBERAL PARTY COALITION BARGAINING IN BRITAIN, 1977–78

As a partial explanation for the modest Liberals' influence over policy, on the one hand, and their achievement in obtaining 'governmental experience', on the other hand, reference to an essay by Alan Beith (1978), provides a convenient point of departure. 'Many of the most valuable policy achievements of the agreement', the Liberal's Chief Whip claims, 'were . . . gained through the process of negotiation'. The attitude, notes the author, had a number of dimensions but these basically added up to an extensive consultation on legislative priorities, access to privileged Whitehall documents and, after the Pact's renewal in July 1977, the ability to discuss government legislation with ministers prior to the Cabinet taking a final decision on its commitments for the coming year.

The above-mentioned observation is undeniably appropriate to the case of Liberal's Economic Spokesman, John Pardoe, who helped re-write that part of the legislation dealing with tax incentives for worker co-ownership schemes. This observation, however, cannot be applied to his Liberal colleagues. Basically, all the Liberal MPs shared the same background in terms of policy preparation while bargaining with Labour ministers. According to the Liberal's economic spokesman, John Pardoe:

> Very few of our policies had been worked out, probably because, after all, the party hadn't been in power for so long and it never looked like being in power, so, it hadn't actually had to prepare its

policies for power. It didn't think about writing its manifesto as though it was a programme for power. It was a programme for opposition.... Our policies were under-researched, we had too small a research department, we never had the resources to do the job properly and we came into the Pact frankly with policies that were hopelessly under-worked.[18]

This preliminary situation, shared by most Liberal MPs during the consultation with Labour ministers, did not preclude the possibility of some Liberal influence over policies, nor did it prevent Liberals acting against Labour policies. Its importance concerns not so much the question 'how' bargaining took place but 'what' was the nature of the government's concessions.

Given that the preference of 'economic recovery' was decisive to the Pact's formation, together with the unequal position of both parties in terms of office control and policy preparation, it is hardly surprising to discover that frequent difficulties existed in the Pardoe–Healey relationship, as described by the former:

I think . . . my negotiations were probably much more detailed and, if you like, much tougher and rougher than my colleagues', because economics was the centre ground of the whole thing . . . [thus] Healey and I had to fight. The only way which the respectability of the Liberal Party could be maintained was if Healey and I had a fight and would be seen to be fighting all the time. The trouble was that the only way in which the Labour Party could maintain that Liberals weren't having too much influence was for Healey also to be seen fighting. So, whether we would have fought because we were that kind of people or not, we were more or less set up to fight. It was a battleground from the start.[19]

At the time when the budget of 1977 came it was only six days after the Pact had been finalised. As a result Pardoe had to commit the Liberal Party to support the government in return for only a modification over petrol tax.

The Liberals could not bring down the government over the economic issues until some improvements had occurred. As the government's negotiations with the TUC for the third stage of the policy of income restraint broke down, for example, the Liberals supported Healey's pay policy while arguing that 'We will stay with it for as long as the Government resolve in the battle against inflation holds, but we remain with it for one purpose only – to bolster that resolve' (Michie and Hoggart 1978: 166). Moreover, the nomination of

Harold Lever to investigate the problems of small businesses without any credit given to the Liberals who were pressing for special attention to the subject, together with Healey's refusal to accept the Liberals' principal demand over the Spring 1978 budget, namely, income tax cuts, demonstrated that the Liberal Party was clearly subordinate to the Labour Party over the economic issue and was obviously receiving an unequal rate of exchange.

This is not to say that Pardoe did not achieve important concessions. The new low tax-rate band of 25 per cent on the first £750 of taxable income exemplifies this point. However, the government concessions on economic issues were not of critical importance to Labour's economic policy. Although the government had lost a budget resolution on income tax due to the Liberals voting with the Conservatives, and the surcharge on employers' national insurance contributions was passed by the House only by the Liberals' abstention (Michie and Hoggart 1978), the pact has been maintained. The extensive consultation with the Labour minister provided Pardoe, however, with some governmental experience.

The 'harmless' nature of the bargaining was confirmed by the Liberal shadow spokeswoman for Employment, Prices and Consumer Protection, Baroness Seear, who co-operated with Roy Hattersley and Albert Booth:

> We were never really very well supplied with information except the information we got from our opposite numbers. . . . The thing I remember very vividly was that we were very opposed to the Dock Work Regulation Act and we managed to hold up the laying of the regulation which brought them into force. That was the kind of way we could operate. We could modify certain things they did. . . . We could get individual things . . . and that was really about all we could do. If we pushed much further than that the Pact would just have been broken.[20]

For a time it appeared that the Liberals' refusal to support the Labour government over the dock labour scheme, levels of income tax, National Insurance contributions and the devaluation of the green pound, might damage the co-operation between the two parties but, after the Liberals had accepted minor modifications to legislation as the upper limit of government concessions, their loyalty could be assumed.

A classic example of the 'weak' position of the Liberals is provided by the negotiations over the devolution issue. The fact that the Liberals had opposed the guillotine on the Scotland and Wales Bill in order to secure two improvements of the Bill, namely, proportional representation and revenue raising powers (Bogdanor 1979: 158), did not preclude the possibility of Liberal support to the guillotine motion for the Second Reading of the Bill. Furthermore, whereas the Pact's negotiations between Steel and Callaghan revealed that there was no commitment from the PLP to support PR to the European Elections, on revenue-raising powers, the government was adamant in refusing to make any concessions (Bogdanor 1979).

As for the importance of these improvements for the Liberals, a question should be asked: did the Liberals have a point at which they were prepared to bring down the government? According to Russell Johnston, a Liberal MP, the answer was:

> No. That made the whole negotiations very weak. I participated in the negotiation over the devolution issue. We had seventeen meetings, John Smith and I. In the end, the problem was that although [the issue] was very important, nevertheless, there was nothing so important . . . that we would have been prepared to pull the plug because that would affect the main political reason for entering the Pact . . . [namely] inflation. And therefore we were in a very weak negotiating position.[21]

The weak 'negotiating position' of the Liberals resulted in a significant concession on revenue-raising powers by Steel as evidenced in a speech made to the annual conference of the Scottish Liberal Party on 19 June 1977.[22] Moreover, since the Liberals lacked a researched policy paper on the issue they used a paper entitled *Scotland and Wales Bill: Conditions for the Resurrection* written by the Outer Circle Policy Unit. The author of the paper, Professor James Cornford, confirmed the weak position of the Liberals during the negotiation:

> Russell Johnston and I . . . went into negotiation [with] Joel Barnett, John Smith and twenty officials . . . in the end, Joel Barnett said; I cannot get this Bill through my backbenchers, my backbenchers will not support this Bill [concerning revenue-raising powers]. And Russell Johnston said; well, if they won't they won't, and he didn't even go outside and said what are we going to do about it. He just gave way.[23]

Given the Liberals' weak 'negotiation position', it is hardly surprising that they were handicapped throughout the negotiations. At the end, 'the only thing that was in the Bill that wouldn't be in the Bill otherwise . . . was the provision for judicial review on the issue of the competence of the Assemblies'.[24]

Up to now it was shown that the Labour Party possessed a relatively high level of bargaining power with respect to the major issues in the bargaining plane. Yet, it is somewhat misleading to contend that the Liberal Party possessed a relatively low level of bargaining power in all aspects of the Pact. On the contrary, Steel's decisive preference of 'obtaining governmental experience', combined with the fact that the party was not forced to modify its alliance strategy following the elite-follower conflicts, call into question any underestimation of the Liberals' bargaining power. To understand the way in which David Steel gained a relatively high level of bargaining power over the decisive preference of 'obtaining governmental experience', it is necessary to appreciate the importance of the extensive consultation with Labour Ministers and the successful mobilisation of the followers' dissatisfaction. At the heart of Steel's strategy were the electoral considerations of the 'realignment of the left'. In order to enhance this idea, he had to obtain governmental experience. Not surprisingly, the major part of the Pact dealt with the institutionalisation of Labour–Liberal regular contacts. The formation of a joint consultative committee, combined with regular consultation between Labour ministers and Liberals MPs created an image of Liberals' involvement in the day-to-day operation of the government. The fact that the terms of the agreement were published also contributed to this aim.

Perhaps one of the factors which enhanced Steel's aim was the fact that the alliance strategy of the Labour government was continuously challenged by Labour backbenchers through massive dissension in parliament, whereas opposition to the renewal of the Pact within the Liberal Party was immediately neutralised. In other words, the Liberal leader could renew the Pact without offence to any incumbent ideological heritage. Furthermore, the government defeats, caused by members of the left-wing faction, gave a basic tactical advantage to the Liberals. Because of the left-wing rebels, Callaghan's Cabinet was not able to embrace economic issues fully without offending the left-wing faction. This strengthened the Liberal's image within the alliance:

> Steel regarded that as an advantage. Steel did not want to be associated with the left-wing of the Labour Party. Politically, the fact that the Labour left-wing voted against it [Lib–Lab matters] was an advantage because it positioned Steel as making a Labour Government respond to him rather than respond to its own left-wing.[25]

Hence, the Liberal's image and the intra-elite conflicts within the Labour Party associated with the left-wing faction were mutually reinforcing. The greater the extent of the internal conflict within the Labour Party, the stronger was Steel's motivation to support the government in order to improve his Party's positioning on the political map. Additionally, Bogdanor's argument that the Pact was not an agreement between the PLP and the Liberal Party but between the parliamentary Liberal Party and the Cabinet (Bogdanor 1979: 156), proved to be of some advantage to the Liberals since it prepared the ground for left-wing dissensions.

It is at this stage of the analysis that a question concerning the collapse of the Pact should be asked. Given that both party leaders successfully neutralised the dissatisfaction of large sections within their parties, why, eventually, did the Pact collapse? The answer to this question lies within the context of the principles which directed the formation of the Pact. After all, the decisive preference of 'economic recovery' was the only convergent principle between the two partners which was formalised in the Pact, thus, naturally, it should have been the potential issue at which one of the partners might bring down the government. Other preferences could not have been as significant as the economic preference to cause the collapse of the Pact. This logic is well explained by the Secretary of State for Employment, Albert Booth:

> Whether or not legislation runs, even complex measures do depend, quite a bit, on what will be the electoral consequences. And that's why I think it was possible for the Labour government to carry a lot of very difficult legislation because being brought down on it in circumstances where you haven't governmental majority means you can go to the country on that measure. So, suppose we had been defeated on the important Employment Protection Act, it would become an election issue, wouldn't it?[26]

Debate within the Liberal Party as to whether they should make the distinction between Labour proposals which had an electorate mandate and those which did not, was intensified due to their inability to impose upon the PLP a commitment for PR to the European Elections. However, since Labour governments tended to implement the major and controversial issues at the beginning of their life-span, it was obvious that the Liberals did not have any of those controversial issues over which they could bring down the government. As Russell Johnston, a Liberal MP, put it:

> We weren't entering a new period of government, and saying this is how the government should run. We were propping up a dying

government and we were taking over policies . . . which were already engrained and trying to do something about things which were already established.[27]

Indeed, prior to the Pact, substantial elements of the Social Contract (which were a range of policies formulated between the Labour Party and the TUC in 1972 and 1973), were already implemented. The Industrial Relations Act, for example, was repealed, the Employment Protection Act was introduced, improvements in pensions and other assistance were given to the retired and the disabled, child benefits were brought in, control of food prices and rents was established and steps were taken to nationalise the shipbuilding and aircraft industries (Jones and Morris: 1986: 270–2). The observation of Coats (1980: 153), that the Pact was not the cause of the Labour Party's inability to pursue the more radical elements in its policy but was one important extra factor for Labour ministers to bear in mind, clearly confirms the view regarding the minor Liberal influence. Moreover, it seemed that Callaghan did not want to pursue the more radical aspects of Labour policies and, as previously stressed, the Pact had provided a convenient excuse.

Following the successful resolution of both partners' internal conflicts, they were not forced to modify their alliance strategies. In this context, it is important to demonstrate how the personal relationships between Callaghan and Steel influenced the subsequent political experience of each party during the termination of the agreement. This involves, first of all, the observation that both leaders coordinated their tactical moves concerning the election to come. Although the final date of the election was determined basically by the Government's defeat in the House of Commons in March 1979, it was in August 1978 that Callaghan decided he should not call a general election in the following autumn.[28] As Lord Donoughue, head of Labour's think-tank, recalled:

Of course, the most important discussion was the one in 1978 when they agreed to break off the negotiation. . . . In summer 1978, Callaghan advised them to break the Pact because we probably will have a general election in the Autumn and he said again, in a fatherly way, to Steel, you must not come into an election with us, you must have an independent electoral position, therefore you must get out of the Pact in advance of the election.[29]

For Steel, the end of the Pact over the preference of 'economic recovery' was in line with his decisive preference of 'obtaining governmental experience'. Whereas Liberal MPs were interested in policy gains, Steel (1980: 115) wanted 'to be able to argue the case for a better way of running Britain and illustrate it as we've never been able to before, by pointing to a successful period of political co-operation'. Thus, for Steel, the Pact's collapse coincided with the period considered sufficient to establish his decisive preferences, namely, 'economic recovery' and the invaluable experience of co-operation with the government. For the decisive preference of 'economic recovery', the period from March 1977 to the end of May 1978 was crucial to achieving it. Hence, one could expect the collapse of the Pact once the visible (i.e. formal) decisive preferences had been achieved.

The discussion so far reveals that the Labour Party enjoyed dominant policy influence over economic issues, whereas the Liberal Party obtained governmental experience. The former superior position was mainly due to the structure of the formal alliance, which did not provide the Liberals with ministerial portfolios. The latter position, on the other hand, was enhanced by the extensive consultation with Labour ministers and the successful mobilisation of followers' dissatisfaction.

THE PS–PCF COALITION BARGAINING IN FRANCE, 1988–91

To understand the relatively high level of bargaining power possessed by the PS during 1988–90, it is necessary to analyse the interparty relationships in the bargaining plane. The passage of the 1989 and the 1990 Budgets provides an appropriate example. In France, there is not simply a single vote on the budget as a whole. Instead, there is a series of votes which determine the expenditure limits of each Ministry, as well as votes on the income component of the budget and on the overall equilibrium level.

The passage of the 1989 budget is a classic example of a government's reliance on an informal alliance. Negotiating each issue separately and on an *ad hoc* basis with the UDC and the PCF enabled the PS government to enjoy three advantages. First, it could pick the least 'expensive' alliance partner available in policy terms. Second, it was able to escape any threats to its stability which might have followed a formal alliance. Third, it avoided the use of Article 49–3 because it won the support on each vote of either the PCF or the UDC.

The government profited from this situation wherever possible by gaining the support of the PCF, or the UDC. As long as the Bills were politically moderate, either the PCF or the UDC (or even both RPR and the UDF) found themselves in situations where a mere refusal would be difficult to justify. Then, the government just had to deal with a few amendments which enabled the external support parties to argue that they have obtained some concessions improving the Bill. Afterwards, either they voted for the text or they refrained from voting, which was enough. Communist abstention, for example, was reached over the education part of the Budget in which increased expenditure was manifested, while the UDC support was obtained for the employment part of the budget as the Minister concerned, Jean-Pierre Soisson, was an *ouverture* Minister. The government just had to keep a constant balance between the two possibilities and was doubly pleased to co-operate with these groups as it avoided using Article 49–3. Guy Carcasson, thus, even summarised this experience as a new sport in France, namely, 'the parliamentary slalom'.[30]

A comprehensive examination of the 1988 budget negotiations, conducted by John Huber (1991: 26), reveals four central features of the bargaining among the government and its informal partners:

1 there was no bargaining before the Bill was presented by the Government to the National Assembly;
2 there was no bargaining or compromise in the Finance Committee;
3 the Government used the rules of legislative procedure to limit the importance of formal amendment activity and debate on the floor, as well as to shape voter perceptions of who should receive credit for particular policy outcomes; and
4 the only forum for negotiating policy concessions was secret meetings between the Government and the leaders of the 'pivot' parties after debate of the Bill on the floor had began.

Undoubtedly, features 1, 2, and 4 were adopted because of the intra-party preoccupations of both the PS, the UDC parliamentary group and the PCF. The strategy of secrecy in the bargaining process, the reduction in the number of participants in the negotiations to the level of parliamentary group leaders, and the contraction of the bargaining plane (i.e. following the elimination of the Finance Committee as a bargaining arena), clearly suggests that the relevant elites aimed at minimising internal dissatisfaction. Such intraparty preoccupations were combined with electoral consideration. By relying on informal, *ad hoc*, coalition the PS could establish a public image of legislative independence while avoiding the cost of dividing the party by calming the fears of its deputies since the budget would not be voted strictly with the UDC. The latter, which was unsure how its strategy of 'constructive opposition' would be seen by the voters, could also escape a deterioration of its image. Furthermore, as its deputies were elected through co-operation with the UDF, the RPR and the UDC, it could avoid problems with the latter parties (Huber 1991: 21–2).

In any event, it seems that the definition of the bargaining plane, as well as the interparty relationships over the 1989 budget, were dominated by the PS. The minor concessions which were recorded in that period exemplifies the argument. The income side of the 1989 budget, for example, was passed by the National Assembly by a vote of 274 to 229, with the Centrists grouping and the Communists abstaining.[31] Whereas the support of the Centrists was won by an agreement to cut the top rate of Value Added Tax to 28 per cent from 33 per cent and a reduction in the *taxe professionelle*,[32] the abstention of the Communists was won by reducing the housing tax on low-income families.

Any attempt to overemphasise the importance of these concessions is bound to be undermined. Dominique Strauss-Kahn, the President of the Finance Committee, explains the nature of the interparty relationships in the bargaining arena as follows:

> I don't think the government had to pay something, but sometimes it accepted amendments which were not in contradiction with what the government wanted. For instance, [in 1988] the government decided itself to decrease the *taxe [professionelle]*, it was my own proposal. . . . So it's not really a price to pay. It's just a kind of good manners. With the Communists [however] we had more difficult negotiation. Probably, you pay less of a price to the Centrists because they are less homogeneous than the Communists.[33]

This is not to say that the PCF and the UDC had no impact on the policy process and its outcome. The influence of both parties was important but not unlimited. Rocard used Article 49–3 to avoid having to accept amendments which were totally unpalatable. Therefore, the relative bargaining power of the PCF and the UDC parliamentary group did not lie in the ability to affect the outcome, but rather some outcomes were designed with consideration of their position. Although Rocard's government was in a minority situation he still retained a certain space in which to operate.

Attention now turns to the interparty relationships over the 1990 budget. Given the extent of the intra-elite conflicts within the PS and the UDC parliamentary group, and the elite-follower conflicts within the PCF, it was hardly surprising that the government did not face the same options as it did in 1988. Regarding the intraparty arena:

> Largely due to the break up of the Mitterand *courant*, the internal party problems within the PS increased noticeably after 1988. The

exchanges between the *fabiusiens* and the *jospinistes* during the preparation of the 1990 budget provide evidence of the increasing tensions within the party. Rocard's strategy at this time was to appear to take neither side, so as to enhance his position as arbitrator. . . . this strategy, was designed to improve Rocard's long-term chances as a future *présidentiable*.

(Elgie 1993: 160)

Regarding Rocard's two potential partners, both the PCF and UDC groups made it clear before even the first budgetary vote in September 1989 that they were unwilling to support the government, thus forcing the use of Article 49–3. For a time it appeared that the gap might be bridged by conducting informal negotiation with the Communists,[34] but after a short period it was clear that the concessions upon which the PCF insisted were unacceptable and were designed to be so as not be seen to support the government on such an important text.

Added to the negative influences of the elite-follower conflicts within the PCF, was the UDC strategy of a formal alliance with their right-wing allies. Not surprisingly, it could also not be seen to support the government on such a critical division. Yet, since the UDC lost their impact as a single bargaining entity, following the internal conflicts, one could expect dissensions over critical divisions. Indeed, this was the case on the first two occasions where Article 49–3 was used to pass the Budget because several UDC deputies, notably, Raymond Barre, refused to censure the government. As a result, on the other two occasions, no censure motion was lodged by the opposition, avoiding any vote and any further embarrassing dissensions.

It is, however, misleading to contend that the break-up of the informal alliance undermined the PS bargaining power. At the outset, Rocard continued to use the two sides of his *majorité stéréo*, the PCF and the UDC, but, the use of Article 49–3 became more frequent. Whereas in the first year this article was used only three times, in the parliamentary session of October–December 1989 it was used to pass four different Bills.[35] Yet, in order to adapt itself to the lack of forthcoming external support, a three fold strategy was initiated. First, an attempt to weaken the internal dissatisfaction during the passage of the 1990 Budget was recorded on several important fiscal issues, including an increase in the wealth tax, where pressure from the PS group forced the government to accept amendments which it would not otherwise have done. Second, a new electoral movement was launched. Third, the government developed its contact with the nineteen independent deputies in an attempt to enlarge its support base.

The latter two aspects deserve some elaboration. Regarding the new electoral movement, the launching of *La France Unie*, an electoral movement founded by Jean-Pierre Soisson, was an attempt by the government to build upon *ouverture* and create a formal alliance with the centreground of French politics. According to one of its members, Jean Marie Daillet:

> He [Jean-Pierre Soisson] phoned me and told me; would you come along with me and try to organise the left-wing of the centre in order to counterbalance the Socialists? The Socialists are in the middle of a big crisis . . . they need a partner. . . . We started with some thirty people; we have a list of MPs which are not very happy inside the party group which they belong to now; they could provide us with parliamentarians who could built up a new group right in the middle of the Assembly. It would be a very peculiar one. It will be very heterodox, almost incoherent. Still, there is a common line for everyone; freedom of speech, freedom of vote.[36]

Since it was a government initiative one might expect that the actual institutionalisation of the movement as a parliamentary group or a political party would take place to ensure the government's survival should the need arise. By June 1990, however, the few Senators and Deputies who rallied to this movement were sufficient to keep the government alive without the need to institutionalise the movement.

Additionally, the government developed its contact with the nineteen independent deputies in an attempt to enlarge its support base. Whereas some of them, such as Bernard Tapie, were elected under the banner of the Presidential majority and rarely voted against the government, others had to be negotiated with and thus concessions had to be made in order to ensure the government majority over critical divisions.

Finally, one might argue that there was also a price to pay for the frequent use of Article 49–3 in terms of the weakness of the government and its majority. However, the government's electoral cost of invoking this Article can hardly be overemphasised since the PCF and the UDC refused to enter serious negotiations with the government (Huber 1991: 27). In fact, this is an understatement. Both parties decided to make ideological and non-credible proposals in 1989. As the electoral costs of invoking the Article were already quite low, following the strategy of the opposition parties, the PS decided that the electoral benefits of avoiding an appearance of disunity outweighed the electoral costs of using the Article.

To sum up, the successful resolution of the intra-elite conflicts within the PS, Article 49–3 and the political situation in which the Article operated contributed to the superior position of the party in the parliamentary bargaining plane. On the other hand, the failure of the PCF to resolve its elite-follower conflicts was translated into an inferior position in the bargaining plane. Furthermore, during the period under examination, it was shown that the UDC parliamentary group could hardly be considered a single bargaining entity. The group was fragmented member by member, with very small groupings revolving around the few key ones. In the light of these circumstances it is hardly surprising that the failure of the UDC parliamentary group to pacify the internal opposition was translated to an inferior position in the bargaining plane.

SUMMARY AND CONCLUSION

This chapter suggests that the resolution of intraparty conflicts relates to the party's bargaining power over the decisive preference which underlies its coalition strategy. A successful resolution of internal conflicts – evident in the cases of the decentralised parties observed – seems more likely to have either no effect, or a positive one, on a party's bargaining power. This, in turn, contributes to the continuation of coalition bargaining and the process of government formation. The failure of elites operating within a centralised party to neutralise internal opposition undermines their bargaining power which, in turn, leads to the termination of coalition bargaining and the process of government formation.

In the Danish case it was shown that the failure of the centralised SD to neutralise the internal opposition was translated into an inferior position in the bargaining plane over its decisive preference. The Liberal Party blocked the major SD plans for 'economic democratisation', tax and housing reforms strongly supported by the trade unions. Additionally, as the SD had twice as many ministers as the Liberal Party, the system of 'contact ministers' enables Liberal ministers to block any initiatives by SD ministers. In the Norwegian case it was shown that a substantial reason for the relatively low level of bargaining power possessed by the SP lay in the failure of the party leader, Johan Jakobsen, to pacify the intra-elite conflicts. During the negotiation over the 1990 budget, for example, the Conservatives made relatively minor concessions to the SP. In the crisis over the EEA issue, the SP parliamentary group militantly opposed the SP Cabinet members, forcing the latter to modify its coalitional behaviour.

In the Italian case it was shown that Lange's (1980: 127) claim, that 'the DC seemed increasingly ready to risk confrontation rather than to make any more concessions to the PCI', is valid. A substantial reason for this lies in the DC's ability to tolerate the activities of its internal opposition. The DC elites were able to establish a type of conformity which allowed for the manifestation of internal dissatisfaction within the party. Throughout the historic compromise, the DC elites were not forced to act in one way or another as a result of rank and file pressures. Whatever has been said or done, dissenting members were able to communicate their positions to their supporters in the party and society, promoting a serious, and undamaging discussion inside the party. The DC elites, for example, did not take into consideration the views of the PCI and the trade unions when drafting their three-year economic plan, nor did they initiate reforms which were formally agreed upon before the formation of the alliance. By contrast, the centralised PCI elites became prisoners of their own party once they imposed the historic compromise without a serious debate. The fact that strong dissent had earlier been banned or at least discouraged, contributed to the evolution of dissatisfaction outside the party, especially in late 1977. This, in turn, led to the PCI's loss of initiative once the militant metalworkers' union (FLN) mobilised Communist activists in the streets of Rome, far away from the repressive mechanisms of the party. Having lost the initiative and being unable to form a formal alliance which would last more than a few months, the PCI failed to establish itself as a reliable actor in Italian politics as it remained unable to propose a reasonable set of short-term reforms and get DC co-operation in generating any serious changes in the country.

In the British case it was shown that the successful resolution of internal conflicts by both party elites contributed to the Labour and Liberal parties gaining a relatively high level of bargaining power over 'economic recovery', and 'obtaining governmental experience', respectively. For the former, the Liberal Party had clearly no choice other than to support the government in the pursuit of 'economic recovery'. As Labour governments tended to implement the major and controversial issues at the beginning of their life-span, it was obvious that the Liberals did not have any of those controversial issues over which they could bring down the government. Whereas the Labour Party dominated the bargaining arena over economic policy, the Liberal Party obtained governmental experience, or at least, an image of such a practice. At the heart of the Liberal leader's strategy were the electoral considerations of the 'realignment of the left'. In order to enhance this idea, the party had to be seen as one which has some governmental experience. Not surprisingly, a major part of the Pact dealt with the institutionalisation of Liberal–Labour regular contacts. The formation of a joint consultative committee, combined with the regular consultation between Labour ministers and Liberal MPs created an image of Liberal's involvement in the day-to-day operation of the government. The fact that the terms of the agreement were published further solidified this image.

In the French case it was shown that the successful resolution of the intra-elite conflicts within the PS, Article 49–3 and the political situation in which the Article operated contributed to the superior position of the party in the parliamentary bargaining plane. By contrast, the failure of the PCF to resolve the elite-follower conflicts internally was translated into an inferior position in the bargaining plane. The minor concessions which were recorded over the 1989 Budget exemplified this point. Over the 1990 Budget, the government was able to legislate even though it lacked a parliamentary majority by using Article 49–3 and relying on the assumption that both the PCF and the UDC parliamentary group were unwilling to fight a general election as they sensed a poor performance. Thus, they were unwilling to join forces to bring the government down.

At the beginning of this chapter I posed the question: 'what are the implications of successful and unsuccessful resolution of intraparty conflicts on a party's bargaining power, and thus, on coalition bargaining and the process of government formation? As shown in Table 7.1, the analysis demonstrates that, in the cases observed, a decentralised party is more likely than a centralised one to resolve conflicts successfully. When intraparty conflicts occur, a decentralised party is most likely to sustain its bargaining power over its decisive preference, and thus to continue the coalition bargaining and the process of government formation. A centralised party which faces internal conflicts is most likely to fail in its attempt to pacify internal opposition. Consequently, it is most likely to face a decline in its bargaining power over its decisive preference, leading to the break up of the coalition bargaining and the process of government formation.

In qualitative political science, it is rare indeed to discover patterns as powerful as those we have just examined. An important omission from our argument, however, will already have occurred to the prudent reader. In unipolar party systems, when the dominant party is located at the median position, single-party minority governments are most likely to be formed (Laver and Schofield 1990). Consequently, there could be no focus to any activities of internal opposition since no (governmental) alternative is likely to be viable. The validity of the

Table 7.1 Bargaining power: the modes of coalition bargaining

Party	Outcome of conflict resolution	Relative bargaining power over the party's decisive preferences	Change of legislative strategy initiated by the party
(i)	*Decentralised parties which face intra-elite conflicts*		
DC	Successful	High	No
Labour Party	Successful	High	No
PS	Successful	High	No
(ii)	*Decentralised parties which face elite-follower conflicts*		
Liberal Party	Successful	High	No
(iii)	*Centralised parties which face intra-elite conflicts*		
SD	Failure	Low	Break-up of alliance
SP	Failure	Low	Break-up of alliance
(iv)	*Centralised parties which face elite-follower conflicts*		
PCI	Failure	Low	Break-up of alliance a few weeks after followers' demonstrations
PCF	Failure	Low	Break-up of alliance a few weeks after followers' demonstrations

Source: Maor (1995a: 83).

patterns discovered here can also be questioned when party elites with-hold information regarding the content of the coalition agreement from members of the parliamentary and extraparliamentary party. Internal opposition leaders are therefore restricted in their ability to use the 'confidential accord' – whose exact content they do not know – as a base point from which a campaign against party strategy could be launched. The next chapter explores precisely such a case.

8 Are centralised parties defenceless against internal conflicts?

The discussion so far has exposed the vulnerability of centralised parties once internal conflicts evolve, especially in cases of elite-follower conflicts. I have argued that a centralised organisation lacks the mechanisms necessary to adjust to dissent among its members, and is therefore at a disadvantage when it enters parliamentary negotiations. When interparty negotiations induce intra-elite or elite-follower conflicts, members may be forced to leave the party or air their dissatisfaction outside the party, as their primary mechanisms for the expression of dissent. A centralised, rigid organisation – especially when confronted with the latter conflict mode – can lead to party disintegration when such a party enters serious coalition negotiations with other parties.

This argument was strongly supported by the comparative analysis so far. However, all cases observed which involved intraparty conflicts within centralised parties have shared one aspect: party elites and members were informed about the content of the coalition agreement or 'understanding'. This is not to say that they were consulted or that a debate within the party had been initiated by the party elites. Rather, it is to stress that, whatever the intraparty consequences of a party's coalition bargaining, once agreement was signed its content had been published in national and party newspapers. In all the cases observed, party members at whichever organisational level in the party could use the coalition agreement as a base point from which a campaign against party strategy could be launched. The question which arises is whether the party elites can withhold sensitive information regarding the coalition agreement from members of the parliamentary and extraparliamentary party.

This chapter illustrate such a case. It analyses modes of conflict manifestation, resolution and bargaining of the Danish RV during 1988–90. In this case intra-elite conflicts emerged in the centralised RV following its co-operation with the CP, SD and the KrF. I hope to show that in an attempt to pacify the conflicts, the party leadership has, among other measures, successfully withheld information regarding the coalition agreement from members of the parliamentary and extraparliamentary party, thus denying them a platform from which a challenge to the party strategy could be launched. This case study illustrates that, once sensitive information regarding the coalition bargaining is withheld, party leadership which operates in a centralised context may take advantage of the intra-elite conflicts following a formation of a formal minority government, demanding more concessions from its coalition partners in order to pacify the internal opposition.

THE RV–CPP COALITION BARGAINING IN DENMARK, 1988–90

Modes of conflict manifestation

To understand why the intra-elite conflicts evolved within the RV it is necessary to appreciate the parliamentary situation which developed after the 1988 elections. A dispute over how to react to possible visits of nuclear warships to Danish ports led to a wider dispute concerning Denmark's NATO and security policy. The minority centre-right coalition led by Poul Schlüter of the CPP was defeated in the *Folketing* on April 1988, over an opposition resolution requiring the government to inform visiting warships that Denmark did not permit nuclear weapons on its territories. This was the twenty-third occasion since coming to power in September 1982 that the four-party coalition had been forced to adopt 'alternative' foreign or defence policies. The coalition, which comprised the CPP, V, CD and KrF, had been guaranteed a majority in domestic and economic matters by the support of the RV, but this party, with a long tradition of pacifism, had voted with the opposition on foreign and defence policy issues. Mr Schlüter had always refused to resign after defeats of this nature, maintaining that they were due to tactical operations of the main opposition party, the SD, designed to force him out of office, but had stated that if the opposition's majority in foreign policy matters ever endangered Denmark's NATO membership he would ask the electorate to decide the issue. As a result of the vote Mr Schlüter reacted by calling a general election in order to ask the electorate for their views on Denmark's full membership of the Western Alliance.

The main result of the May 1988 election was a drop in the Conservatives' vote from around 23 to 19 per cent (see Appendix 2.1). Nevertheless, Poul Schlüter began negotiating with the RV over a formation of a government coalition. The evidence and arguments presented by a large number of commentators suggest that Schlüter's aim was to put an end to the 'alternative majority'. However, a choice of a CPP-led minority government with the V, RV, CD and the KrF imposed certain constraints on the RV. According to the KrF leader, Flemming Kofod-Svendsen:

> As far as I know, the *Radical Venstre* would not like there to be two great parties and three small parties in government. They wanted there to be only three parties because they hoped they could profile themselves better. . . . But Schlüter mentioned that he had to choose a government between the four parties [namely], the Conservatives, the Venstre, the *Radical Venstre* and the Centre Democrats, and the three [i.e. the Conservatives, the Venstre and the Radical Venstre].[1]

Additionally, one of the main factors which enhanced the formation of the CPP–V–RV coalition was the consensus-oriented strategy of the CD and the KrF. This strategy is well described by the CD founder and Member of *Folketing*, Erhard Jacobsen:

> For the moment, for instance, we do not have a great sympathy or great admiration for the government but we just have to realise that nobody else could form a government, and therefore we will not do anything to harm the government. But, of course, if the government put forward a proposal directly against what we think is right . . . we will vote against it and they know that. . . . We are not part of the government background but, on the other hand, we will guarantee that we will never take part in an action against the government with the intention of overthrowing the government because who would form another government?[2]

As it was probably reasonable to assume that the KrF strategy would not deviate significantly from that of the CD, Schlüter could consider both parties as 'sleeping partners'. Since the CPP–V–RV coalition had still no majority in the *Folketing* it had to seek the support of either the SD or the FrP. This parliamentary situation has created a dilemma for the RV's leadership. On the one hand, the party's views concerning security and foreign matters were much closer to the SD than to its coalitional partners, on the other hand, as part of the government, the party could not vote against the government. This dilemma was a major factor which contributed to the evolution of intra-elite conflicts within the RV. Jørgen Estrup, a member of the RV's parliamentary group who led the internal opposition, explained:

> The only really major split I can think of at the moment is the one we had last May or June just after the election, when there were discussions about forming the present government. . . . I was part of the reason for the split because I did not think it was a very good idea to form the present government, because . . . there was not any formal agreement between the three parties. So, I was a bit frightened that [we would have] too many cleavages and there would be too many problems that would have to be solved in that way and it would not be possible to follow a straight track to solve the rather big economic problem.[3]

A debate as to whether to co-operate with the CPP and the V surfaced between the RV's prospective ministers, namely, Niels Helveg Petersen, Jens Bilgrav Nielsen, Ole Vig Jensen and Lone Dybkjær, and the party's parliamentary group, most notably, Jørgen Estrup, Elizabeth Arnold and, to a lesser extent, the leader of the group, Marianne Jelved. The attitudes of the latter group had a number of dimensions, or 'cleavages' as Estrup termed, but these basically added up to controversial questions concerning security and foreign affairs and the mechanisms which would enable their successful resolution.

Given the seriousness of the discussions over the formation of the CPP–V–RV formal alliance, it is hardly surprising that the 'voice' option was taken up; members of the RV's parliamentary group had appealed to the prospective members of cabinet with the aim of changing their intention to co-operate with the CPP and the Liberal Party. However, 'for voice to function properly it is necessary that individuals possess reserves of political influence which they can bring into play when they are sufficiently aroused' (Hirschman 1970: 71–2). This argument can be used to explain a further appeal of the parliamentary group to RV party activists and the mobilisation of the activists' support to enhance the former's objectives. One political editor reviewed an attempt of the parliamentary group's leader in mid-1989 to mobilise the activists' support towards accepting decisions against the party lines as follows:

> I guess the Radical Left has a number of more serious problems with their roots or even with the organs in the party. They just had a meeting [in their] main body with some 200 members [in which]

they put forward a programme for an economic [policy] which on two essential points is quite opposite to what the government wants. . . . They put forward a programme which said they wanted a new pension [plan] which the government does not [want], and it was part of the agreement, when the Radical Left entered the government, that they could not put forward proposals on a new pension [plan]. And they [members of the parliamentary group] do not want to flatten out the taxes [whilst] the government wants to make them more flat, to take away [the] progressive [element]. So it is quite different from what the party stands for in the government. This proposal was put forward in the meeting by the leader of the parliamentary group, Marianne Jelved, and it was agreed by the vast majority.[4]

The successful mobilisation of the RV's activists against the party's positions did not imply that an elite-follower conflict evolved. Rather, it was the parliamentary group that initiated the conflict and led the internal opposition. The mobilisation of party activists was therefore simply a manifestation of the parliamentary group's ability to mobilise party members against the elites' line.

Modes of conflict resolution

However inconsistent the strength of the RV's parliamentary group may have been throughout 1989–90, it prompted determined action from the RV's cabinet members during coalition bargaining and the process of government formation. In order to neutralise and pacify the intra-elite dissatisfaction, a confidential agreement, signed between the RV's Minister of Environment, Lone Dybkjær, and the V's Minister of Foreign Affairs, Uffe Ellemann-Jensen, contained two key elements. First:

There was actually a list of all those decisions of the parliament where the government had been in minority and it was an agreement about what could happen in the coming period for the new government if those items were brought up again. Would they cause trouble or could we somehow manage with them.[5]

Besides this document, in which twenty-three controversial matters and the preferable strategy to tackle them were specified, there was also an accord which introduced a mechanism of co-operation between the government and the SD over security and foreign policy matters. According to Jørgen Estrup:

There was a document spelling out what could be done with respect to forming the future decisions on foreign policy, so that you could be sure that there would be a majority backing them. Since the new government would have been a minority government, it would need to have at least the Social Democrats to accept its policy, and that was one of the crucial things for my party that you could make a formal instrument to ensure that the Social Democrats would be backing the foreign policy. There was a document specifying that you could form some kind of a committee, or at least a body, that would make an expert analysis on foreign policy, security policy, which would support the discussion in parliament and be an instrument for forming, thus, consensus decisions.[6]

It should be obvious from the content of the confidential agreement that the main objective of the RV in joining the government was to develop a broad co-operation with the CPP and the Liberal Party over economic policy, and with the SD over foreign affairs and security policy. To illustrate whether this aim has been realised, however, requires an evaluation of the co-operation with the SD and the derived consequences in terms of RV's bargaining power.

Modes of coalition bargaining

Logically, one can expect that the break up of the alternative majority would be immediately manifested by a decrease in the SD's participation in the winning sides in final votes. This, in turn, may indicate a decline in RV's bargaining power, at least over issues of foreign affairs and security policy. However, an analysis of the final votes in the *Folketing* suggests that the SD participation on the winning side dropped marginally from 68 per cent in the first session of 1987–88 to 64 per cent in the second session (Damgaard and Svensson 1989: 743). Given the facts that the SD position on the winning side remained almost unchanged (during the period examined) and that the SD voting strategy was coordinated with that of the RV, it can be argued that although the alternative majority was formally broken up following the inclusion of the RV in the government no significant change in the level of co-operation between the RV and the SD was recorded.

The setting up of the parliamentary forum on foreign affairs and security policy in November 1988 (which was mentioned in the Dybkjær–Ellemann-Jensen agreement) furthermore exemplifies the type of structural constraint imposed on the governmental decision-making process by the centralised RV. This committee has restricted the room for manoeuvre of the other coalition partners, including the Conservative Party, thus maintaining the RV position in the bargaining arena. Some insight of the operation of the forum and the RV position can be gained through Jørgen Estrup's description that 'We have not had any real trouble in parliament with foreign policy because we had the possibility to discuss it with the Social Democrats in the committee'.[7] It is therefore reasonable to argue that the parliamentary forum which was established as a result of the Dybkjær–Ellemann-Jensen agreement was a critical factor in maintaining a relatively high level of RV–SD co-operation. This, in turn, implies that RV's bargaining power was not undermined as a result of the internal conflict: the RV was able to maintain co-operation with its governmental partners over economic policy, and with the SD over foreign and security policy.

Naturally, the fact that the Dybkjær–Ellemann-Jensen agreement was a confidential one (even members of the RV's parliamentary group were not allowed to see the agreement) calls into question the importance of the CPP and V's concessions.[8] Furthermore, there is no reason to believe that the Schlüter-led government changed its attitude, evident from 1982 to 1988, towards the importance of foreign affairs and security policy for its survival. Economic issues still seemed to prevail over all other issues. The fact that general elections were called in December 1990 over the issue of a tax reform illustrates this point (Maor 1991). To be on the safe side, therefore, the analysis concludes that the RV's relative bargaining power was not undermined by the intra-elite conflicts due to their successful resolution.

SUMMARY AND CONCLUSION

Intra-elite conflicts within the centralised RV, following a formal minority government with the CPP and the V, were manifested by 'voices' within the parliamentary and extraparliamentary party. A substantial reason for the lack of the 'exit' mode lies in the strategy implemented by the party leadership during the coalition bargaining and the process of government formation. First, decisions against the government line by party members did not trigger off reactions of the RV's cabinet members although they were approved unanimously in party bodies. Second, a confidential agreement was signed among the coalition partners. The agreement included a list of controversial matters and the preferable strategy to tackle them, and the establishment of a parliamentary body responsible for coordination of activities between the government and the RV.

The signing of a confidential accord between the coalition partners implies that the RV leadership successfully withheld information regarding the coalition agreement from members of the parliamentary and extraparliamentary party. By doing so, it denied them a platform from which a challenge to the party strategy could be launched. With no serious challenge to the party's legislative strategy, the party leadership was able to take advantage of the intra-elite conflicts following a formation of a formal minority government, demanding more concessions from its coalition partners in order to 'pacify' the internal opposition.

9 Conclusions and implications

The comparative study of intraparty conflicts and coalition bargaining in nine European parties has attempted to demonstrate that, contrary to the traditional argument according to which the more centralised the party structure the easier it is for the party to remain in the coalition, the case cannot be made for an equivalent comparison when one breaks free from the assumption that a party is a unitary actor. Taking seriously the view that internal relationships are not only a matter of democracy but also a matter of manageability, this study bears out this argument in detail. But, an extended view can emphasise the fact that our conclusion bore a direct impact on coalition stability. The first priority must be to anticipate possible criticisms of the theoretical framework and to answer these with a restatement of its logic.

There are two varieties deserving particular attention. The first is the objection that the study focuses on intraparty conflicts which emerge following coalition bargaining; other sources of conflicts, such as personal or opposition of principal, are being neglected. A second claim concerns two assumptions – namely, minimal size and minimal number of coalition members – which are needed to be incorporated into the theoretical framework. For the former, intraparty conflict was strictly defined in the context of coalitional behaviour mainly because the focus of the thesis was on internal conflicts which emerge as a result of an interparty relationship. This is not to say that other sources of internal conflicts are less important. It is rather to stress that the organisational characteristics which significantly affect the elites' ability to neutralise internal dissatisfaction do not depend on the conflict's source. The arguments developed here, thus, are valid whatever the source of the internal conflict is.

The second objection should be similarly evaluated in the light of the thesis's logic. The advantage of decentralised parties in pacifying internal dissatisfaction combined with the disadvantage of the centralised parties to perform the same task, seem relevant whatever the size of a coalition, and whatever the number of partners involved. The size of a coalition (i.e. whether minority or majority status) and the number of coalition partners might affect the likelihood of such conflicts, as well as their intensity and extent. Yet the analysis does not aim to predict the evolution of internal conflicts. On the contrary, all the hypotheses are conditioned by the evolution of intraparty conflicts. Once such conflicts occur, whatever the size of the coalition and the number of its partners, one can rely on the insight of the thesis in order to predict the modes of conflict resolution and its derived consequences in terms of a party's bargaining power. Before exploring the impact of our conclusion on the study of coalition stability I summarise the study's argument.

ORGANISATIONAL DETERMINANTS OF COALITION BARGAINING

The concern of the preceding chapters has been to deal with political parties as complex organisations and to strike a middle course, between non-comparison and over-abstraction, by applying a theoretical model to a relatively large number of cases in different party systems. Political conflicts, it was argued, are to be seen essentially as bargaining situations. Political parties in multiparty systems face a bargaining problem which refers to the need for party elites to reach some settlement in parliament, but, at the same time, the wish to settle on terms favourable to themselves.

The bargaining problem indicates that the fundamental relationships considered here are those between intraparty conflict and a party's bargaining power, and their effect on the party's coalition bargaining. With a practicable political context for the formation of a coalition strategy, it was further argued that the way power is distributed within the party is an intervening variable because intraparty relationships are mainly matters of manageability rather than solely a matter of democracy. In other words, the distribution of power within the party and the nature of the intraparty conflicts affect the ability of the party elite to pacify and neutralise internal opposition.

Intuitively, it is tempting to accept Groenning's (1968) and Panebianco's (1988) argument that the more centralised parties are, the stronger they are as coalition actors. However, the study suggested that the value of the institutional mechanisms to mobilise internal dissatisfaction have been underestimated by both scholars. At the heart of the study's strategy lay the notion that it is decentralised parties that are characterised by diffused mechanisms for internal dissent, as well as the ability to establish new mechanisms. As long as dissenting activities take place within those channels, these parties tend to possess more defences with respect to internal challenges than centralised parties.

It is important at this point to reiterate the status of those explanatory generalisations about to be made. They do not claim, nor are they designed to imply, a general theory of party politics. They are *de facto* generalisations, to be assumed as relevant mainly to the cases examined here within the period chosen. It is, furthermore, an addition to the modest stock of systematic middle-level observations with appropriate theoretical formulations.

The central *de facto* generalisation pursued over the foregoing pages, 'the organisational determinants of coalition bargaining', the thesis of which now merits a recapitulation: *Everything else being equal, when intraparty conflicts occur, the strength of a party in the parliamentary bargaining arena (i.e. its relative bargaining power) lies in its organisational decentralisation.* When intraparty conflicts occur, organisational decentralisation allows the party to handle intra-elite and elite-follower conflicts in a variety of manageable ways without forcing members to leave the party. As a result, the party can enter into conflict-inducing coalition negotiations with other parties without risking its hold on its own members. A centralised organisation, however, lacks the mechanisms necessary to adjust to dissent among its members, and is therefore at a disadvantage when it enters parliamentary negotiations. When interparty negotiations induce intra-elite or elite-follower conflicts, members may be forced to leave the party, or air their dissatisfaction outside the party as their primary mechanisms for the expression of dissent. A centralised, rigid organisation – especially when confronted with the latter conflict mode – can lead to party disintegration when such a party enters serious coalition negotiations with other parties.

Thus, the study gives rise to the following set of generalisations:

1 Conflicts within a decentralised party are most likely to be manifested by 'voices' within the parliamentary and party arenas whereas conflicts within a centralised party are most likely to be manifested by 'exit' or 'voices' outside these arenas.
2 Elites within a decentralised party are most likely to emphasise 'decisive preferences' during coalition life-span and tolerate factional activities and the formation of new factions in an attempt to pacify internal opposition. Elites within a centralised party which face intra-elite conflicts are most likely to emphasise 'decisive

preferences', and impose structural constraints on the day-to-day operation of the government coalition or the party. Elites within a centralised party which face elite-follower conflicts are most likely to emphasise 'decisive preferences', initiate 'articulation of ends' and impose a transition period before a formal alliance is concluded.

3   A decentralised party is more likely than a centralised one to resolve conflicts successfully. When intraparty conflicts occur, a decentralised party is most likely to sustain its bargaining power over its decisive preference and, thus, to continue the coalition bargaining and the process of government formation. A centralised party which faces internal conflicts is most likely to face a decline in its bargaining power over its decisive preference, leading to the breakup of the coalition bargaining and the process of government formation.

These are relevant arguments, for they have, I believe, a reasonable logic. It complements Maor's (1992) study of intraparty conflicts and coalition bargaining in Denmark and Norway which concludes that centralised parties may avoid intraparty conflicts by forming legislative (i.e. informal, *ad hoc*) coalitions. The validity of this argument can be questioned however when – as shown in the case of the centralised RV – party elites withhold information regarding the content of the coalition agreement from members of the parliamentary and extraparliamentary party. Internal opposition leaders are therefore restricted in their ability to use the 'confidential accord' – whose exact content they do not know – as a base point from which a campaign against party strategy could be launched. The validity of these arguments can be also questioned when applied to party systems which are significantly dominated by one party (Maor 1995a, 1997b). In unipolar systems, especially when the dominant party is located at the median position, single-party minority governments are most likely to be formed (Laver and Schofield 1990). By negotiating each issue separately and on an *ad hoc* basis, such governments can in each case pick the least 'expensive' coalition partner available. 'Expensive' refers to the potential threat of the partner to the party's cohesion and stability. Thus, in cases of single-party minority government which negotiate each issue separately, internal conflicts seem less likely to occur. Even if they do occur, there could be no focus to its activities since no (governmental) alternative is likely to be viable due to the format of the party system.

So far, the thesis has established that intraparty conflicts bore a direct impact on a party's coalition bargaining in minority situations. The interesting question is what this conclusion really entails? Does it bear an impact on other aspects of coalition behaviour?

ORGANISATIONAL DETERMINANTS OF COALITION STABILITY

The idea this study raises is that there is a need for scholars of cabinet durability to concern themselves with party attributes. Cabinet durability – the length of time an incumbent cabinet government survives in office without an election, government's resignation and changes in party membership of cabinet or Prime Minister – has long been viewed as a critical indicator of coalition maintenance (Laver and Schofield 1990: 145). Several approaches have been suggested as factors affecting cabinet durability.

The 'regime attributes' approach has concentrated on the relationship between cabinet stability and a number of features of the political system in general, such as the 'size' or fragmentation of the party system (Duverger 1964; Sartori 1976: 178; Strøm 1990b). Another tradition, the 'coalition attributes' approach, looks at properties of particular coalitions that might contribute to their stability, the most obvious of which is majority status (Warwick 1979; Laver 1974; Dodd 1976; Sanders and Herman 1977). A third possibility is to look at the structure of the bargaining system within which coalitions must exist (Dodd 1976). Another attempt, the 'events' approach, takes into account the fact that the actual downfall of a cabinet is typically the product of a particular 'critical' or 'terminal' event that is liable to occur at any time during its life (Browne *et al.* 1986).

Undoubtedly, Paul Warwick's (1979, 1994) studies of cabinet durability are the most important works on the topic. In the first study, Warwick (1979) reported that approximately 50 per cent of the variance in cabinet duration is explained by the conjunction of the independent variable; cabinet majority status, number of governing parties, minimal winning cabinet status, and an index of ideological cleavage among cabinet actors. However, a large number of abovementioned models, which are based on structural variables, failed to improve upon prediction of cabinet duration. This, in turn, leads to the assertion that while such factors may contribute substantially to some coalition processes of formation and payoffs allocation, they should not be expected to affect significantly cabinet durability. In the second study, Warwick (1994) focuses on the role of ideology in making or breaking cabinet coalitions. Contrary to much of the literature, he argues that ideological diversity, rather than properties such as size or fractionalisation, is the most important determinant of cabinet duration. In other words, bargaining complexity, as reflected in the availability of attractive coalition alternatives, is not an important factor in explaining cabinet durability.

In light of Warwick's (1994) stress on intraparty and environmental constraints on bargaining, I suggest a future research agenda for students of politics who deal with cabinet durability – the 'party attributes' approach. Put simply, cabinet durability may be dependent, among others, on the distribution of power within a party. The fact that a decentralised party is more likely than a centralised one to resolve internal conflicts successfully implies that such a party can enter into conflict-inducing coalition negotiations with other decentralised parties without risking its hold on its members. A relatively stable cabinet may be a very likely outcome of such negotiations. A centralised organisation, however, lacks the mechanisms necessary to adjust to dissent among its members and is therefore at a disadvantage when it enters conflict-inducing coalition negotiations with other parties. When interparty negotiations induce internal conflicts, a rigid organisation may lead to party disintegration – the likely outcome of which is government collapse. Thus, under conditions of conflict-inducing coalition negotiations during the stages of coalition formation and maintenance, a coalition of decentralised parties may be more likely to produce a durable and stable cabinet compared with a coalition which includes, among others, a centralised party.

This argument implies that in order to avoid internal conflicts centralised parties must look for a bargaining arena which does not induce conflicts. Such an arena could be constructed once an informal, *ad hoc* alliance is selected. A few illustrations suffice. The Danish SD formed informal minority governments with the CPP, KrF, CD and the RV during 1975–78, as it was unable to build a majority with the parties on its left. A classic example of these legislative alliances was the agreement between SD and its partners over the passage of the 1976 budget, which introduced heavier penalties for breaches of current collective wage agreements and a complete wage and price freeze. Although Anker Jørgensen subsequently went back on the first part of this agreement, following strong opposition from the central federation of labour (LO), the proposals for wage and price freezes were passed in December 1975 with the support of the four parties mentioned above.

Given the *ad hoc* nature of informal minority governments, the SD leadership could select the least 'expensive' co-operation partner available. Two examples concerning the inclusion of the Radical Liberals in some of the 1977 alliances and its exclusion from others spring to mind. On the one hand, co-operation between SD, V, RV and CPP, in April, resulted in the adoption of an emergency Bill incorporating the government's 6 per cent norm for annual pay increases for a two-year period. Similarly, on 6 September 1977, the government, supported by these parties, secured parliamentary approval for a package of increases in indirect taxes on petrol, tobacco and spirits. On the other hand, the RV was excluded from an agreement among the SD, V, KrF, CPP, and the CD over a four-year extension of the defence budget in March 1977. As these were many feasible partners, SD elites could oppose the demands of the RV and the extreme left-wing parties without risking legislative defeat over this issue. As long as SD elites formed informal alliances, the party maintained a relatively high level of bargaining power. The ability to choose partners meant that the bargaining arena might have been characterised by a relatively high level of complexity, yet it did not induce conflicts within the alliance partners.

The legislative behaviour of the Norwegian Labour Party (DNA) during Odvar Nordli's and Gro Harlem Brundtland's terms of office in 1976–81 and 1986–89, respectively, provides a further set of illustrative examples. During both periods the DNA formed informal minority governments. This strategy reduced potential negative 'influences' stemming from the party's coalition bargaining. The internal opposition, especially during Nordli's period, could therefore not rally itself over the issue of coalition strategy since the party committed itself to the least binding interparty co-operation. This direction is confirmed by a Labour Party MP, Bjørn Tore Godal:

> There has been strong tendency in the Labour Party to avoid any organised co-operation with anybody in a formal agreement. Not since the 1930s has our party gone into a formal agreement with any other party. It's really the basic belief that we are strong enough in our own right.[1]

This parliamentary strategy was duly implemented during 1976–81 and 1986–89. For the former period, potential alliance partners were mainly the Centre Party, which lost nine seats (around 43 per cent of its share) in the 1977 election, the Socialist Left Party (SV), which lost fourteen seats (around 88 per cent of its share), and the Liberal Party (V), which maintained its two seats in the *Storting*. For the latter period, potential alliance partners were mainly the SP, which increased its share of the seats from eleven to twelve in the 1981 and

1985 elections, the KrF, which improved its share of the seats from fifteen to sixteen, and the SV, which improved its share of the seats from fifteen to sixteen, during the same elections.

External support from the SP was clearly expected during the redistribution of wealth in favour of the rural population which began in 1976. During 1986–89, however, support from the SP, which was usually accompanied by support from the KrF, was perhaps less to be expected, but none the less evident on several occasions. In June 1986, for example, the government's austerity measures were approved by the *Storting* after an agreement with the SP and KrF. Similarly, the 1987 budget was approved in revised form in December 1986 with the support of SP and KrF. In December 1987 the 1988 budget was again approved with the support of SP and KrF. Additionally, in April 1988 the *Storting* passed legislation, effectively freezing wages and dividends, which had been proposed by the government and was supported by SP. Finally, in June 1988, the parliament approved a new law which served to regulate the Oslo stock exchange, which had been proposed by the government and was supported by the SP.

What is most interesting here is the relative bargaining power of the Labour Party during the periods specified above. During 1976–81 the Prime Minister, Odvar Nordli, could summarise the DNA's bargaining power as follows:

> You cannot co-operate with different parties without giving something, but I could give those gifts from the programme of the Labour Party. If you find it as the right time, it's all right. So, I must say, in the five years I was Prime Minister of a minority government, I had no great problems in parliament.[2]

The dominant policy influence of the DNA was evident in the wave of economic democratisation reforms passed in the 1970s. These reforms included improvement of working conditions, enhancing industrial democracy and the decentralisation of banking, all of which exemplify the relatively high level of bargaining power possessed by the DNA during this period (Esping-Andersen 1985: 224).

Minor concessions to the coalition partners – the SP and KrF – were also evident during 1986–89. SP in particular was, from the perspective of Labour Party elites, considered to be a most co-operative party. As Einar Førde, leader of the DNA parliamentary group, put it:

> By far the easiest party to negotiate with is the Centre Party for a very pure and simple reason; that is, because it is an extreme case

[of] a pragmatic party oriented towards their own interests. They will always make a deal on the judgement of what they get. There was very little ideology in it and it was very clearly a case of take-and-give relations.[3]

The Labour Party, in short, could rely on the external support of the Centre Party which was forthcoming after minor modifications of DNA proposals. As long as DNA elites formed informal alliances, the party maintained a relatively high level of bargaining power. As in the case of the Danish SD, the ability to choose partners meant that the bargaining arena might have been characterised by a relatively high level of complexity, yet it did not induce conflicts within the alliance partners.

The argument illustrated here, but yet to be proven by a cross-country quantitative analysis, is that the most attractive strategy for a decentralised party may be a formation of formal alliances whereas the most attractive strategy for a centralised party may be a formation of informal alliances. 'Attractive' refers to avoiding internal conflicts, possessing a relatively high level of bargaining power and maintaining a relatively stable alliance. This conclusion, if proven, contradicts a well-known theory of minority government which suggests that formal external support agreements are the least attractive legislative strategy for minority governments that want to maximise their policy influence (Strøm 1990b: 108). This theory is based on the assumption that a party is a unitary actor. Viewing a party as a complex organisation, however, reveals a different picture. The preceding chapters demonstrated that Strøm's theory cannot be applied to the cases investigated which involve decentralised parties. When entering into a formal agreement, such parties were able to maintain a durable alliance, and at the same time, possess a relatively high level of bargaining power.

The discussion so far raises two basic questions:

1 Why do some centralised parties form formal alliances?
2 Why do some decentralised parties form informal alliances?

For the former, centralised anti-system or protest parties might seek legitimacy through a formal alliance with a governmental party (for instance, the PCI during 1976–79). Additionally, a centralised party which occupies a governmental position might be willing to commit itself to formal co-operation in order to 'share' the 'burden' of economic crisis (for instance, the SD during 1978–79). Regarding decentralised parties, an informal alliance might be the plausible strategy to be implemented by a new party which would like to avoid being identified (in ideological terms) with a governmental party. A classic example is the informal alliance between the new Democratic Renewal Party and the Social Democratic Party in Portugal during 1985–87. Additionally, a 'bad' past experience of co-operation might lead to the formation of an informal alliance. This reason seems most relevant in the case of the external support provided by the Socialist Party to the Social Democrats in Portugal during 1985–87, as a result of the 'turbulent' co-operation between both parties during 1983–85. Another case is when a parliamentary situation enables a decentralised party to take for granted the external support of other decentralised parties. A classic example is the relationship between the CPP–V–RV government and the external support parties, CD and the KrF, in Denmark during 1989–90.[4]

Finally, the above discussion of the institutional determinants of coalition stability leaves us with a surprisingly favourable impression of specific types of alliances. To be sure, minority situations tend to cause internal conflicts due to the complex process of constructing legislative majorities and the probable co-operation with untraditional partners. Yet, decentralised parties which form formal alliances and centralised parties which form informal alliances enjoy substantial advantages in terms of bargaining power and are likely to maintain a relatively stable alliance. Clearly, other alliances are in most respects inferior to the above-mentioned alliances.

CLOSING THE LACUNA OF COALITION BARGAINING

During the early 1990s, a surge in the study of intraparty politics was evident. Such a surge just leaves us with a new beginning – it has to be followed up and made to bear fruit. The aim of this thesis was to raise new promises and to back them with an appropriate theoretical framework. Furthermore, the use of a cross-national perspective was fundamental to the thesis' strategy. Beyond the genuine interest in the relationships between intraparty politics and coalitional behaviour, the choice of the Danish, Norwegian, Italian, British and the French cases was motivated by the desire to demonstrate the utility of middle-level comparison.

The institutional determinants of coalition bargaining is therefore a generalisation of resolutely modest ambition; it is not presumed to apply to parties beyond its geographic and temporary limits. Yet a determination to delimit clearly the study's conclusion does not eliminate the possibility that its approach would be equally illuminating when applied to another cross-national assortment of cases. The conclusions, which aim at contributing to the field of coalitional behaviour, were formulated in general terms. In fact, the effort to close the lacuna of coalitional behaviour might well be helped by the core argument developed here which was examined by a core method (i.e. cross-national comparison). The thesis, therefore, tries to avoid the sterile abstraction inherent in universal comparison in search of law-like generalisations, without simultaneously accepting the chaos of a comparative school consisting primarily of one-nation expertise.

In all of these studies far greater stress could be placed on parties as complex organisations. Ultimately, it is absurd to explain the behaviour of any party by abstracting it from the changing social reality in which it operates. However, it is equally important for the student of parties to appropriate a measure of autonomy from the society around it. A substantial view underlying this study was that although parties are constrained constitutionally and socially by popular sentiment and cleavage structure, they are regularly able to exercise a significant degree of political independence. The thesis also accepts the notion that party behaviour grows out of the independence of its elites as bargaining actors.

A focus on political parties as organisations in the study of coalitional behaviour, which de-emphasises the 'rational actor' assumptions still so prevalent in the field, would discard their continued characterisation as office-seeking players. It would judge the internal dynamics of political parties as themselves influential to the outcome of political processes. While it would not of necessity have to proceed from the standpoint of the distribution of power within the party organisation, a detailed knowledge of any party elites' perception of their political mandate over time and their emphasis on certain political goods over others could contribute to a more subtle understanding of these dynamics. Plausible explanations concerning why parties do not appear to respond to certain coalition pressures, despite the penalties that apparent passiveness entails, and yet exhibit remarkable sensitivity to other demands, regardless of their limited policy benefits, might well result from the effort.

Lastly, in carrying through this project, the principal intention has not been to present only another study of coalitions in Western Europe but rather to attempt something more ambitious by taking a fresh look at coalition politics from an intraparty perspective. Inevitably, in view of the complexities of the subject, such an approach has to inductive in its methodological design. The reliance on the method of elite interviewing has enabled us to relate internal conflict, which were manifested formally, as well as strifes which occurred behind 'closed doors', to coalitional behaviour. Yet, the logic of inquiry was deductive in nature. After the model was constructed, the field research began. If one takes into consideration this research strategy, as well as the scope of the analysis, one must first of all adjust to the loneliness of the undertaking.

Appendix 1.1

List of elite interviews

Italy (interviews conducted in October 1989)

1 Alessandro Natta, PCI, President of the parliamentary group.
2 Giorgio Napolitano, PCI, Member of Parliament.
3 Gianni Cervetty, PCI, Member of Parliament.
4 Giovanni Berlinguer, PCI, Member of Parliament.
5 Flaminio Piccoli, DC, President of the parliamentary group.
6 Gerardo Bianco, DC, Member of Parliament.
7 Luigi Gui, DC, Minister of Interior 1974–1976.
8 Mario Segni, DC, Member of Parliament.
9 Raffaele Valensis, MSI, Member of Parliament.
10 Francesco Giulio Baghino, MSI, Member of Parliament.
11 Giovanni Malagodi, PLI, Member of Parliament.
12 Luigi Preti, PSDI, President of the parliamentary group.
13 Alberto Ciampaglia, PSDI, Member of Parliament.
14 Matteo Matteotti, PSDI, Member of Parliament.
15 Silvano Labriola, PSI, Member of Parliament.
16 Giorgio La Malfa, PRI, Member of Parliament.

Norway (interviews conducted in October 1990)

1 Surlien Rakel, SP, Minister of Environment 1983–1986.
2 Ragnhild Queseth Haarstad, SP, Member of *Storting*.
3 Alice Ruud, V, Party Secretary 1980–1986.
4 Tor Mikkel Wara, FrP, Member of *Storting*.
5 Lars Roar Langslet, CP, Minister of Cultural Affairs 1981–1986.
6 Oddrun Pettersen, DNA, Member of *Storting*.
7 Bjørn Tore Godal, DNA, Member of *Storting*.
8 Sissel Ronbeck, DNA, Minister of Environment 1986–1989.
9 Jens Holvard Bratz, CP, Minister of Industry 1981–1985.

10 Carl I. Hagen, FrP, party leader.
11 Jen Simonsen, FrP, Member of *Storting*.
12 Anne Enger Lahnstein, SP, Leader of the Parliamentary Group, 1986–1990.
13 Kåre Willoch, CP, Prime Minister 1981–1986.
14 Svein Gronnern, CP, party secretary.
15 Hans J. Rosjorde, FrP, Member of *Storting*.
16 Tora A. Houg, SV, Member of *Storting*.
17 Willian Engseth, DNA, Minister of Municipal and Labour Affairs 1988–1989.
18 Jon Lilletun, KrF, Member of *Storting*.
19 Einar Førde, DNA, parliamentary leader 1981–1989.
20 Jo Benkow, CP, President of the *Storting*.
21 Per Ditlev-Simonsen, CP, Minister of Defence 1989–1990.
22 Anders Aune, FFF, Member of *Storting*.
23 Ole Gabriel Ueland, SP, Member of *Storting*.
24 Theo Koritzinski, SV, Member of *Storting*.
25 Arne Synnes, KrF, head of parliamentary Secretariat.
26 Svein Sundsbo, SP, Minister of Agriculture 1985–1986.
27 Thor E. Gulbrandsen, DNA, Member of *Storting*.
28 Hanna Kvanmo, SV, party leader 1976–1989.
29 Fridtjof F. Gundersen, FrP Member of *Storting*.
30 Per-Kristian Foss, CP, Member of Parliament.
31 Gunnar Berge, DNA, Finance Minister 1986–1989.
32 Oddmund H. Hammerstad, CP, Member of *Storting*.
33 Lise Enger Gjorv, DNA, Member of *Storting*.
34 Odvar Nordli, DNA, Prime Minister 1976–1981.
35 Inge Staldvik, DNA, Member of *Storting*.
36 Egil Sundar, editor of *Aftenposten* 1975–1989.
37 Kirsti Kolle Grondahl, DNA, Minister of Religious Affairs and Education 1986–1989.
38 Royseland Borghild, KrF Member of *Storting*.
39 John Dale, SP Party Secretary.

UK (interviews conducted in February 1990)

1 William Rodgers, Lab., Transport Secretary 1976–1979.
2 Harold Laver, Lab., Member of the House of Lords.
3 John Smith, Lab., Member of the House of Commons.
4 Lord Mackie, Lib., Member of the House of Lords.
5 John Frazer, Lab., Member of the House of Commons.
6 Russell Johnston, Lib., Member of the House of Commons.

7 Teddy Taylor, Con., Member of the House of Commons.
8 James Cornford, policy adviser for the Liberal Party.
9 Albert Booth, Lab., Employment Secretary 1976–1979.
10 John Morris, Cons., Member of the House of Commons.
11 John Pardoe, Lib., Economic Spokesman.
12 Andrew Gifford, Lib., Party leader's assistant.
13 Merlyn Rees, Lab., Member of the House of Commons.
14 Lord Hooson, Lib., Member of the House of Lords.
15 George Robertson, Lab., Member of the House of Commons.
16 Tom McNally, Lab, Callaghan's private secretary.
17 Denis Howell, Lab., Member of the House of Commons.
18 Alan Beith, Lib., Liberals' Chief Whip.
19 Jack Jones, TUC leader 1976–1979.
20 Timothy Raison, Con., Member of the House of Commons.
21 Richard Holme, an adviser of the Liberal party leader.
22 James Gardiner, Con., Member of the House of Commons.
23 James Molyneaux, Ulster Unionist, Party leader.
24 Baroness Seear, Lib., Member of the House of Lords.
25 David Owen, Lab., Secretary of State for Foreign and Commonwealth Affairs.
26 James Prior, Con., Member of the House of Lords.
27 James Lamond, Lab., Member of the House of Commons.
28 Lord Donoghou, Head of Labour's think-tank.
29 Stanley Orme, Lab., Social Security Secretary 1976–1979.
30 Peter Shore, Lab., Environment Secretary 1976–1979.

Denmark (interviews conducted in May 1989)

1 Ahm Agner, Political Editor, *Politiken.*
2 Benke Kim, FrP, Member of *Folketing.*
3 Bennedsen Dorte, SD former Minister of Education, 1978–1982.
4 Buksti A. Jacob, SD, head of the economic research department.
5 Christensen Arne, V, former Minister of Commerce, 1977–1978.
6 Dam Hans, editor, *Berlingske Tidende.*
7 Dybkjær Lone, RV, Minister of Environment, 1988–1990.
8 Elizabeth Arnold, RV, Member of *Folketing.*
9 Elmquist Bjørn, V, Member of *Folketing.*
10 Engaard Knud, V, former Minister of Interior, 1978–1979, 1986–1988, former Minister of Energy, 1982–1986, former Minister of Economic Affairs, 1987–1988, Minister of Defence, 1988–1993.
11 Erling Olsen, SD, former Minister of Housing, 1977–1982.
12 Estrup Jørgan, RV, Member of *Folketing.*

13 Frandsen Aage, SF, Member of *Folketing*.
14 Gade Steen, SF, Member of *Folketing*.
15 Glistrup Mogens, FrP, former leader, 1972–1988.
16 Glonborg Knud, KrF, Member of *Folketing*.
17 Gredal Eva, SD, former Minister of Social Affairs, 1975–1977.
18 Grove Henning, CPP, former Minister of Fisheries, 1982–1986.
19 Hansen Bent, SD, former chief editor of the SD daily newspaper *Aktuelt*, former Minister of Social Affairs, 1982.
20 Hansen Jens Kristian, SD, former Minister of Public Works, 1982
21 Helveg-Petersen Niels, RV, leader, Minister of Economic Affairs, 1988–1990.
22 Herman Leif, SF, Member of *Folketing*.
23 Hjortnæs Karl, SD, former Minister of Justice, 1973, former Minister of Taxation, 1980–1981, former Minister of Fisheries, 1981–1982.
24 Jakobsen Erhard, CD, former Minister of Economic Coordination, 1987–1988.
25 Jakobsen Svend, SD, former Minister of Inland Revenue, 1975–1977, former Minister of Fisheries, 1977–1979, former Minister of Finance, 1979–1982.
26 Jelved Marianne, RV, leader of the parliamentary group.
27 Kent Kirk, CPP, Member of *Folketing*.
28 Kofod-Svendsen Flemming, KrF, leader, former Housing Minister, 1987–1988.
29 Kofoed-Anker Niels, V, former Minister of Agriculture, 1977–1978, 1982–1986.
30 Lykketoft Mogens, SD, former Minister of Taxation, 1981–1982, former Minister of Inland Revenue, 1982.
31 Nyrup Rasmussen Poul, SD, Member of Folketing.
32 Pedersen Thor, V, former Minister of Housing, 1986–1987, Minister of Interior, 1988–1993.
33 Petersen Gert, SF, leader.
34 Pundic Herbert, editor, *Politiken*.
35 Rahbeak Moller Kjeld, SF, Member of *Folketing*.
36 Stilling Pedersen Inger, KrF, Member of *Folketing*.
37 Strange Ebba, SF, Member of *Folketing*.
38 Voight Pelle, SF, Member of *Folketing*.

France (interviews conducted in April 1990)

1 Jean Auroux, PS, Member of the National Assembly.
2 Raymond Barre, UDC, Member of the National Assembly.

3 Dominique Boudis, UDC, Member of the National Assembly.
4 Jean-Michel Belorgey, PS, President of the Cultural and Social Affairs Committee.
5 Huguette Bouchardeau, PS, Member of the National Assembly.
6 Jean-Christophe Cambadelis, PS, Member of the National Assembly.
7 Michel Cointat, RPR, Member of the National Assembly.
8 Jean-Marie Daillet, UDC, Member of the National Assembly.
9 Jean-Louis Debre, RPR, Member of the National Assembly.
10 Francois Fillon, RPR, Member of the National Assembly.
11 Yves Freville, UDC, Member of the National Assembly.
12 Claude Labbe, RPR, Member of the National Assembly.
13 Alain Lamassoure, UDF, Member of the National Assembly.
14 Didier Mathus, PS, Member of the National Assembly.
15 Michel Pezet, PS, Member of the National Assembly.
16 Yann Piat, UDF, Member of the National Assembly.
17 Dominique Strauss-Kahn, PS, President of the Finance and Economic Committee.
18 Jean-Pierre Worms, PS, Member of the National Assembly.
19 Gabriel Kaspereit, RPR, Member of the National Assembly.
20 Gerard Longuet, UDF, Member of the National Assembly.

Appendix 2.1

Party composition of the *Folketing*, 1971–88

	1971	1973	1975	1977	1979	1981	1984	1987	1988
Social Democrats (%)	37.3	25.6	29.9	30.0	38.3	32.9	31.6	29.3	29.8
	(70)	(46)	(53)	(65)	(68)	(59)	(56)	(54)	(54)
Conservatives (%)	16.7	9.2	5.5	8.5	12.5	14.5	23.4	20.8	19.3
	(31)	(16)	(10)	(15)	(22)	(26)	(42)	(38)	(34)
Liberals (%)	15.6	12.3	23.3	12.0	12.5	11.3	12.1	10.5	11.8
	(30)	(22)	(42)	(21)	(22)	(20)	(22)	(19)	(21)
Radical Liberals (%)	14.4	11.2	7.1	3.6	5.4	5.1	5.5	6.2	5.6
	(27)	(20)	(13)	(16)	(10)	(9)	(10)	(11)	(10)
Communists (%)	1.4	3.6	4.2	3.7	1.9	1.1	0.2	0.9	0.8
	(0)	(6)	(7)	(7)	(0)	(0)	(0)	(0)	(0)
Justice Party (%)	1.7	2.9	1.8	3.3	2.6	1.4	1.5	0.5	–
	(0)	(5)	(0)	(6)	(5)	(0)	(0)	(0)	–
Socialist People's Party (%)	9.1	6.0	5.0	3.9	5.9	11.3	11.5	14.6	13
	(17)	(11)	(9)	(7)	(11)	(21)	(21)	(27)	(23)
Left Socialists (%)	1.6	1.5	2.1	2.7	3.7	2.7	2.7	1.4	0.6
	(0)	(0)	(4)	(5)	(6)	(5)	(5)	(0)	(0)
Christian People's Party (%)	2.0	4.0	5.3	3.4	2.6	2.3	2.7	2.4	2.0
	(0)	(7)	(9)	(6)	(5)	(4)	(5)	(4)	(4)
Progress Party (%)	–	15.9	13.6	14.6	11.0	8.9	3.6	4.8	9.0
		(28)	(24)	(26)	(20)	(16)	(6)	(9)	(16)
Centre Democrats (%)	–	7.8	2.2	6.4	3.2	8.3	4.6	4.8	4.7
		(14)	(4)	(11)	(6)	(15)	(8)	(9)	(9)
Common Cause (%)	–	–	–	–	–	–	–	2.2	1.9
								(4)	(0)
Others (%)	0.2	–	–	0.9	0.4	0.2	0.1	1.5	1.3
	(0)			(0)	(0)	(0)	(0)	(0)	(0)

Source: Keesing's Contemporary Archives, 1971–88.

Appendix 2.2

Party composition of Danish governments, 1971–91

Period	Parties (seats)**	Per cent of seats in parliament held by parties in government*
Oct. 1971–Oct. 1972	Social Democrats (70)	39
Oct. 1972–Dec. 1973	Social Democrats (70)	39
Dec. 1973–Feb. 1975	Liberals (22)	12
Feb. 1975–Aug. 1977	Social Democrats (53)	30
Feb. 1977–Aug. 1978	Social Democrats (65)	36
Aug. 1978–Oct. 1979	Social Democrats (65) Liberals (21)	48
Oct. 1979–Dec. 1981	Social Democrats (68)	38
Dec. 1981–Sep. 1982	Social Democrats (59)	33
Sep. 1982–Jan. 1984	Conservatives (26) Liberals (20) Centre Democrats (15) Christian People's Party (4)	36
Jan. 1984–Sep. 1987	Conservatives (42) Liberals (22) Centre Democrats (8) Christian People's Party (5)	43
Sep. 1987–June 1988	Conservatives (38) Liberals (19) Centre Democrats (9) Christian People's Party (4)	39
June 1988–Dec. 1990	Conservatives (35) Liberals (22) Radical Liberals (10)	37
Dec. 1990–	Conservatives (30) Liberals (29)	33

* Percentages are calculated on the basis of all 179 members of the *Folketing*, i.e. including the two MPs from Greenland and the two from the Faroe Islands.
** The Prime Minister's party is given first in the case of coalition governments.
Source: Keesing's Contemporary Archives, 1971–91.

Appendix 2.3

Party composition in the *Storting*, 1969–85

	1969	1973	1977	1981	1981*	1985
Norwegian Labour Party (%)	46.5	35.3	42.3	37.1	37.2	40.0
	(74)	(62)	(76)	(65)	(66)	(71)
Conservative Party (%)	19.6	17.4	24.8	31.8	31.7	30.4
	(29)	(29)	(41)	(54)	(53)	(50)
Christian People's Party (%)	9.4	12.2	12.4	9.4	9.4	8.3
	(14)	(20)	(22)	(15)	(15)	(16)
Centre Party (%)	10.5	11	8.6	6.6	6.6	6.6
	(20)	(21)	(12)	(11)	(11)	(12)
Liberal Party (%)	9.4	3.5	3.2	3.9	3.9	3.1
	(13)	(2)	(2)	(2)	(2)	(0)
Liberal People's Party (%)	–	3.4	1.4	0.6	0.5	0.5
		(1)	(0)	(0)	(0)	(0)
Norwegian Communist Party (%)	1	–	0.4	0.3	0.3	0.2
	(0)		(0)	(0)	(0)	(0)
Socialist People's Party (%)	3.5	–	–	–	–	–
	(0)					
Socialist Electoral Alliance (%)	–	11.2	–	–	–	–
		(16)				
Socialist Left Party (%)	–	–	4.2	5	4.9	5.5
			(2)	(4)	(4)	(6)
Red Electoral Alliance (%)	–	0.4	0.6	0.7	0.7	0.6
		(0)	(0)	(0)	(0)	(0)
Progress Party (%)	–	5	1.9	4.5	4.5	3.7
		(4)	(0)	(4)	(4)	(2)
Others (%)	0.0	0.5	0.2	0.1	0.1	0.4
	(0)	(0)	(0)	(0)	(0)	(0)

* Second results in 1981 account for a re-run election in the constituencies of Troms and Buskerud.
Source: Keesing's Contemporary Archives, 1969–85.

Appendix 2.4

Party composition of Norwegian governments, 1969–90

Period	Parties (seats)	Per cent of seats in parliament held by parties in government
Oct. 1965–Sep. 1969	Centre Party Conservatives Liberals Christian People's Party	53
Sep. 1969–Mar. 1971	Centre Party Conservatives Liberals Christian People's Party	50
Mar. 1971–Oct.1972	Labour Party	49
Oct. 1972–Oct. 1973	Christian People's Party Centre Party Liberals	26
Oct. 1973–Jan. 1976	Labour Party	40
Jan. 1976–Sep. 1977	Labour Party	40
Sep. 1977–Jan. 1981	Labour Party	49
Feb. 1981–Oct. 1981	Labour Party	49
Oct. 1981–June 1983	Conservatives	34
June 1983–Sep. 1985	Conservatives Christian People's Party Centre Party	51
Sep. 1985–May 1986	Conservatives Christian People's Party Centre Party	49
May 1986–Sep. 1989	Labour Party	45
Sep. 1989–Oct. 1990	Conservatives Christian People's Party Centre Party	37

Source: Keesing's Contemporary Archives, 1969–90.

Party composition of the Chamber of Deputies, 1968–83

	1968	1972	1976	1979	1983
Christian Democrats (%)	39.1	38.8	38.7	38.3	32.9
	(266)	(267)	(262)	(262)	(225)
Communists (%)	26.9	27.2	34.4	30.4	29.9
	(177)	(179)	(228)	(201)	(198)
Socialists (%)	14.5	9.6	9.6	9.8	11.4
		(61)	(57)	(62)	(73)
Social Democrats (%)	5.1	3.4	3.8	4.1	
	(91)	(29)	(15)	(20)	(23)
Republicans (%)	2.0	2.9	3.1	3.0	5.1
	(9)	(14)	(14)	(16)	(29)
Liberals (%)	5.8	3.9	1.3	1.9	2.9
	(31)	(21)	(5)	(9)	(16)
Radicals (%)	–	–	1.1	3.5	2.2
			(4)	(18)	(11)
Italian Social Movement (%)	4.4	8.7	6.1	5.3	6.8
	(24)	(56)	(35)	(30)	(42)
Monarchists (%)	1.3	–	–	–	–
	(6)				
Proletarian Democracy	–	–	1.6	0.8	1.5
			(6)	(0)	(7)
Others (%)	6.0	4.0	0.8	4.1	2.7
	(26)	(4)	(4)	(12)	(6)

Source: *Keesing's Contemporary Archives*, 1968–83.

Appendix 2.6

Party composition of Italian governments, 1968–80

Period	Parties (seats)	Per cent of seats in parliament held by parties in government
Feb. 1966–June 1968	DC, PSI, PSDI, PSI	61
June 1966–Nov. 1968	DC	42
Dec. 1968–July 1969	DC, PSU, PRI	58
Aug. 1969–Feb. 1970	DC	42
Mar. 1970–July 1970	DC, PSI, PSDI, PRI	58
Aug. 1970–Mar. 1971	DC, PSI, PSDI, PRI	58
Mar. 1971–Jan. 1972	DC, PSI, PSDI	56
Feb. 1972–Feb. 1972	DC	42
June 1972–June 1973	DC, PSDI, PLI	50
July 1973–Mar. 1974	DC, PSI, PSDI, PRI	58
Mar. 1974–Oct. 1974	DC, PSI, PSDI	56
Nov. 1974–Jan. 1976	DC, PRI	44
Feb. 1976–Apr. 1976	DC	42
July 1976–Jan. 1978	DC	41
Mar. 1978–Jan. 1979	DC	41
Mar. 1979–Mar. 1979	DC, PSDI, PRI	41
Aug. 1979–Mar. 1980	DC, PSDI, PLI	46

Source: Keesing's Contemporary Archives, 1968–80.

Appendix 2.7

Party composition of the House of Commons, 1970–79

	1970	Feb. 1974	Oct. 1974	1979
Conservatives (%)	46.4	37.9	35.9	43.9
	(330)	(297)	(277)	(339)
Labour (%)	43.1	37.2	39.2	36.9
	(288)	(301)	(319)	(269)
Liberal Party (%)	7.5	19.3	18.3	13.8
	(6)	(14)	(13)	(11)
Scottish Nationalists (%)	1.1	2.0	2.9	1.6
	(1)	(7)	(11)	(2)
Plaid Cymru (%)		0.6	0.6	0.4
		(2)	(3)	(2)
Others (%)	1.4	3.0	3.1	3.3
	(6)	(14)	(12)	(12)

Source: Keesing's Contemporary Archives, 1970–79.

Appendix 2.8

Party composition of the National Assembly, 1978–88

	1978	1981	1986	1988
PS (1st ballot %)	–	–	31.6 (206)	–
PS-MRG (1st ballot %)	24.98 (112)	37.5 (285)	–	35.87 (276)
MRG (1st ballot %)	–	–	0.4 (20)	–
PCF (1st ballot %)	20.61 (86)	16.2 (44)	9.8 (35)	11.32 (27)
Ecologists (1st ballot %)	2.18 (0)	1.1 (0)	–	0.35 (0)
RPR (1st ballot %)	22.52 (145)	20.8 (88)	11.21 (76)	19.8 (128)
UDF (1st ballot %)	21.37 (120)	19.2 (62)	8.31 (53)	18.49 (130)
RPR-UDF (Joint List)	–	–	21.46 (147)	–
FN (1st ballot %)	–	–	9.8 (35)	9.65 (1)
Others (1st ballot %)	5.01 (11)	5.2 (7)	6.4 (21)	4.86 (13)

Source: Keesing's Contemporary Archives, 1978–88.

Appendix 3.1

The membership of the PCI: total membership, party adherence rate, new recruits, non-renewals, and PCI votes as percentage of total vote cast, 1963–79

Year	Membership total (000s)	Adherence rate*	New recruits (000s)	Non-renewals (000s)	PCI Share of vote ** (per cent)
1963	1,613	4.72	130	147	25.3
1964	1,636	4.78	139	116	
1965	1,611	4.66	122	148	
1966	1,571	4.51	108	148	
1967	1,530	4.36	102	143	
1968	1,496	4.20	98	133	27.0
1969	1,496	4.16	101	101	
1970	1,498	4.12	106	103	
1971	1,510	4.11	113	100	
1972	1,576	4.24	151	88	27.2
1973	1,611	4.32	137	99	
1974	1,644	4.38	133	100	
1975	1,715	4.54	156	84	
1976	1,798	4.72	172	90	34.4
1977	1,796	6.70	127	128	
1978	1,772	4.46	100	124	
1979	1,742	4.38	92	122	30.4

* The adherence rate measures the percentage of party members as a ratio of the total electorate, 21 years and older.
** National elections were held in 1946, 1953, 1963, 1972, 1976 and 1979.
Source: Barbagli and Corbetta (1982b: 80).

Appendix 4.1

Christian Democratic Party national membership,
1945–80

Year	Membership
1963	1,621,620
1964	1,676,222*
1965	1,613,314*
1966	1,641,615
1967	1,621,866
1968	1,696,402
1969	1,743,651*
1970	1,738,996
1971	1,814,580
1972	1,827,925
1973	1,879,429*
1974	1,843,515
1975	1,732,501
1976	1,366,187
1977	1,301,707
1978	1,355,423
1979	1,383,650
1980	1,385,141

* Figures for these four years are estimated because of missing membership data from one or more provinces.
Source: © Leonardi, R. and Wertman, D., *Italian Christian Democracy: The Politics of Dominance*. Reprinted with permission of St. Martin's Press, Incorporated.

Appendix 4.2

The Lib–Lab Pact: A Joint Statement by the Prime Minister and the Leader of the Liberal Party

We agreed today the basis on which the Liberal Party would work with the government in the pursuit of economic recovery.

We will set up a joint consultative Committee under the Chairmanship of the Leader of the House, which will meet regularly. The Committee will examine Government policy and other issues prior to their coming before the House, and Liberal policy proposals.

The existence of this Committee will not commit the Government to accepting the views of the Liberal Party, or the Liberal Party to supporting the Government on any issue.

We agree to initiate regular meetings between the Chancellor and the Liberal Party economic spokesman, such meetings to begin at once. In addition, the Prime Minister and the Leader of the Liberal Party will meet as necessary.

We agree that legislation for Direct Elections to the European Assembly in 1978 will be presented to Parliament in this Session. The Liberal Party re-affirm their strong conviction that a proportional system should be used as the method of election. The Government is publishing next week a White Paper on Direct Elections to the European Assembly which sets out the choices among different electoral systems, but which makes no recommendation. There will now be consultation between us on the method to be adopted and the Government's final recommendation will take full account of the Liberal Party's commitment. The recommendation will be subject to a free vote of both Houses.

We agree that progress must be made on legislation for devolution, and to this end consultations will begin on the detailed memorandum submitted by the Liberal Party today. In any future debate on proportional representation for the devolved Assemblies there will be a free vote.

We agree that the Government will provide the extra time necessary to secure the passage of the Housing (Homeless Persons) Bill, and that the Local Authorities (Works) Bill will now be confined to provisions to protect the existing activities of Direct Labour Organizations in the light of local government reorganization.

We agree that this arrangement between us should last until the end of the present Parliamentary Session, when both Parties would consider whether the experiment has been of sufficient benefit to the country to be continued.

We also agree that this understanding should be made public.

10 Downing Street

23 March 1977

Source: Steel (1989: 129–30)

Notes

1 THE PROBLEM, THE PARADOX, THE MODEL

1 The following research concerns have emerged in the literature:

   (i) *Representation* (Rae 1971; Taagepera and Shugart 1989; Lijphart 1990; Doron and Maor 1989, 1991);

   (ii) *Party Policies* (Budge *et al.* 1987; Budge and Keman 1990; Laver and Schofield 1990; Laver and Budge 1992; Austen-Smith and Banks 1988; Baron 1993);

   (iii) *The Nature of Parliamentary Government* (Austen-Smith and Banks 1990; Laver and Shepsle 1990a, b); and

   (iv) *The Institutions of Government Decision Making* (Laver and Shepsle 1996).

2 Although the ordering of these two variables can be the other way around all hypotheses investigated here take as their starting point the emergence of internal conflicts.

3 Cohesion at the price of loss of control defeats their purpose (Barber 1960). In a very real sense the leaders may be prisoners of their own party, so it is a mistake to count every high cohesion vote as an indicator of elites' effectiveness.

4 Party elites are thus assumed capable of strategic behaviour. For an elaboration of their objectives and behavioural options, see: Barber (1960).

5 This is not to say that dissatisfied members within such organisations simply want voice for its own sake. It is rather to stress that those who seriously seek to change party strategy can opt for the exit option. They can also attempt to mobilise public opinion by expressing their dissatisfaction outside the party. Whether they choose to do so remains to be seen (i.e. in the empirical analysis).

2 THE INTRAPARTY AND CONSTITUTIONAL CONTEXTS

1 Policy development refers to the locus of power in determining the party's position on substantive issues of government. Our concern is limited to the determination of party policy and not to its implementation when the party is in government. Execution of political line refers to

the management of the party's affairs between Party Conferences. Candidate selection refers to the selection of parliamentary or legislative candidates. Leadership selection refers to the election of the national party leader. Funding allocation refers to decisions regarding the distribution of party funds. Party press refers to the handling of literature distribution (party newspaper and documents) and electronic broadcasts (radio, television and internet site). Discipline refers to decisions of rewards and punishments taken to motivate party actors to conform to party line.

2 The rivalries between potential PS presidential candidates is often considered the cause of the conflicts within the party. Yet, factionalism within the PS was not only subordinated by presidentialisation. During the 1980s it was further mitigated by the ideological and sociological heterogeneity of the 'tendencies' themselves, the factions lacking clear enough boundaries to pose a threat to the leadership (Cayrol and Ysmal 1982; Cayrol and Ignazi 1983).

3 For the adverse economic conditions, see: Blanchard *et al.* (1986: Appendix 1).

4 Class voting patterns were given credit for the relatively stable levels of popularity between elections and the inability of a third party to make any inroad into the two party's respective vote. See, for example, Rose and McAllister (1986: 1), Pulzer (1975) and Butler and Stokes (1969).

5 The notion of 'a decade of dealignment' to describe the process that had set in during the 1970s, Särlvik and Crewe (1983) claim, was due to the revelation of an apparent decline over time in the relationship between partisan support and social class. Therefore, none of the major occupational groups in the 1970s provided the same degree of solid and consistent support for the two major parties as was the case in the earlier post-war era. An alternative explanation which focuses on the housing and transport markets, suggests that people involved in 'collective' modes of consumption, such as council tenants and public transport users are, as a result of their own distinctive interests more likely to incline to the left than people involved in more 'individual' modes of consumption such as home-owners and car-owners (Dunleavy 1979).

6 *H.C. Deb.* vol. 915, col. 1493–1755. On the usage of guillotine during 1974–1979, see: Stout (1981).

7 The *Guardian*, 18 February, 1977.

8 *H.C Deb*. vol. 926, col. 1361–1366.

9 The *Guardian,* 5 March, 1974, p. 1.

10 These tendencies in French politics are derived from changes within French society. Perhaps most important in the cleavage structure is the rapid religious decline occuring in a political context strongly constrained by religion (Berger 1987: 112). Beyond the electoral advantages to the Left of the rapid collapse of religious structures over the past two decades, the real significance lies in an increased capacity for mobilisation and the enlarged organisational resources that accrue to the Left due to the Catholics that have shifted massively to the Left. An interesting research suggests, moreover, that ideology came first in importance, religion second, class third and region fourth (Lewis-Beck 1984: 443).

Undoubtedly, the largest beneficiary from these processes was the Socialist Party as it moved to the centre in mid-1980s.

3 MODES OF CONFLICT MANIFESTATION IN CENTRALISED PARTIES

1 Regarding governmental parties, Jones (1991: 177) has argued that, of all the factors which impinge upon the head of government's influence in West European political systems, party politics is the most important. He states that ' . . . Party is the critical resource and constraint: The key to the power of both the prime minister and the other actors and institutions'.

2 Bent Hansen, interview with the author, Copenhagen, May 1989.

3 *Keesing's Contemporary Archives*, 1977, p. 28269.

4 *Keesing's Contemporary Archives*, 1978, p. 29331.

5 *Keesing's Contemporary Archives*, 1978, p. 29331.

6 *Facts on File*, Vol. XXXVII, 1977, p. 426.

7 *Keesing's Contemporary Archives*, 1980, p. 30030.

8 Bent Hansen, interview with the author, Copenhagen, May 1989.

9 *Keesing's Contemporary Archives*, 1978, p. 29332.

10 Svend Jakobsen, interview with the author, Copenhagen, May 1989.

11 Bent Hansen, interview with the author, Copenhagen, May 1989.

12 Karl Hjortnæs, interview with the author, Copenhagen, May 1989. Although in the interview there is a reference to 'majority government', the SD-V alliance was a minority government since it did not enjoy a majority in the legislature. However, this government was considered by many politicians to be a 'majority' government since it was only one MP short of a majority and, practically, there was no alternative viable coalition.

13 Svend Jakobsen, interview with the author, Copenhagen, May 1989.

14 Karl Hjortnæs, interview with the author, Copenhagen, May 1989.

15 Svend Jakobsen, interview with the author, Copenhagen, May 1989.

16 Svend Jakobsen, interview with the author, Copenhagen, May 1989.

17 Käre Willoch, interview with the author, Oslo, October 1990. See also Willoch (1990).

18 Anne Enger Lahnstien, interview with the author, Oslo, October 1990.

19 John Dale, interview with the author, Oslo, October 1990.

20 *Keesing's Contemporary Archives*, 1989, p. 36901; Jen Simonsen, interview with the author, Oslo, October 1990; Fridtjof F. Gundersen, interview with the author, Oslo, October 1990.

21 Tor Mikkel Wara, interview with the author, Oslo, October 1990.

22 Carl Hagen, interview with the author, Oslo, October 1990.

23 Graziano (1980), for example, argues that in Italy, political convergence is likely to occur, if at all, through a struggle for hegemony and would result in a pattern of politics both more participatory and dynamic than classic consociational democracy.

24 Alessandro Natta, interview with the author, Rome, October 1989.

25 Giorgio Napolitano, interview with the author, Rome, October 1989.

26 Giorgio La Malfa, interview with the author, Rome, October 1989.

27 Silvano Labriola, interview with the author, Rome, October 1989.
28 Giorgio Napolitano, interview with the author, Rome, October 1989.
29 *Keesing's Contemporary Archives*, 1977, p. 28493.
30 Giorgio Napolitano, interview with the author, Rome, October 1989.
31 Draft theses for the Fifteenth Congress of the PCI, December 1978, Translated in: Lange and Vannicelli (1981: 174).
32 *The Times*, 20 October, 1988.
33 *The Times*, 23 November, 1988.
34 *The Economist*, 17 September, 1988, p. 62.
35 *Keesing's Contemporary Archives*, 1988, p. 36706.

4 MODES OF CONFLICT MANIFESTATION IN DECENTRALISED PARTIES

1 *Keesing's Contemporary Archives*, 1976: 27711, 1977: 28180.
2 Flaminio Piccoli, interview with the author, Rome, October 1989.
3 Raffaele Valensise, interview with the author, Rome, October 1989.
4 *Keesing's Contemporary Archives*, 1977, p. 28493.
5 *Keesing's Contemporary Archives*, 1978, p. 29006.
6 Gerardo Bianco, interview with the author, Rome, October 1989.
7 *Keesing's Contemporary Archives*, 1976, p. 27718.
8 *Keesing's Contemporary Archives*, 1976, p. 27898.
9 Stanley Orme, interview with the author, London, March 1990.
10 Tom McNally, interview with the author, London, February 1990.
11 John Pardoe, interview with the author, London, February 1990.
12 David Owen, interview with the author, London, March 1990.
13 Lord Donoughue, interview with the author, London, March 1990.
14 Richard Holme, interview with the author, London, February 1990.
15 Peter Shore, interview with the author, London, March 1990.
16 *Keesing's Contemporary Archives*, 1977, p. 28356.
17 Alan Beith, interview with the author, London, February 1990.
18 George Gardiner, interview with the author, London, February 1990.
19 Teddy Taylor, interview with the author, London, February 1990.
20 *H.C. Deb.* Vol. 939, col. 197–204, 207–14, 747–654.
21 John Pardoe, interview with the author, London, February 1990.
22 Lord Hooson, interview with the author, London, February 1990.
23 *The Economist*, 17 September, 1988, p. 62.
24 *The Economist*, 23 July, 1988, p. 24.
25 Dominique Strauss-Kahn, interview with the author, Paris, May 1990.
26 Mitterrand, F. 'Lettre à tout les français', *Libération*, 7 April, 1988.
27 Jean-Pierre Worms, interview with the author, Paris, May 1990.
28 See the remarks by Méhaignerie in *Le Monde*, 3 July, 1990: 'There is less difference between the centre-left and the centre-right than between, on the one hand, the right and the centre-right and, on the other hand, the left and the centre-left'.
29 Jean-Pierre Worms, interview with the author, Paris, May 1990.
30 Guy Carcassone, letter sent to the author dated 5 July, 1990.
31 Guy Carcassone, letter sent to the author dated 5 July, 1990.
32 Jean-Pierre Worms, interview with the author, Paris, May 1990.

33 *The Times*, 19 March, 1990, p. 7.
34 Dissatisfaction from Rocard's alliance strategy was manifested also within the party base. Leftist militants, for example, called for a repositioning of the party to the left after the disappointing returns in many districts in the May 1989 Municipal elections (Huber 1991: 26). However, the dominant mode of the conflicts within the PS was, undoubtedly, an intra-elite one.
35 *Keesing's Record of World Events*, 1988, p. 36706.
36 *Keesing's Record of World Events*, 1989, p. 37262.

5 MODES OF CONFLICT RESOLUTION IN CENTRALISED PARTIES

1 *Keesing's Contemporary Archives*, 1978, p. 29331.
2 Svend Jakobsen, interview with the author, Copenhagen, May 1989.
3 Svend Jakobsen, interview with the author, Copenhagen, May 1989.
4 *Nationen*, 6 October, 1989, p. 2.
5 *Keesing's Contemporary Archieves*, 1989, p. 36985.
6 Ole Gabriel Ueland, interview with the author, Oslo, October 1990.
7 Ole Gabriel Ueland, interview with the author, Oslo, October 1990.
8 Enrico Berlinguer's speech to the PCI conference of Intellectuals, Rome, 1 January, 1977. Translated in: Lange and Vannicelli (1981: 50).
9 *The Times*, 20 October, 1988.
10 *The Times*, 23 November, 1988.

6 MODES OF CONFLICT RESOLUTION IN DECENTRALISED PARTIES

1 *Keesing's Contemporary Archives*, 1976, p. 27927.
2 Flaminio Piccoli, interview with the author, Rome, October 1989.
3 Peter Shore, interview with the author, London, March 1990.
4 Tom MacNally, interview with the author, London, February 1990.
5 David Owen, interview with the author, London, March 1990.
6 William Rodgers, interview with the author, London, February 1990.
7 *H.C. Deb.* vol. 965, col. 583–88.
8 Guy Carcassone, letter sent to the author dated 5 July, 1990.

7 MODES OF COALITION BARGAINING

1 Svend Jakobsen, interview with the author, Copenhagen, May 1989.
2 Knud Engaard, interview with the author, Copenhagen, May 1989.
3 Borghild Royseland, interview with the author, Oslo, October 1990.
4 Per Ditlev-Simonsen, interview with the author, Oslo, October 1990.
5 John Dale, interview with the author, Oslo, October 1990.
6 Giorgio Napolitano, interview with the author, Rome, October 1989.
7 *Keesing's Contemporary Archives*, 1979, p. 29685.

8 *Keesing's Contemporary Archives*, 1979, p. 29685.
9 Alessandro Natta, interview with the author, Rome, October 1989.
10 Chiaromonte is quoted in: Di Giulio and Rocco (1979: 61).
11 Flaminio Piccoli, interview with the author, Rome, October 1989.
12 Silvano Labriola, interview with the author, Rome, October 1989.
13 Giorgio Napolitano, interview with the author, Rome, October 1989.
14 Giorgio La Malfa, interview with the author, Rome, October 1989.
15 Giorgio Napolitano, interview with the author, Rome, October 1989.
16 Raffaele Valensise, interview with the author, Rome, October 1989; Francesco Giulio Baghino, interview with the author, Rome, October 1989.
17 Raffaele Valensise, interview with the author, Rome, October 1989.
18 John Pardoe, interview with the author, London, February 1990.
19 John Pardoe, interview with the author, London, February 1990.
20 Baroness Seear, interview with the author, London, February 1990.
21 Russell Johnston, interview with the author, London, February 1990.
22 Cited in: Bogdanor (1979: 158).
23 James Cornford, interview with the author, London, February 1990.
24 James Cornford, interview with the author, London, February 1990.
25 Richard Holme, interview with the author, London, February 1990.
26 Albert Booth, interview with the author, London, February 1990.
27 Russell Johnston, interview with the author, London, February 1990.
28 A letter, dated 31 May, 1990, from Lord Callaghan to the author.
29 Lord Donoughue, interview with the author, London, March 1990.
30 Guy Carcassone, letter sent to the author dated 5 July, 1990.
31 *Facts on File* vol. XLVIII, 1988, p. 793.
32 This was a business tax set up in 1976 whose rate varied according to a firm's capital.
33 Dominique Strauss-Kahn, interview with the author, Paris, May 1990.
34 Raymond Douyere, Socialist Deputy charged with negotiations with the PC, Interview with Robert Elgie, Paris, May 1990.
35 Guy Carcassone, letter sent to the author dated 5 July, 1990.
36 Jean-Marie Daillet, interview with the author, Paris, May 1990.

8 ARE CENTRALISED PARTIES DEFENCELESS AGAINST INTERNAL CONFLICTS?

1 Flemming Kofod-Svendsen, interview with the author, Copenhagen, May 1989.
2 Erhard Jakobsen, interview with the author, Copenhagen, May 1989.
3 Jørgen Estrup, interview with the author, Copenhagen, May 1989.
4 Anger Ahm, interview with the author, Copenhagen, May 1989.
5 Jørgen Estrup, interview with the author, Copenhagen, May 1989.
6 Jørgen Estrup, interview with the author, Copenhagen, May 1989.
7 Jørgen Estrup, interview with the author, Copenhagen, May 1989.
8 The confidentiality of the agreement is confirmed by: Elizabeth Arnold, interview with the author, Copenhagen, May 1989; Jørgen Estrup, interview with the author, Copenhagen, May 1989; Lone Dybkjær, interview

with the author, Copenhagen, May 1989; Marianne Jelved, interview with the author, Copenhagen, May 1989.

9 CONCLUSIONS AND IMPLICATIONS

1 Bjørn Tore Godal, interview with the author, Oslo, October 1990.
2 Odvar Nordli, interview with the author, Oslo, October 1990.
3 Einar Førde, interview with the author, Oslo, October 1990.
4 For more examples of interparty co-operation in the context of government–opposition relationship, see: Maor and Smith (1993a, b). For examples of interparty co-operation which takes place in interlinked political markets, see: Maor (1995b) and Maor (1997a, b).

Bibliography

Aarebrot, F. (1982) 'Norway: Centre and Periphery in a Peripheral State', in: S. Rokkan and D.W. Urwin (eds) *The Politics of Territorial Identity*, London: Sage, pp. 75–111.

Aberbach, J.D., Putnam, R.E. and Rockman, B.A. (1981) *Bureaucrats and Politicians in Western Democracies*, Cambridge, Mass.: Harvard University Press.

Almond. G.A. and Verba, S. (1963) *The Civic Culture: Political Attitudes and Democracy in Five Nations*, Princeton: Princeton University Press.

Anderson, L. (1968) 'Organizational Theory and the Study of the State and Local Parties', in: W.J. Crotty (ed.) *Approaches to the Study of Party Organisation*, Boston: Allyn and Bacon, pp. 375–403.

Andersen, P.C. (1975) *Kristen Politik*, Odense: Odense Universitetsforlag.

Andreotti, G. (1981) *Diari 1976–79: gli anni della solidarieta*, 2nd edition, Milan: Rizzoli.

Austen-Smith, D. and Banks, J. (1988) 'Elections, Coalitions, and Legislative Outcomes', *American Political Science Review*, 82(1): 405–22.

Austen-Smith, D. and Banks, J. (1990) 'Stable Governments and the Allocation of Policy Portfolios', *American Political Science Review*, 84: 891–906.

Bacharach, S.B. and Lawler, E.J. (1981) *Bargaining: Power, Tactics and Outcomes*, San Francisco: Jossey-Bass.

Barbagli, M., Corbetta, P., Parisi, A., Hans, M. and Schadee, A. (1979) *Fluidita Elettorale e Classi Sociali in Italia*, Bologna: Il Mulino.

Barbagli, M. and Corbetta, P. (1982a) 'After the Historic Compromise: A Turning Point for the PCI', *European Journal of Political Research*, 10(3): 213–40.

Barbagli, M. and Corbetta, P. (1982b) 'The Italian Communist Party and the Social Movements 1968–1976', *Political Power and Social Theory: A Research Annual*, Vol. 3, Greenwich, Conn.: JAI Press, pp. 77–112.

Barber, J.D. (1960) 'Leadership Strategies for Legislative Party Cohesion', *Journal of Politics*, 2(28): 347–67.

Bardi, L. and Morlino, L. (1992) 'Italy', in: R.S. Katz and P. Mair (eds) *Party Organisations: A Data Handbook on Party Organisations in Western Democracies, 1960–90*, London: Sage, pp. 458–618.

Bardi, L. and Morlino, L. (1994) 'Italy: Tracing the Roots of the Great Transformation', in: R.S. Katz and P. Mair, (eds) *How Parties Organise:*

Change and Adaptation in Party Organisations in Western Democracies, London: Sage, pp. 242–77.

Barnes, S.H. (1977) *Representation in Italy*, Chicago: University of Chicago Press.

Baron, D.P. (1993) 'Government Formation and Endogeneous Parties', *American Political Science Review*, 87(1): 34–47.

Beith, A. (1978) 'The Working of the Lib–Lab Arrangement' in: *Probleme von Koalitionsregierungen in Westeuropa*, Bonn: Liberal-Verlag GmbH, pp. 29–38.

Bell, D.S. and Criddle, B. (1988) *The French Socialist Party: The Emergence of a Party of Government*, Oxford: Clarendon.

Bendix, P. (1974) 'Valget, Som en Politiker Ser Det' in: *Decembervalget 1973*, Copenhagen: Schultz.

Berger, S. (1987) 'Religious Transformation and the Future of Politics', in: C.S. Maier (ed.) *Changing Boundaries of the Political: Essays on the Evolving Balance Between the State and Society, Public and Private in Europe*, Cambridge: Cambridge University Press, pp. 107–50.

Bergman, T. (1993) 'Formation Rules and Minority Governments', *European Journal of Political Research*, 23: 55–66.

Bille, L. (1992) 'Denmark', in: R.S. Katz and P. Mair (eds) *Party Organisations: A Data Handbook on Party Organisations in Western Democracies, 1960–90*, London: Sage, pp. 199–272.

Bille, L. (1994) 'Denmark: The Decline of the Membership Party?', in: R.S. Katz and P. Mair (eds) *How Parties Organise: Change and Adaptation in Party Organisations in Western Democracies*, London: Sage, pp. 134–57.

Blanchard, O., Dornbusch, R. and Layard, R. (eds) (1986) *Restoring Europe's Prosperity*, Cambridge, Mass.: MIT Press.

Bogdanor, V. (1979) *Devolution*, Oxford: Oxford University Press.

Bogdanor, V. (1983) *Multi-Party Politics and the Constitution*, Cambridge: Cambridge University Press.

Bogdanor, V. (1984) 'The Government Formation Process in the Constitutional Monarchies of North-West Europe', in: D. Kavanagh and G. Peele (eds) *Comparative Government and Politics*, Boulder: Westview Press, pp. 49–72.

Browne, E., Frendreis, J. and Gleiber, D. (1986) 'The Process of Cabinet Dissolution: An Exponential Model of Duration and Stability in Western Democracies', *American Journal of Political Science*, 30(2): 628–50.

Budge, I and Laver, M. (1986) 'Office Seeking and Policy Pursuit in Coalitition Theory', *Legislative Studies Quarterly*, 11: 485–506.

Budge, I., Robertson, D. and Hearl, D. (eds) (1987) *Ideology, Strategy and Party Change: Spatial Analyses of Post-war Election Programmes in Nineteen Democracies*, Cambridge: Cambridge University Press.

Budge, I., Robertson, D. and Hearl, D. (eds) (1987) *Ideology, Strategy and Party Change: Spatial Analyses of Post-war Election Programmes in Nineteen Democracies*, Cambridge: Cambridge University Press.

Budge, I. and Keman, H. (1990) *Parties and Democracy: Coalition Formation and Government Functioning in Twenty States*, Oxford: Oxford University Press.

Budge, I. and Keman, H. (1990) *Parties and Democracy: Coalition Formation and Government Functioning in Twenty States*, Oxford: Oxford University Press.

Butler, D. and Stokes, D. (1969) *Political Change in Britain*, London: Macmillan.

Callaghan, J. (1987) *Time and Change*, London: Collins.

Castles, F.G. (1978) *The Social Democratic Image of Society: A Study of the Achievements and Origins of Scandinavian Social Democracy in Comparative Perspective*, London: Routledge.

Cayrol, R. and Ysmal, C. (1982) 'Les Militants du PS', *Projet*, May 1982, pp. 572–86.

Cayrol, R. and Ignazi, P. (1983) 'Cousins ou Frères? Attitude politique et conceptions du parti chez les militants socialistes francais et italiens', *Revue Français de Science Politique*, 33(4): 629–50.

Cervetti, G. (1977) 'A Mass Debate on the Party, the Movement and the Political Picture', *The Italian Communists*, 2: 119–28.

Charlot, M. (1986) 'L'emergence du Front National', *Revue Français de Science Politique*, 36(1): 30–45.

Chiaromonte, G. (1986) *Le Scelte della Solidarieta Democratica*, Roma: Editori Riuniti.

Coats, D. (1980) *Labour in Power?: A Study of the Labour Government 1974–1979*, London: Longman.

Cole, A.M. (1988) 'La France Unie? Francois Mitterrand', in: Gaffney, J. (ed.) *The French Presidential Elections of 1988: Ideology and Leadership in Contemporary France*, Aldershot: Dartmouth, pp. 81–100.

Cole, A.M. (1989a) 'Factionalism, The French Socialist Party and the Fifth Republic: An Explanation of Intraparty Decisions', *European Journal of Political Research*, 17(1): 77–94.

Cole, A.M. (1989b) 'The French Socialist Party in Transition', in: *Modern and Contemporary France*, no. 37, April.

Crewe, I., Särlvik, B. and Alt J. (1977) 'Partisan Dealignment in Britain 1964–1974', *British Journal of Political Science*, 7(2): 129–90.

Damgaard, E. (1973) 'Party Coalitions in Danish Law-Making 1953–1970', *European Journal of Political Research*, 1(1): 36–66.

Damgaard, E. (1974) 'Stability and Change in the Danish Party System over Half a Century', *Scandinavian Political Studies*, 9: 104–25.

Damgaard, E. (1990) 'Parlamentarimens danske tilstande', in: E. Damgaard, D. Anckar, H. Rommetvedt, A. Sannerstedt and M. Sjolin (eds) *Parlamentarisk forandring i Norden*, Oslo: Universitetforlaget, pp. 15–44.

Damgaard, E. and Svensson, P. (1989) 'Who governs? Parties and Policies in Denmark', *European Journal of Political Research*, 17(6): 734–45.

Di Giulio, F. and Rocco, E. (1979) *Un Ministro-Ombra si confessa*, Milan: Rizzoli.

Di Palma, G. (1977) *Surviving Without Governing: The Italian Parties in Parliament*, Berkeley: University of California Press.

Dodd, L.C. (1976) *Coalitions in Parliamentary Governments*, Princeton, NJ: Princeton University Press.

Doron, G. and Maor, M. (1989) *Barriers to Entry into Israeli Politics*, Tel Aviv: Papirus (in Hebrew).

Doron, G. and Maor, M. (1991) 'Barriers to Entry into a Political System: A

Theoretical Framework and Empirical Application from the Israeli Experience' *Journal of Theoretical Politics*, 3 (2): 175–88.

Dunleavy, P. (1979) 'The Urban Basis of Political Alignment' *British Journal of Political Science*, 9(4): 409–44.

Duverger, M. (1964) *Political Parties*, London: Methuen.

Eckstein, H. (1966) *Division and Cohesion in Democracy: A Study of Norway*, Princeton, NJ: Princeton University Press.

Elgie, R. (1993) *The Role of the Prime Minister in France, 1981–91*, Houndmills: Macmillan.

Elgie, R. and Maor, M. (1992) 'Accounting for the Survival of Minority Governments: An Examination of the French Case (1988–1991)', *West European Politics*, 15: 57–75.

Elklit, J. (1991) 'Party Behaviour and the Formation of Minority Coalition Governments: Some Recent Danish Experiences', *Paper prepared for presentation at the ECPR Joint Sessions of Workshops*, Colchester, Essex: March.

Epstein, L.D. (1980) *Political Parties in Western Democracies*, New Brunswick, NJ: Transaction Books.

Erskine May (1976) *Treaties on the Law, Privileges, Proceedings and Usage of Parliament*, Sir David Lidderdale (ed.) 19th edition, London: Butterworths.

Esping-Andersen, G. (1985) *Politics Against Markets: The Social Democratic Road to Power*, Princeton, NJ: Princeton University Press.

Facts on File, 1970–90.

Fitzmaurice, J. (1986) 'Coalition Theory and Practice in Scandinavia', in: G. Pridham (ed.) *Coalitional Behaviour in Theory and Practice: An Inductive Model for Western Europe*, Cambridge: Cambridge University Press, pp. 251–77.

Frears J.R. (1991) *Parties and Voters in France*, London: Hurst & Company.

Galli, G. (1976) *Storia del PCI*, second edition, Milan: Bompiani.

Graziano, M. (1980) 'The Historic Compromise and Consociational Democracy: Toward a New Democracy?', *International Political Science Review*, 1(3): 345–68.

Groennings, S. (1968) 'Notes Toward Theories of Coalition Behavior in Multiparty Systems: Formation and Maintenance', in: S. Groennings, E.W. Kelley and M. Leisersen (eds) *The Study of Coalition Behavior: Theoretical Perspectives and Cases from Four Continents*, New-York: Holt, Rinehart and Winston, pp. 445–65.

Hatfield, M. (1978) *The House the Left Built: Inside Labour Policy Making, 1970–1975*, London: Victor Gollancz.

Healey, D. (1989) *The Time of my Life*, London: Michael Joseph.

Heidar, K. (1988) 'Party System Change in Norway and Denmark 1970–1988: Spring time for "Frozen Cleavages"?' *Paper presented at the Joint Sessions of Workshops of the ECPR, Rimini, Italy.*

Heidar, K. (1990a) 'Nar Partiene Kommer Pa Trygd – Far Partimedlemmene Da Statsstipend?', Paper Prepared for the Nordic Congress of Political Science, Rekjavik.

Heidar, K. (1990b) 'A New Party Leadership?', *Working Paper*, Oslo: Institutt for Statsvitenskap, Universitetet i Oslo.

Hellman, S. (1988) *Italian Communism in Transition: The Rise and Fall of the*

Historic Compromise in Turin, 1975–1980, New York: Oxford University Press.

Hine, D. (1979) 'The Italian Socialist Party under Craxi: Surviving but not Reviving', *West European Politics*, 2(3): 133–48.

Hine, D. (1980) 'Surviving or Reviving: The Italian Socialist Party under Craxi', in: P. Lange and S. Tarrow (eds) *Italy in Transition: Conflict and Consensus*, London: Frank Cass, pp. 133–48.

Hirschman, A.O. (1970) *Exit. Voice and Loyalty: Responses to Decline in Firms, Organisations and States*, Cambridge, Mass.: Harvard University Press.

Huber, J.D. (1991) 'Parliamentary Rules and Party Behavior during Minority Government in France', *Paper prepared for presentation at the ECPR Joint Sessions of Workshops, Colchester, Essex, 1991.*

Jacobs, F. (1989) 'Norway', in: F. Jacobs (ed.) *Western European Political Parties: A Comprehensive Guide*, Harlow: Longman, pp. 585–608.

Janda, K. (1980) *Political Parties: A Cross National Survey*, New York: The Free Press.

Jones, G. (1991) 'West European Prime Ministers in Perspective', *West European Politics*, 14(2), 163–78.

Jones, J. and Morris, M. (1986) *A–Z of Trade Unionism and Industrial Relations*, London: Sphere Books.

Jørgensen, A. (1989) *Bolgensen: Fra mine dagboger 1972–1975*, Copenhagen: Fremad.

Jørgensen, A. (1990) *Braendingen: Fra mine dagboger 1978–1982*, Copenhagen: Fremad.

Kaarsted, T. (1988) *Rageringen, vi aldrig fik. Regeringsdannelsen i 1975 og dens baggrund*, Odense: Odense University Press.

Katz, R.S. and Mair, P. (1992) 'Introduction: The Cross-National Study of Party Organisations', in: R.S. Katz and P. Mair (eds) *Party Organizations: A Data Handbook on Party Organizations in Western Democracies, 1960–90*, London: Sage, pp. 1–20.

Katz, R.S. and Mair, P. (1995) 'Changing Models of Party Organization and Party Democracy: The Emergence of the Cartel Party', *Party Politics*, 1(1): 5–28.

Kavanagh, D. (1983) 'Organisation and Power in the Liberal Party', in: V. Bogdanor (ed.) *Liberal Party Politics*, Oxford: Clarendon Press, pp. 123–42.

Keesing's Contemporary Archives, 1968–91.

Kirchheimer, O. (1966) 'The Transformation of Western European Party Systems' in: J. LaPalombara and M. Weiner (eds) *Political Parties and Political Development*, Princeton, NJ: Princeton University Press, pp. 177–200.

Kogan, M. and Kogan, D. (1982) *The Battle for the Labour Policy*, London: Fontana.

Kuhnle, S., Strøm, K. and Svåsand, L. (1986) 'The Norwegian Conservative Party: Setback in an Era of Strength', *West European Politics*, 9(3): 448–71.

Lane, Jan-Erik and Ersson, S.O. (1994) *Politics and Society in Western Europe*, 2nd edition, London: Sage.

Lange, P. (1975) 'The PCI at the Local Level: A Study of Strategic Performance', in: D.L.M. Blackmer and S. Tarrow (eds) *Communism in Italy and France*, Princeton, NJ: Princeton University Press, pp. 259–304.

Lange, P. (1980) 'Crisis and Consent, Change and Compromise: Dilemmas of Italian Communism in the 1970s', in: P. Lange, and S. Tarrow (eds) *Italy in Transition: Conflict and Consensus*, London: Frank Cass, pp. 110–32.

Lange, P. and Tarrow, S. (eds) (1980) *Italy in Transition: Conflict and Consensus*, London: Frank Cass.

Lange, P. and Vannicelli, M. (eds) (1981) *The Communist Parties of Italy, France and Spain: Postwar Change and Continuity*, London: Allen and Unwin.

LaPalombara, J. (1977) 'Italian Elections as Hobson's Choice' in: R. Howard Penniman (ed.) *Italy at the Polls: The Parliamentary Elections of 1976*, Washington, D.C.: American Enterprise Institute for Public Policy Research, pp. 1–40.

LaPalombara, J. (1981) 'Two Steps Forward, One Step Back: The PCI's Struggle', in: H.R. Penniman (ed.) *Italy at the Polls: The Parliamentary Elections of 1979*, Washington, D.C.: American Enterprise Institute for Public Policy Research, pp. 104–40.

Lægreid, P. and Olsen, J.P. (1986) 'The Storting – A Last Stronghold of the Political Amateur', in: E.N. Suleiman (ed.) *Parliaments and Parliamentarians in Democratic Politics*, New York: Holmes and Meier, pp. 176–222.

Laver, M. (1974) 'Dynamic Factors in Government Coalition Formation', *European Journal of Political Research*, 2(3): 259–70.

Laver, M. and Budge, I. (1992) *Party Policy and Coalition Government*, London: Macmillan.

Laver, M. and Schofield, N. (1990) *Multiparty Government: The Politics of Coalition in Europe*, Oxford: Oxford University Press.

Laver, M. and Shepsle, K.A. (1990a) 'Government Coalitions and Intraparty Politics', *British Journal of Political Science*, 4(4): 489–508.

Laver, M. and Shepsle, K.A. (1990b) 'Coalitions and Cabinet Government', *American Political Science Review*, 84(3): 873–90.

Laver, M. and Shepsle, K.A. (eds) (1994) *Cabinet Ministers and Parliamentary Government*, Cambridge: Cambridge University Press.

Laver, M. and Shepsle, K.A. (1996) *Making and Breaking Governments: Cabinets and Legislatures in Parliamentary Democracies*, Cambridge: Cambridge University Press.

Leonardi, R. (1981) 'Political Power Linkages in Italy: The Nature of the Christian Democratic Party Organization' in: K. Lawson (ed.) *Party Linkages in Comparative Perspective*, New Haven: Yale University Press, pp. 243–65.

Leonardi, R. and Wertman, D. (1989) *Italian Christian Democracy: The Politics of Dominance*, New York: Macmillan.

Lewis-Beck, M.S. (1984) 'France: The Stalled Electorate', in: R.J. Dalton, S.C. Flanagan and P.A. Beck *Electoral Change in Advanced Industrial Democracies: Realignment or Dealignment?*, Princeton, NJ: Princeton University Press.

Lijphart, A. (1990) 'The Political Consequences of Electoral Laws, 1945–85', *American Political Science Review*, 84: 481–96.

Lindblom, C.E. (1965) *The Intelligence of Democracy: Decision Making through Mutual Adjustment*, New York: Free Press.

Lowi, T.J. (1971) *The Politics of Disorder*, New York: Norton Co.

Luebbert, G.M. (1986) *Comparative Democracy: Policymaking and Governing Coalitions in Europe and Israel*, New York: Columbia University Press.

Machin, H. (1990) 'Political Leadership', in: P.A. Hall, J. Hayward and H. Machin (eds) *Developments in French Politics*, London: Macmillan, pp. 95–113.

Malatesta, S. (1978) 'Tanti modi di dire no', *Panorama*, 24 June, pp. 38–40.

Mannheimer, R. and Sani, G. (1987) *Il Mercato Elettorale: Identikit dell' Elettore Italiano*, Bologna: Il Mulino.

Maor, M. (1991) 'The 1990 Danish Election: An Unnecessary Contest?', *West European Politics*, 14(3): 209–14.

Maor, M. (1992) 'Intraparty Conflict and Coalitional Behaviour in Denmark and Norway: The Case of "Highly Institutionalized" Parties' *Scandinavian Political Studies* 15(2): 99–116.

Maor, M. (1995a) 'Intra-Party Determinants of Coalition Bargaining', *Journal of Theoretical Politics*, 7(1): 65–91.

Maor, M. (1995b) 'Party Competition in Interlinked Political Markets: The European Union and its Member States', in: K. Dowding and D. King (eds) *Preferences, Institutions and Rational Choice*, Oxford: Clarendon Press, pp. 114–33.

Maor, M. (1997a) 'Towards Political Union: Assessing Two Strategies of EPU', in S. Stavridis, E. Mossialos, R. Morgan and H. Machin (eds) *New Challenges to the European Union: Policies and Policy-Making*, Aldershot: Dartmouth, pp. 43–66.

Maor, M. (1997b) *Political Parties and Party Systems: Comparative Approaches and the British Experience*, London: Routledge.

Maor, M. and Smith, G. (1993a) 'Government–Opposition Relationships as a Systemic Property: A Theoretical Framework', paper presented at the annual ECPR Joint Session, Leiden, April 1993.

Maor, M. and Smith, G. (1993b) 'On the Structure of Party Competition: The Impact of Maverick Issues', in: T. Bryder (ed.) *Party Systems, Party Behaviour and Democracy*, Copenhagen: Copenhagen University Press, pp. 40–50.

Marradi, A. (1982) 'Italy: From "Centrism" to Centre-Left Coalitions', in: Browne and Dreijmanis (eds) *Government Coalitions in Western Democracies*, New York: Longman, pp. 33–70.

McClosky, H. Hoffmann, P.J. and O'Hara, R. (1960) 'Issue Conflict and Consensus among Party Leaders and Followers', *American Political Science Review*, 54(2): 406–27.

McKelvey, R.D. and Schofield, N. (1987) 'Generalized Symmetry Conditions at a Core Point', *Econometrica*, 4: 923–33.

Merkel, W. (1985) *Die Sozialistische Partei Italians*, Bochum: Brockmeyer.

Michie, A. and Hoggart, S, (1978) *The Pact: The Inside Story of the Lib–Lab Government. 1977–78*, London: Quartet Books.

Mitterrand, F. 'Lettre à tout les français', *Libération*, 7 April, 1988.

Neumann, S. (1956) 'Towards a Comparative Study of Political Parties', in S. Neumann (ed.) *Modern Political Parties*, Chicago, IL.: Chicago University Press, pp. 395–421.

Norton, P. (1980) *Dissension in the House of Commons 1974–1979*, Oxford: Clarendon Press.

Olsen, J.P. (1983) *Organized Democracy: Political Institutions in a Welfare State – The Case of Norway*, Bergen: Universitetsforlaget.

Olson, M. (1965) *The Logic of Collective Action*. Cambridge, Mass.: Harvard University Press.

Outer Circle Policy Unit (1977) *Scotland and Wales Bill: Conditions for the Resurrection*, London: The Outer Circle Policy Unit.

Owen, D. (1986) *A United Kingdom: An Argument and a Challenge for a Better Britain*, Harmondsworth: Penguin.

Paci, M. (1978) *La Struttura Sociale Italian*, Bologna: Il Mulino.

Paggi, L. and D'Angelillo, M. (1986) *I Comunisti Italiani e il Riformismo*, Torino: Einaudi.

Panebianco, A. (1988) *Political Parties: Organization and Power*, Cambridge: Cambridge University Press.

Parisi, A. and Pasquino, G. (1980) 'Changes in Italian Electoral Behaviour: The Relationships Between Parties and Voters', in: P. Lange and S. Tarrow (eds) *Italy in Transition: Conflict and Consensus*, London: Frank Cass, pp. 6–30.

Pasquino, G. (1980) 'Italian Christian Democracy: A Party for all Seasons', in: P. Lange and S. Tarrow (eds) *Italy in Transition: Conflict and Consensus*, London: Frank Cass, pp. 88–109.

Pasquino, G. (1985) 'Partiti, Societa Civile e Istituzioni', in G. Pasquino (ed.) *Il Sistema Politico Italiano*, Bari: Laterza, pp. 1–30.

Pasquino, G. (1987) 'Party Government in Italy: Achievements and Prospects', in: R.S. Katz (ed.) *Party Governments: European and American Experiences*, Berlin, New York: De Gruyter, pp. 202–42.

Pasquino, G. (1988) 'Mid-Stream and Under-Stress: The Italian Communist Party', in: M. Waller and M. Fennema (eds) *Communist Parties in Western Europe: Decline or Adaptation*, Oxford: Basil Blackwell, pp. 26–46.

Pedersen, M.N. (1988) 'The Defeat of All Parties: The Danish Folketing Election, 1973' in: K. Lawson and P.H. Merkl (eds) *When Parties Fail: Emerging Alternative Organizations*, Princeton, NJ: Princeton University Press, pp. 257–81.

Poggi, G. (ed.) (1968) *L'organizzazione partitica del PCI e della DC*, Bologna: Il Mulino.

Powell, B. (1982) *Contemporary Democracies: Participation, Stability and Violence*, Cambridge, Mass.: Harvard University Press.

Pridham, G. (1988) *Political Parties and Coalitional Behaviour in Italy*, London: Routledge.

Przeworski, A. and Teune, H. (1970) *The Logic of Comparative Social Inquiry*, New York: Wiley.

Pulzer, P. (1975) *Political Representation and Elections in Britain*, London: Allen and Unwin.

Punnett, R.M. (1994) *British Government and Politics*, 6th edition, Aldershot: Dartmouth.

Putnam, R.D. (1973) *The Belief of Politicians: Ideology, Conflict and Democracy in Britain and Italy*, New Haven: Yale University Press.

Putnam, R.D. (1975) 'The Italian Communist Politicians' in D.L.M. Blackmer and S. Tarrow (eds) *Communism in Italy and France*, Princeton, NJ: Princeton University Press, pp. 173–220.

Rae, D. (1971) *The Political Consequences of Electoral Laws*, 2nd edition, New

Haven: Yale University Press.
Ranger, J. (1986) 'Le Decline du Parti Communiste Francais', *Revue Francais de Science Politique*, vol. xxxvi, no. 1, pp. 46–63.
Robertson, D. (1976) *A Theory of Party Competition*, London: Wiley.
Rokkan, S. (1968) 'Electoral Systems', in: D.L. Sills (ed.) *International Encyclopedia of the Social Science*, New York: Macmillan, pp. 6–21.
Rokkan, S. (1970) *Citizens, Elections, Parties*, New York: David McKay.
Rommetvedt, H. (1990) 'Parties and Governments in Norway', *Paper prepared for presentation at the ECPR Joint Sessions of Workshops*, Bocum, Germany.
Roscue, J. (1982) *The Italian Communist Party 1976–81: On the Threshold of Government*, London: Macmillan.
Rose, R. and McAllister, I. (1986) *Voters Begin to Choose: From Closed-Class to Open Elections in Britain*, London: Sage.
Rose, R. and Mackie, T.T. (1988) 'Do Parties Persist or Fail? The Big Trade-off Facing Organizations', in: K. Lawson and P.H. Merkl (eds) *When Parties Fail: Emerging Alternative Organizations*, Princeton, NJ: Princeton University Press, pp. 533–560.
Rostow, D. (1956) 'Scandinavia: Working multiparty Systems' in: S. Newmann (ed.) *Modern Political Parties*, Chicago: University of Chicago Press, pp. 169–93.
Sanders, D. and Herman, V. (1977) 'The Stability and Survival of Governments in Western Democracies', *Acta Politica*, 12: 346–77.
Sani, G. (1977) 'Le elezioni degli anni 1970: terremoto o evoluzione?', in: A. Parisi and G. Pasquino (eds) *Continuita e Mutamento Elettorale in Italia*, Bologna: Il Mulino, pp. 67–102.
Särlvik, B. (1983) 'Coalition Politics and Policy Output in Scandinavia: Sweden, Denmark and Norway', in: V. Bogdanor (ed.) *Coalition Government in Western Europe*, London: Heinemann, pp. 97–152.
Särlvik, B. and Crewe, I. (1983) *Decade of Dealignment: The Conservative Victory of 1979 and Electoral Trends in the 1970s*, Cambridge: Cambridge University Press.
Sartori, G. (1976) *Parties and Party Systems: A Framework for Analysis, Volume I*, Cambridge: Cambridge University Press.
Schain, M.A. (1987) 'The National Front in France and the Construction of Political Legitimacy', *West European Politics*, 10(2): 229–52.
Schelling, T. C. (1960) The Strategy of Conflict. Cambridge, Mass.: Harvard University Press.
Schofield, N. (1986) 'Existence of a Structurally Stable Equilibrium for a Noncollegial Voting Rule', *Public Choice*, 51(3): 267–84.
Sjöblom, G. (1968) *Party Strategies in a Multiparty System*, Lund: Studentlitteratur.
Steel, D. (1980) *A House Divided: The Lib–Lab Pact and the Future of British Politics*, London: Weidenfeld and Nicolson.
Steel, D. (1989) *Against Goliath: David Steel's story*, London: Weidenfeld and Nicolson.
Stout, M.L. (1981) 'Guillotine Procedure and the Structure of Conflict in the British House of Commons', *Unpublished Ph.D dissertation*, London: The University of London.

Strøm, K. (1990a) 'A Behavioural Model of Competitive Political Parties', *American Journal of Political Science*, 34(2): 565–98.

Strøm, K. (1990b) *Minority Government and Majority Rule*, Cambridge: Cambridge University Press.

Svåsand, L. (1992) 'Norway', in: R.S. Katz and P. Mair (eds) *Party Organisations: A Data Handbook on Party Organisations in Western Democracies, 1960–90*, London: Sage, pp. 732–80.

Svåsand, L. (1994) 'Change and Adaptation in Norwegian Party Organisations', in: R.S. Katz and P. Mair (eds) *How Parties Organize: Change and Adaptation in Party Organizations in Western Democracies*, London: Sage, pp. 304–31.

Svensson, P. (1982) 'Party Cohesion in the Danish Parliament During the 70s', *Scandinavian Political Studies*, 5: 17–42.

Taagepera, R. and Shugart, M.S. (1989) *Seats and Votes: The Effects and Determinants of Electoral Systems*, New Haven: Yale University Press.

Tarrow, S. (1981) 'Three Years of Italian Democracy', in: H.R. Penniman (ed.) *Italy at the Polls: The Parliamentary Elections of 1979*, Washington, DC: American Enterprise Institute for Public Policy Research, pp. 1–33.

Tarrow, S. (1983) 'Historic Compromise or Bourgeois Majority: Eurocommunism in Italy, 1976–1979', in: H. Machin (ed.) *National Communism in Western Europe: A Third Way to Socialism?*, London: Methuen, pp. 124–53.

Urwin, D.W. (1987) 'Norway: Parties between Mass Membership and Consumer-Oriented Professionalism', in: A. Ware (ed.) *Political Parties: Electoral Change and Structural Response*, Oxford: Basil Blackwell, pp. 183–204.

Vacca G. (1987) *Tra Compromesso e Solidarieta: La politica del Pci negli anni '70*, Rome: Editori Riuniti.

Valen, H. (1981) *Valg og Politikk: Et Samfunn i Endring*, Oslo; NKS-Forlaget.

Valen, H. (1988) 'Norway: Decentralization and Group Representation', in: T. Gallagher and M. Marsh (eds) *Candidate Selection in Comparative Perspective: The Secret Garden of Politics*, London: Sage, pp. 210–35.

Valen, H. and Katz, D. (1964) *Political Parties in Norway*, Oslo: Universitetsforlaget.

Valen, H. and Rokkan, S. (1974) 'Norway: Conflict Structure and Mass Politics in a European Periphery', in: R. Rose (ed.) *Electoral Behaviour: A Comparative Handbook*, New York: Free Press, pp. 315–70.

Verba, S. (1971) 'Cross-National Survey Research: The Problem of Credibility', in: I. Vallier (ed.) *Comparative Methods in Sociology: Essays on Trends and Applications*, Berkeley: University of California Press, pp. 339–56.

Warwick, P.V. (1979) 'The Durability of Coalition Governments in Parliamentary Democracies', *Comparative Politics*, 11(4): 465–98.

Warwick, P.V. (1994) *Government Survival in Parliamentary Democracies*, Cambridge: Cambridge University Press.

Webb, P.D. (1994) 'Party Organizational Change in Britain: The Iron Law of Centralization?', in: R.S. Katz and P. Mair (eds) *How Parties Organize: Change and Adaptation in Party Organizations in Western Democracies*, London: Sage, pp. 109–33.

Wertman, D.A. (1979) 'La Partecipazione Intermittente. Gli Iscritti e la Vita di Partito', in: A. Parisi (ed.) *Democristiani*, Bologna: Il Mulino, pp. 61–84.

Wertman, D.A. (1981) 'The Christian Democrats: Masters of Survival', in: H.R. Penniman (ed.) *Italy at the Polls: The Parliamentary Elections of 1979*, Washington, DC: American Enterprise Institute for Public Policy Research, pp. 64–103.

Willoch, K. (1990) *Statsminister*, Oslo: Schibsted.

Wright, W.E. (1971) 'Comparative Party Models: Rational Efficient and Party Democracy', in: W.E. Wright (ed.) *A Comparative Study of Party Organization*, Columbus: Merrill.

Wright, V. (1989) *The Government and Politics of France*, 3rd edition, London: Unwin Hyman.

Index